ENDORPHINOMICS

Also by Steve Moeller

Effort-less Marketing for Financial Advisors

ENDORPHINOMICS

The Science of Human Flourishing

| HEALTH | WEALTH | HAPPINESS |

STEVE MOELLER

Endorphin Zone New Media
Tustin, California

ENDORPHINOMICS: THE SCIENCE OF HUMAN FLOURISHING

Professional Edition
All rights reserved.
Copyright © 2014 by Steven W. Moeller.
Endorphinomics™ and Endorphin Zone™ are trademarks of Steve Moeller.

Second edition 2014 (c6.52, i5.0)
No part of this book may be reproduced or transmitted in any form or by any means, electronic or mechanical, including photocopying, recording, or by any information storage and retrieval system, without permission in writing from the publisher. For information, email info@endorphinzone.com or address correspondence to:
Endorphin Zone New Media
1131 East Main St., Suite 203
Tustin, CA 92780
800-678-1701 or info@endorphinzone.com
www.endorphinzone.com

Publisher's Cataloging-in-Publication data
Moeller, Steve.
Endorphinomics: the science of human flourishing / Steve Moeller. –Professional ed., 2nd ed.
p. : ill. ; cm.
"Healthier, Wealthier, Happier."

ISBN: 978-0-9899222-0-3

1. Self-actualization (Psychology) 2. Well-being. 3. Success. I. Title.
BF637.S4 M64 2014
158.1

Art direction by Eddie Bryant
Cover concept by Brooke Moeller
Cover design by Alexander Vulchev
Interior design by GKS Creative
Edited by Karen Risch
Technical illustrations by Krista Donnelly
Whimsical illustrations by Phil Boyd

For Martin Seligman, Mihaly Csikszentmihalyi, Ed Diener, David Myers, Barbara Fredrickson, Sonya Lyubomirsky, and all the other visionaries in the emerging science of human flourishing. Your discoveries are contributing to the evolution of human consciousness and will help transform our planet into a more peaceful, prosperous, and sustainable world for all.

CONTENTS

Introduction	1
STEP ONE - Commit to Flourishing	**13**
1 The Truth About Money and Happiness	15
2 The Purpose of Positive Emotions	39
3 Endorphins Each Day Keep the Doctors Away	65
STEP TWO - Discover Your Flourishing Self	**89**
4 Optimize Your Personal Operating System	91
5 Define Your Personal Powers	113
6 Discover Your Life's Purpose	139
7 Pursue Your Passions in Positive Places	165
8 Identify Positive People	189
STEP THREE - Envision A Flourishing Future	**215**
9 Visualize Your Ideal Work and Play	217
10 Optimize Your Personal Finances	239
11 Build Wealth for Financial Freedom	257
STEP FOUR - Align Your Life With Your Vision	**281**
12 Go Confidently in the Direction of your Dreams	283
Acknowledgments	307
Appendix	309
About the Author	311
Join the Endorphin Zone Community	312
Quick Order Form	314

ENDORPHINOMICS

Introduction

*The constitution only gives you the right to pursue happiness.
You have to catch it yourself.*
—**Anonymous**

One of the most breathtaking scenic drives on Earth, the Sea-to-Sky highway carries you from Vancouver to Whistler. After it leaves the city, the road hugs the edge of Howe Sound, and then it follows the wildly cascading Squamish River. Not a single billboard mars the pristine wilderness. Instead, soaring granite cliffs, massive boulders, fir trees, aspen groves, and dense green shrubs line the way.

One crisp summer morning, I drove this wilderness highway, heading back to the Vancouver airport after delivering a speech at the elegant Chateau Whistler. Cruising along, soaking up the inspiring scenery, the wind whipped my hair, and rock and roll blasted from my car's stereo.

Then, rounding a bend, I gasped at an awesome sight in front of me: a grove of aspens backlit by the sun. Each of thousands of leaves were crowned with a golden halo, and Lion's Bay glistened behind them, creating a spectacular scene.

I had to pull over to savor the experience.

Leaping out of the car, I headed straight for a granite slab overlooking the view. Ancient glaciers had carved the granite into a perfect seat for me, where I sat transfixed by the sparkling leaves. The natural beauty sent a shiver down my spine, a silly grin lit up my face. A squirrel scolded me for invading her territory, and a Steller's jay called in the distance.

Closing my eyes and relaxing into the coolness of my rock throne, I luxuriated in every detail.

A profound feeling of awe, beauty, and joy—a deep connection with nature—overcame me. For a few magical moments, I experienced a transcendent, euphoric state of consciousness, and a voice whispered inside my head,

Aaaaaaaaah. This is it. This is what life's all about.

Have you ever felt this way? It's rare, isn't it? But not unattainable. Most of us experience it at least once in a while, whether we're outside in nature, listening to or playing music, running, skiing, riding a bike, creating or enjoying art, making love, cooking, or eating, or . . . the list is endless, and each experience particular to whoever's having it.

Psychologist Abraham Maslow called these magical moments "peak experiences," and they're the most intense type of what I call "endorphin moments." Not every endorphin moment feels as grand or memorable as my experience at Lion's Bay. Positive emotions range from sublime contentment to powerful, transcendent spiritual awakenings—the ultimate peak experiences that transform lives and, sometimes, civilizations.

In the pages ahead, you'll learn how to experience more frequent endorphin moments and positive emotions in your life, and how to eliminate harmful stress. You'll discover how experiencing more positivity in your life will release your inner brakes so you can *flourish*.

Optimize Your Life with Endorphinomics™

Endorphins are chemical messengers that relieve pain and create a mild state of euphoria. *Economics* is a social science that studies the acquisition (or creation), allocation, management, and consumption of resources.

So *Endorphinomics* ("en-door-fin-NOM-icks"), then, is about how to synergistically integrate and utilize all your resources to optimize your quality of life—so you're constantly experiencing a mild state of euphoria.

The information and suggestions in this book offer a framework for understanding and achieving the "good life," living a life you love. It's based on decades of research and my experience in a range of fields, including anthropology, career counseling, comparative religions, economics, future studies, indigenous wisdom, life coaching, management consulting, medicine, neuroscience, philosophy, physiology, peak performance, personal finance, positive psychology and social science. Whew!

But, since I wrote this book for laypeople and I don't want to overwhelm you with data, you won't find footnotes or citations in it. If you want to pursue anything you read here more in depth, a full bibliography is available at EndorphinZone.com.

Though I've studied widely and am constantly looking at the latest findings, I'm not a scientist or a psychologist, nor do I play one on TV. I'm a business consultant, author, workshop leader, and life coach who specializes in money and happiness. My processes have helped thousands of people enhance their incomes and their quality of life.

But, my interest in what eventually became Endorphinomics began long before my professional pursuits, back when I was a boy, growing up in Northern California.

My Own "Rich Dad, Poor Dad" Paradox

Born into an unhappy family, I often heard my mom and dad argue. They eventually divorced when I was four. Shortly after that, Dad remarried, giving me a new stepmom and, soon, a new half brother and half sister. Dad was conservative, uptight, and hard working. He was highly organized and demanding. (We liked to say he was "very

German.") He put in long hours at his orthodontics practice and spent the weekends remodeling older homes. He didn't laugh much, and he had no close friends. He was a classic type-A workaholic.

Although Dad's profession bought him luxury cars, custom homes, and long vacations, he was perennially unhappy, tense, and stressed.

Meanwhile, in my other family, things were different. When I was six years old, my mom married Ralph, a happy-go-lucky salesperson. My new stepfather was exactly the opposite of my dad. He was warm, loving, loose, unstructured, joyful, and fun. He loved partying and had an aversion to hard labor, believing that work and sobriety were okay as long as you did them in moderation.

Mom and Ralph were liberal Democrats who had an extended family of far-out friends: artists, boozers, carpenters, civil-rights attorneys, comedians, commies, "courtesans," designers, jazz musicians, intellectuals, mechanics, novelists, philanderers, philosophers, reporters, socialists, surgeons, seafarers, television producers, writers, and other assorted brilliant, underemployed bohemians. Since few of their friends had "real jobs" and making money wasn't a high priority, they weren't usually burdened with any.

During the fourteen years I lived with mom and Ralph, we shared our home with more than fifty different people who were "getting their acts together." Earning enough money to support all of us kids and the constant parade of live-in guests was a never-ending challenge for Ralph.

The common thread connecting this ragtag community was Alan Watts, the famous British philosopher, author, and speaker who popularized Eastern religions and philosophies in the West, especially Zen Buddhism. Alan was in my parents' close circle of friends and was a mentor and role model for me. He opened many hearts and minds to see there's more than one way to interpret and understand our life experiences.

Every Sunday during my formative years, Alan's resonant voice and mind-expanding ideas filled our home via his "lectures" on KPFA radio. Alan was a master communicator who earned a living with his wisdom, speeches, humor, and books. He was the only adult I knew who I wanted to emulate.

That pronounced dichotomy between my two families, and possibly Alan Watts' influence, led me to an important life decision when I was thirteen. One day, while walking home from junior high school, my mind wandered to the often paradoxical differences between my "rich" but unhappy father and my "poor" but happy stepfather.

Aha! Suddenly, it occurred to me to do something that now seems obvious: consciously take only the best from both of my fathers and my families.

The Beginning of Something Big

On the spot, I vowed to live my best possible life, one that included love, happiness, friendships, fun, and financial success but excluded stress, anxiety, and poverty. I decided to pursue the perfect balance between personal happiness and financial success, the balance that leads to what I now call "flourishing."

In my innocence, though, I didn't yet grasp what most adults already know: not many people find this balance. Finding role models who are living a balanced, happy, fulfilled, and prosperous life can be extremely difficult.

Throughout high school, I searched for the secrets to the good life. I went to Turkey on an exchange program to discover if people in poorer societies were more or less happy. My Turkish family and friends seemed just as happy (and unhappy) as people I knew at home. I read voraciously and attended dozens of personal development workshops, steadily evolving in the direction of my quest.

By my late thirties, I felt I'd learned enough to take a life-changing step. I established a consulting, training, speaking, and writing business—*and that's when my real learning started.*

Over the next fifteen years, I researched, developed, and taught a yearlong business and personal development program for financial advisors, helping to transform hundreds of advisors and a few major investment companies to a more holistic, client-centered, and sustainable business model.

I learned through tangible experience about the awesome power of vision to guide, inspire, and rapidly produce positive change. Diving deep to really understand what I was seeing, I studied many religions and philosophies, and I followed business management and personal development gurus. To get a look outside my Western "mindset," I adventured to indigenous communities in the High Andes and the rainforests of the Upper Amazon, where the local Yachak and Uwishin healers taught me to use my imagination and intuition to make positive changes in my life and the lives of others.

Eventually, I discovered Martin Seligman's seminal book, *Authentic Happiness,* which revealed to me that serious scientists were finally looking at the phenomena of human flourishing. I read other books on the subject and enrolled in Seligman's training program on the science of happiness. I attended a few conferences, where I met many of the leading lights of this exciting new field.

Over the next few years, I synthesized the most important things I'd learned from the scientists and the shamans, then shared it with my clients and people in my audiences. It was a natural blending of heart and mind for me.

Is This Book for You?

Not everyone appreciates my philosophy of pursuing financial success *and* happiness. In fact, I've had a few people walk out of my workshops. In Massachusetts, one participant wrote on his evaluation, "This happiness crap won't go over here in Boston. It sounds like a California cult to me."

INTRODUCTION

Honestly, it never occurred to me that seeking happiness would be controversial!

The quality-of-life movement isn't a California cult or West Coast fad. Thousands of senior scientists, economists, business people, policy makers, and government officials are actively working, right now, to define and encourage human flourishing. Around the world, hundreds of millions of people yearn for more meaningful and fulfilling lives. I wrote this book for them. Maybe for you.

Ten specific groups will get the most out of this book. See if one describes you.

1. *Life transitioners* are contemplating or facing a major life change or question, such as the loss of a loved one, divorce, a new career, starting or graduating from school, moving to a new area, or retiring. This book is an encouraging gift for anyone going through a time of upheaval or reinvention.
2. *Upgraders* are frustrated with their current situation. They have a vague sense that their current lives are somehow suboptimal. They're dissatisfied or stressed, yearning for more, and seeking the right direction for their lives.
3. *Optimizers* are happy with their lives but want to be even happier. They're always looking for ways to improve their lives and make a more significant contribution to our world.
4. *Consultants, therapists, financial advisors, and life coaches* help others evolve, grow, and change. They can use this book to help clients align their outer lives more closely with their authentic selves. Many client-centered financial advisors will use it to help their investors envision their ideal retirement. There are additional resources for people who want to use this book in their business at EndorphinZone.com.

5. *Participants* in my workshop webinars, coaching programs, classes, and other communities of people who are actively seeking ways to apply this information in their lives.
6. *Scientists and educators,* including psychology instructors, teachers, and researchers, can use this book as an introduction to applied positive psychology for themselves or their students. I invite scientists to challenge and test my conclusions and recommendations. I'll add your findings when I revise this book.
7. *Entrepreneurs, managers, and human resources professionals* will find support for their associates and employees in increasing teamwork, innovation, and productivity while lowering stress.
8. *Book study groups* include any group of people who want an evidence-based process for helping each other flourish.
9. *Healthcare professionals* will discover practical ways to teach their patients to reduce their stress while boosting their immune systems, health, and sense of purpose.
10. *Pleasure readers* may not be in any of the groups above but will enjoy reading this book for entertainment, inspiration, and self-improvement.

If you're in any of these groups and want more substance than typical self-help books, you'll find solid science behind everything I present here. No matter why you're reading this book, I'm thrilled you've made that decision.

Your Role and Mine

Buddhists believe that when the student is ready, the teacher will appear. Think about this: everything you've done in your life so far has prepared you to apply the information in this book! It's your logical next step.

Before we begin, let's clarify our roles and identify some possible obstacles. My role is to entertain, inspire, and encourage you while providing useful information and practical exercises. I've invested one hundred percent of my best insights and experiences in this book. Your role is to invest one hundred percent of your attention and energy into—no, not just reading this book, but instead *becoming your best-possible self and living a flourishing life.*

To do that you need to do the work: read, think, discuss, and act. Commit to overcoming every obstacle between you and a life you love.

Health, wealth, abundance, and happiness are your natural states. I believe learning to flourish is a kind of healing, getting back to your true nature. In his book, *Coyote Healing,* Dr. Lewis Mehl-Madrona shares this wisdom from a Native American healer:

> *"Seventy percent of healing is from the patient's intention to get well, twenty percent is from God and the divinely inspired personal transformation, and the remaining ten percent is from the show that the medicine man puts on to make people think something happened."*

The stories, information, and exercises in this book are the "show." But your intentions will determine if this book is just light entertainment or a deep healing that reconnects you with your higher self.

How to Get the Most From This Book

Divided into four sections, this book will guide you through my four-step process:

1. **commit to flourishing,**
2. **discover your flourishing self,**
3. **envision a flourishing future, and**
4. **align your life with your vision.**

To achieve the greatest benefits, read this book and do the exercises with one or more people you care about. Consider creating a group that meets periodically to discuss this book. Coach and encourage each other as you complete the exercises, discuss your insights, and take action on them. (You can download a guide for establishing a study group at EndorphinZone.com.)

I recommend you read *Endorphinomics* more than once. Each time you do it, you'll gain deeper insights. These insights and new knowledge will physically change your brain, establishing new neural connections and networks. Rewiring your brain is the first step to optimizing your life.

On your first reading, focus on the big picture, how the concepts and information make you feel and think. Highlight passages that are meaningful for you. Invite your family and friends to join you in each chapter's Endorphin Events. Creating positive experiences, on purpose, will start you on an upward spiral of positivity. Then, to reinforce your new knowledge and insights, answer the last question on the Endorphin Events pages.

As you become more and more fluent in the ideas, principles, and practices of Endorphinomics, remember that teachers always learn more than their students. So, if you really want to "own" this material, teach it to others. Something amazing happens when we learn, share, and act together. Each of us will flourish while helping others flourish, in an upward spiral of human flourishing.

INTRODUCTION

By reading this far, you've taken the first step on your journey to a more successful and happier life. However, anything of real value can be achieved only with focused effort over time. So be patient: start with small steps and simple exercises. Discuss your insights and questions with your inner circle. Your positive emotions will guide you in the right direction.

Now, turn the page and take the first step on your journey to a flourishing life.

STEP ONE

Commit to Flourishing

1

The Truth About Money and Happiness

> *Money is a good servant but a bad master.*
> —Sir Francis Bacon

When I first met Toby, he seemed perfectly happy. We'd both addressed his firm's annual conference at a posh Aspen resort, and although the audience had listened politely to my presentation, they'd been mesmerized by Toby.

At the awards ceremony that evening, I learned why. The firm's president recognized Toby with the Top Producer award because he had (drum roll, please) "GENERATED OVER THREE MILLION DOLLARS OF GROSS REVENUE IN THE PREVIOUS YEAR!"

During his acceptance speech, Toby boasted, "You ain't seen nothin' yet." He fired up his peers by promising them, "Within three years, I'm going to generate over five million dollars." Enthusiastically, he concluded, "Each of you can get rich, just like me, if you're willing to sacrifice and do what it takes." His colleagues responded with thunderous applause, stomping, and then a standing ovation.

Over dinner, Toby and I chatted about changes happening in the investment industry, and after dessert, he lowered his voice to share a secret.

"I've got an important project that I need some help with. Can you come over to my office in Newport Beach next week?"

Although he'd surprised me, I readily agreed. He'd certainly piqued my curiosity: why would a guy of his stature need my help?

When I arrived at his address a week later, the elevator doors opened into a jaw-droppingly luxurious penthouse. From the reception area, you could see Santa Catalina Island, rising out of the Pacific, twenty-six miles off the coast. Classical music and the musky scent of leather furniture filled the air. Persian carpets adorned the marble floors. It reminded me more of a palace than an office.

Toby was far, far wealthier than any of my previous clients, and to be honest, I found it not only perplexing but a little intimidating.

As I approached the reception desk, a sharply dressed young woman rose and greeted me warmly.

"You must be Steve." She smiled and shook my hand. "I'm Monique, one of Toby's assistants."

Maybe she sensed some of my hesitance as she walked me to Toby's office, because she assured me that Toby was eager to meet with me.

As I entered his office, Toby, a bear of a man, was pacing nervously, clutching a cordless phone to his ear. Family photos and a cabinet full of awards made his office feel more like a den than a high-powered broker's office. But the three monitors displaying market data reassured me he was wired into Wall Street.

He took off his glasses and pointed with them toward a couch facing the ocean. Settling in, I stared out the window, watched cottony clouds hanging over Catalina, and wondered what on earth I was doing in this man's office.

An Unexpected Request

Ending his call, Toby turned toward me and announced, "I just bought my wife a fully loaded Lincoln Navigator, the biggest and most expensive SUV on the market. They're almost impossible to get."

After congratulating him on his purchase, I complimented him on his office, and we both admired the awesome view. We made some small talk, and then he abruptly shifted gears. "Look, I know you're busy, so I'll get right to the point. This is strictly confidential." He raised an eyebrow and asked, "Can I trust you with what I'm about to say?"

When I nodded, he took a deep breath and revealed, "Steve, I need your help. I can't take this any longer."

"I—I'm not sure I know what you mean," I stammered.

"This," he said, waving his arm to show that he meant his office, his business, his life. "I worked my butt off to build my business. For the first ten years I owned my business, but for the last seven, it's owned me."

He paused to let his words sink in. "It's true, though. I'm running as fast as I can. I'm working sixty or seventy hours a week." Rubbing his forehead, he went on. "The more successful I get, the harder I have to work. It's hopeless. I've got to get out."

He searched my face for some reaction, which I did my best to hide.

"I should be happy," he continued. "I'm taking home almost two million dollars a year. But my wife's threatening divorce. My daughter's in rehab and my son just got out of jail. My doctor says that if I don't slow down, I'll probably die of a heart attack. *Frigging success is killing me.*"

I wanted to tell him, *Forget your five-million-dollar goal, and just take some time off.* "Seems like you need a vacation," I volunteered.

"Damn right," he shot back. "I need a long one, but if I'm not generating income, my bills will eat me alive. Do you know how much it costs to run an office like this? I can't afford a vacation!

And, meanwhile, I don't have anyone I can talk to about this. My wife, my company, and the other reps all think I've got it made. Everyone looks up to me."

I tried to look sympathetic, but to be honest, I had no idea what I could do for him, since my specialty was helping people in his profession do exactly what he'd done.

"I don't feel successful, I feel exhausted," he confided. "That's why I wanted to meet with you, Steve. Can you help me find someone who will buy my business?"

My Personal Tipping Point

Later, riding the elevator down, I noticed how my stomach had tightened. Toby's words rang in my head as I tried to make sense of them. It was hard to believe that someone earning so much money, with every trapping of success imaginable, could be so miserable—and that I could do so little to help him. Sure, I'd promised to pass along any leads I might have for a buyer, but really, was that all I had to offer?

Toby's confession had sparked some serious conflicts for me, so I drove to the beach to think.

Before Toby's cry for help, I'd been coaching and training investment advisors to build highly profitable businesses much like his. That's what they wanted, and that's why they paid me. That afternoon, it struck me like a ton of bricks that my advice could make my clients miserable—even while their income was going through the roof! That thought had never occurred to me before. I felt numb and couldn't think straight. I walked out on Balboa Pier, where anglers dangled their lines in the water. As I passed a father and son reeling in a bonito, a scary thought flashed through my mind: *My current business model needs a major upgrade.*

That short conversation with Toby had sensitized me to reflect on my own experience and beliefs. It prompted me to start asking my friends and clients about their quality of life. I soon discovered "successful miserable people" all around me. Many of them were winning awards from their companies, but not from their families.

I knew how to help Toby improve his business, but I didn't know how to improve his quality of life, and his predicament led me to make a new commitment: to learn how to help my clients have it all—health, wealth, and happiness—which was exactly what I wanted for myself. I embarked on a journey to learn as much as possible about the "good life" and how to achieve it. That proved to be a challenge.

Back then, in the mid-nineties, there was a lot of research on depression, stress, and mental illness. But there were few empirical studies available for lay people on happiness and human flourishing. Only a few scattered scientists had studied what values, beliefs, and behaviors create joyful, prosperous, satisfying, stress-free, and meaningful lives.

Happiness: The Meaning and Purpose of Life

Most of the available information on success consisted of unscientific claims by self-help gurus. The lack of scientific research on happiness was particularly puzzling because Western civilization has been fascinated with it for thousands of years. The Greek philosophers thought deeply about it. More than 2,300 years ago, Aristotle said, "Happiness is the meaning and purpose of life, the whole end and aim of human existence." He was right. We're hardwired to pursue pleasure, positive emotions, and positive states.

Unless we're seriously broken, we believe everything we do will lead us to more happiness. We put energy into increasing our incomes, pursuing romance, and acquiring possessions only because we believe they will make us happy.

Happiness is the one thing we pursue for its own sake. It's the holy grail of Western civilization.

Happiness, experiencing positive emotions often and negative emotions rarely, is a major component of a flourishing life. So here's an important question: if happiness is so important to us, how much "happiness training" have we had? For most of us, the answer is none. Even though we all dream of happiness, few of us know exactly what it is or how to achieve it. Because of our lack of knowledge, many of us, like Toby, pursue the good life by pursing financial success.

Toby's biggest mistake was believing the American happiness myth: *If I work hard, put up with a lot of stress, and make a lot of money, someday I'll be happy.*

But his single-minded approach to happiness brought stress and frustration—unhappiness. In fact, the more money he made, the harder he had to work and the more stressed he became. Happiness eluded him.

"Miswanting": A Common Problem

Harvard psychologist Daniel Gilbert has discovered that humans are terrible at accurately predicting how we'll feel in future situations. He calls chasing something we think will make us happy—but doesn't—"miswanting."

Toby had a bad case of miswanting. And he's not the only one who believes the American happiness myth. Survey after survey shows that most Americans believe they can buy happiness. Researchers at the University of Michigan recently asked a representative sampling of citizens what would improve the overall quality of their lives, and the top answer was "more money."

Today, more and more of our best and brightest young people believe the American happiness myth. In 1969, only about four in ten incoming college students ranked "being well off financially" as very important or essential. Back then, "developing a meaningful philosophy of life" was most important to eight out of ten new students.

Now, almost eight out of ten incoming students say that "being well off financially" is their most important goal. Meanwhile the percentage of these students who ranked "developing a meaningful philosophy of life" as their most important goal dropped nearly in half!

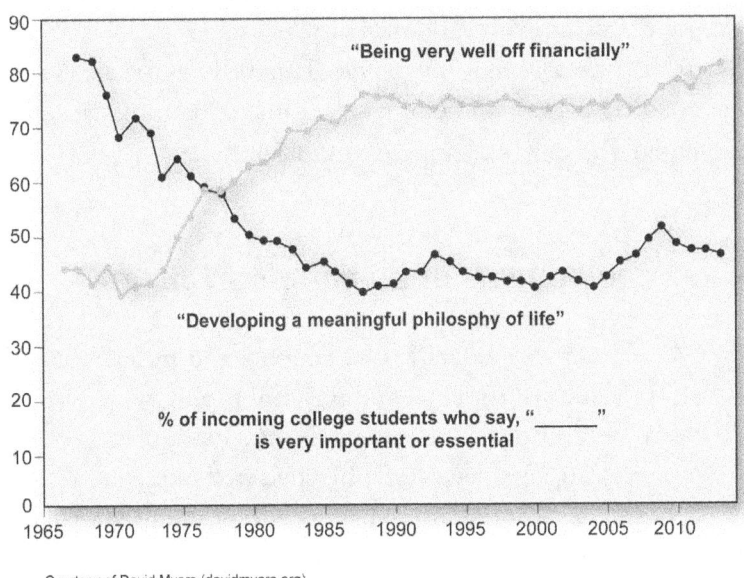

Courtesy of David Myers (davidmyers.org)

Figure 1.1. Changing Priorities for College Students

Know this: it takes more than a solid income to truly flourish. Still, more and more people, it seems, endorse this simplistic equation: money = success and happiness.

Happiness and Flourishing

Aristotle's concept of happiness was broader than wealth, possessions, or just feeling good in the moment. The Greek word he used was *eudaimonia*, which means "happy spirit." It's usually translated into English as "well-being" or "flourishing." It's about becoming your best possible self: happy, fulfilled, successful, virtuous, and a solid contributor to your community. It includes the important concept of personal growth.

The concept of *Endorphinomics* expands Aristotle's multi-dimensional concept of happiness to *include* wealth and personal finance. It's about evolving and thriving in every domain of your life.

Flourishing is the opposite of languishing. Languishing means living a life that feels stuck, hollow, and empty; it means not coming close to your full potential, for success, happiness, and fulfillment.

The key components of human flourishing:

1. *Objective well-being* refers to the tangible and measurable aspects of your life: your mental and physical health, your income, net worth, education, nutrition, environmental quality, etc. People experiencing high levels of objective well-being are referred to as *healthy and wealthy,* and as having a high standard of living.
2. *Subjective well-being* refers to internal states that are difficult to assess, including positive emotions and positive evaluations of your life. People who experience high frequencies of positive thoughts and feelings, and low frequencies of negative thoughts and feelings, are referred to as *happy.*

Breaking subjective well-being down even further, positive *emotions* are triggered by positive thoughts and experiences. Positive *evaluations*, such as life satisfaction, meaningfulness, and fulfillment aren't based solely on how we feel in the moment. They also require conscious deliberation and assessment.

For instance, to determine your current life satisfaction, simply ask yourself, *All things considered, on a scale of one to ten, how satisfied am I with my life?* (One is miserable. Ten is ecstatic.)

Take a moment, right now, to rate your current life satisfaction.

Your answer is based on your evaluation of your past, present, and future, and it is dependent on your definition of success, which reflects your beliefs and expectations. If your thoughts, behaviors, and results are aligned with your beliefs, values, and expectations, you'll feel positive about your life and give yourself a high score. If they fall short of your expectations, you'll feel dissatisfied with your life.

The concept of flourishing that I will use throughout this book, includes objective and subjective well-being, and an important third component; growing, evolving and striving to *fulfill your potential*.

Flourishing is About Living Your Best Possible Life					
1. Objective Well-Being		2. Subjective Well-Being		3. Fulfilling Your Potential	
(Measureable)		(Emotional & Thoughtful)		(Subjective & Objective)	
Internal	External	Positive Emotions	Positive Evaluations	Personal Growth	Contribution to Others
Body mass Blood pressure Cholesterol Education Mental health Nutrition Physical fitness	Income Net worth Possessions Residence Safety Sustainability Virtuous behavior	Subconscious responses to stimuli. Attraction Autonomy Engagement Competence Connection Happiness Interest Joy Love Optimism Pleasure Security	Based on learned "success criteria" Achievement Fulfillment Meaning Success	Adaptation Character strengths Intrinsic rewards Learning Psycho. Integration Purpose Skill develop. Spirituality Values clarification	Community involvement Creativity Generativity Healing Helping Innovation Leadership Mentoring Preserving eco-systems Supporting causes Teaching
Healthy	Wealthy	Happy	Satisfied	Self-Actualized	Successful

Figure 1.2. The Components of Human Flourishing

Now that you know the components of a happy and successful life, you can see where Toby missed the boat. He pursued just one dimension of a multidimensional "target." Fortunately, scientists are discovering exactly what it takes to flourish on purpose.

The Science of Human Flourishing

In 1998, the American Psychological Association elected Martin Seligman as their president. Seligman is a visionary leader with a long track record of successfully promoting new ideas and raising funds for psychological research. In his spare time, he has penned more than twenty books.

As president, Seligman articulated a powerful new mission for his peers. During his acceptance speech, he called for an expansion of psychology from fixing what's wrong with people to enhancing what's right with them. He presented his vision of a ". . . science that emphasizes the understanding and building of the most positive qualities of an individual: optimism, courage, work ethic, future-mindedness, interpersonal skill, the capacity for pleasure and insight, and social responsibility."

Seligman defined the mission for a new positive psychology that identifies and nurtures the factors that empower individuals, communities, and entire societies to flourish.

To accomplish this, Seligman founded the Positive Psychology Network, a community of scientists all over the world. They conduct research in three key areas: positive emotions, positive character traits, and positive organizations. Notice the emphasis on *positive*. Their common goal is to develop a body of scientific knowledge for living *the good life* based on universal truths of human nature. So, from Sigmund Freud's initial focus on the worst pathologies of the human mind, psychology has evolved to a more profound purpose: empowering individuals and communities to achieve their highest potential.

Positive psychology has captured the imagination of many of the best and brightest visionaries in science, business, and government. That's because they see its potential to foster a second renaissance that could ultimately transform Earth into a thriving, peaceful, and sustainable planet. To this end, thousands of psychologists are collaborating with scientists in other fields, such as biology, neurology, physiology, endocrinology, psychiatry, pharmacology, genetics, sociology, finance, and economics. Slowly but surely, they're deciphering the Endorphin Code.

Money, Happiness, and Quality of Life

What, then, have the researchers found out about the relationship between money and happiness? What might they say to Toby? Here's something to consider: when we think about earning money, the same reward circuits light up as when we think about having great sex! No doubt you've experienced earning money or receiving a big check and getting a rush of joy and excitement, just like most people do. It's no wonder they say sex and money make the world go round.

Of course, you can earn a huge income and be unhappy, like Toby. But, on average, people who earn more money are happier and healthier than people who earn less money.

To state the obvious, not having enough money for adequate shelter, food, healthcare, and clothing is stressful. As the comedian Woody Allen quipped, "Money is better than poverty, if only for financial reasons." Small problems, like a toothache or a flat tire, become major problems when you can't afford to fix them. That's why increasing income for poor people rapidly reduces their stress and increases their happiness. An additional $10,000 for someone earning $15,000 a year will create more happiness than for someone earning $250,000 a year. And it's not just a matter of proportion.

Nobel Prize–winning psychologist Daniel Kahneman and economist Angus Deaton, both at Princeton, found that once people achieve a comfortable middle class income of about $75,000 a year in America, additional earnings' impact on moment-by-moment happiness plateaus. The $75,000 level of income enables us to live a reasonably stress-free and pleasant life. Of course, this is an average. Each of us has an income comfort zone that is largely determined by our parents' values and socioeconomic status. And, of course, if you live in an expensive city, or have a big family, you'll need to earn more to be stress-free.

Seligman sums up the impact of rising income on our emotional state this way: "Once the basics like food, shelter, and clothing are paid for, more money creates surprisingly little increase in happiness."

After you have enough to pay for basic living costs, the benefits of earning more money shift from reducing hunger and stress to increasing life satisfaction. Your moment-by-moment sense of security and stability doesn't continue to improve, but your assessment of your "success," continues to rise as you earn more money, although at a slowing pace. An extra $10,000 for those earning $250,000 a year won't make any difference in their stress, security, and nutrition. But, they will perceive themselves as slightly more successful, which will boost their self-esteem and life satisfaction, a bit.

Having adequate financial resources softens the pain of life's misfortunes, such as illness, divorce, and caring for a dependent family member. More income increases positive emotions and reduces stress, until you have "enough." Then additional income continues to enhance your assessment of your "success." But, as Toby discovered, earning your way into the top one percent doesn't guarantee happiness or life satisfaction, especially if making it causes too much stress.

The Plight of Successful Miserable People

In economically advanced countries, the mass media relentlessly promotes wealth, consumption, and pleasure as the path to a good life. Our cultural heroes are the rich and famous. This cultural value motivates many people to pursue high-paying careers, but not every road to wealth leads to a satisfying, low-stress life.

Lawyers now earn the highest average incomes of any profession in America—even more than doctors do. But, things aren't all that rosy in Lawyerland. In a recent poll, fifty-two percent of practicing attorneys described themselves as dissatisfied with their lives. And out of more than a hundred careers surveyed, attorneys were the most likely to become clinically disabled because of stress and major depression.

Clearly, not all attorneys are unhappy, and many are very happy with their chosen career. Still, law now has the highest percentage of "successful miserable people" of any profession. Even so, there are more law students now than ever before. Apparently, they don't know these distressing facts about their future occupation.

Sudden wealth doesn't guarantee happiness, either. A windfall usually boosts happiness a little bit, for little a while, but researchers have discovered only a tiny long-term, positive impact on winners' happiness. On the downside, we've all heard the stories of those who've won a lottery or received a large legal settlement, and then crashed financially.

"For many people, sudden money can cause disaster," according to Susan Bradley, who's a certified financial planner in Palm Beach, Florida, and the author of *Sudden Money: Managing a Financial Windfall*. She says, "Often they can keep the money and lose family and friends–or lose the money and keep the family and friends—or even lose the money and lose the family and friends."

So if high incomes and easy money aren't guaranteed paths to a happy, flourishing life, maybe these people just don't have *enough*. What about the super wealthy?

Are the super-wealthy super-happy?

Ed Diener, a leader in the positive psychology movement, studied *Forbes* magazine's four hundred richest Americans. Diener's team asked these centi-millionaires and billionaires to rate their life satisfaction from "extremely dissatisfied" to "extremely satisfied" on a scale from one to seven. The respondents' average satisfaction rating was 5.8, only slightly more than the average American. Of special note, about three out of ten *Forbes* responders were less happy than average.

Then, in a telling comparison, Diener invited indigenous people from the plains of East Africa to participate in the same survey: The Maasai live in semi-nomadic tribes, farming deserts and scrublands. They reside in dung huts, herd cattle, have no electricity or running water, and use little or no money. But they were almost exactly as happy as the wealthiest Americans were. Their average life satisfaction was 5.7!

Intrinsic Values Enhance Our Subjective Well-Being

Clearly, wealth doesn't guarantee happiness or life satisfaction. Nor does its absence guarantee misery. Then why do people like Toby put up with so much stress to earn more money than they need? It's because of their values.

Richard Ryan and Edward Deci study the connection between people's values and motivations, and their well-being. Building on the work of earlier psychologists, they've defined two types of values that motivate us in opposite directions: *intrinsic*, or inner-directed values, and *extrinsic*, or externally directed values.

We all have a combination of both type of motivations, but the happiest and most satisfied people place the greatest value on intrinsic motivations. These "hard-wired" motivations are part of our evolutionary programming and are communicated to us via our emotions. They prod us to satisfy universal human needs, wants, and aspirations.

Scientists have discovered that, to feel happy and satisfied, we must pursue and satisfy these six intrinsic motivations:

1. security (physical and psychological),
2. community (affiliation and helping others),
3. close and intimate relationships (connection and love),
4. physical fitness (health, strength, endurance, flexibility, and vitality),

5. personal growth (toward integration and inner calm, the authentic self), and
6. self-esteem (feeling of self-worth or self-acceptance).

Intrinsically motivated people evaluate their lives based on how they feel about themselves, listening to their inner guides when deciding where to direct their life energies. They seek positive emotional states and, because they're social and altruistic, they long to contribute to a better world. Highly intrinsic people think outside the box and are often extremely creative or unconventional. Mahatma Gandhi is a classic example of an intrinsically motivated person.

Extrinsically motivated people evaluate their lives by the size of their "toys," their paychecks, net worth, and *the approval of others*. They get their cues externally, from other people and from data, when deciding where to direct their life energies. The dominant values of popular American culture are mostly extrinsic. But extrinsic motivations aren't innately rewarding; they don't satisfy universal human needs and wants. These values are mostly based on trying to meet the expectations of our parents, spouses, and peers:

1. wealth (money and material possessions),
2. power (control over others),
3. image (physical attractiveness, looking good), and
4. status and social recognition (fame, approval, fan club).

A big problem with extrinsic values is they don't motivate you to evolve or contribute to others—two areas crucial to happiness and satisfaction. Extrinsically motivated people are self-focused and, in extreme cases, narcissistic. Most of them are men. Donald Trump's public image exemplifies extrinsic values.

Innate Versus Learned Motivations	
Intrinsic Values & Motivations (Internally-Directed)	Extrinsic Values & Motivations (Externally-Directed)
In-Born Intuitions	Learned After Birth
Adaptation Affiliation Connection Contribution Growth towards Actualization Health & Fitness Vitality	Control Fame Image Influence Possessions Power Status Wealth
More Satisfying	Less Satisfying

Figure 1.3. Intrinsic Versus Extrinsic Values/Motivations

Each of us has a unique blend of both sets of values. The priority you assign to these competing "values clusters" shapes the quality of your life. Substantial research shows that pursuing and achieving intrinsic values makes people happier and more satisfied than pursuing and achieving extrinsic ones.

Intrinsically motivated people tend to be calmer and have more peak experiences. They have better and longer-lasting relationships, and they are less anxious, tense, stressed, and depressed. They experience better health and vitality and are less likely to abuse drugs and alcohol.

Clearly, happiness comes from within. That's why "following your bliss" is crucial if you want to flourish. Positive emotions guide you on an effort-less path to your naturally healthy, happy, successful self. But you need balance between these two sets of values. If you put all of your energy into pursuing intrinsic rewards, it can lead to financial disasters and dependency. Not valuing money creates more stress and unhappiness than valuing it appropriately. Balance is essential!

There's the paradox: although striving too hard for fame or fortune can make you miserable, more money can also make you happier and more satisfied. It all depends on your motivations and beliefs, and what you're doing to earn the money. To flourish, you must follow your own path and not stress yourself out to win the approval of others.

Rising Income and Happiness

Money is a funny thing. No matter how much we have, we never seem to have enough. In one survey, the average American said they needed about forty percent more income to be happy.

Our natural desire for more is based on our almost limitless capacity to adapt to changes in life circumstances. When we experience a positive change, like an increase in income, we enjoy a temporary rush of positive emotions. But we soon adapt to the new normal. Then our emotional state returns to its natural set point.

To experience another rush of happiness, we need another raise. Then we adapt again on a never-ending "hedonic treadmill" of rising income and improving standard of living, but stable happiness. It's like an addiction. The more we get, the more we want. This is the main reason that rising income has such a small impact on emotional state. We adapt easily to a new standard of living.

Further, it's human nature to compare ourselves with people above our current income level. When he was listed in *Forbes* magazine as one of America's wealthiest people, a famous Wall Street investment banker was horrified. The problem? He was on the bottom of the list. When his peer group moved up-market, his expectations changed, and his satisfaction with his life plummeted.

Relative difference, not total income, determines how satisfied we are with our earnings. Our satisfaction with our finances rises and falls depending on which social group we use for comparison.

The two psychological phenomena above, adaptation and social comparison, can be clearly seen in a curious discovery. Since 1957, the purchasing power of Americans almost tripled, rising from about $12,000 a year to about $33,000 in 2011 (in inflation-adjusted dollars). However, during that same time period, the percentage of people telling the University of Chicago's National Opinion Research Center that they were "very happy" declined from thirty-five percent to twenty-nine percent.

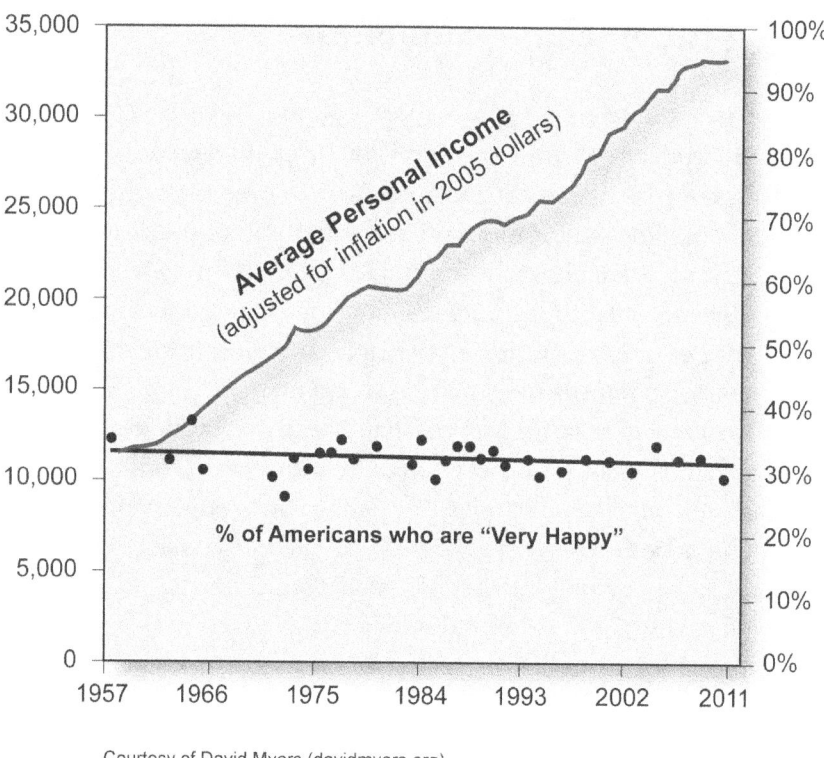

Courtesy of David Myers (davidmyers.org)

Figure 1.4. Income and Happiness.

The reason we don't all experience a surge in happiness is that everyone's income is going up, so we don't feel we're making progress where it counts: in comparison with peers. Our shared higher levels of affluence become the new normal, and our emotional state returns to its baseline level.

Americans aren't alone. Richard Easterlin and his colleagues at the University of Southern California studied thirty-seven rich and poor countries around the world. The results were the same wherever they looked: over the long term, increasing a nation's wealth doesn't increase its citizens' happiness. (If the country starts out in dire poverty, rising living standards will reduce stress and, therefore, increase happiness a bit.)

The bottom line is that it's not how much money you make; it's what you do with your life that determines how happy, secure, and satisfied you are. If money is important to you, chances are good you'll earn an above-average income. You'll probably become wealthy. Strive to do it with balance. As you acquire wealth, be sure to make money a good servant, and don't ever let it become your master.

The Key to Wealth and Happiness

About five years after my conversation with Toby, I held one of my annual Endorphin Fests in Alta, Utah. One successful investment advisor, Barry, came as the guest of a good friend. He seemed authentic, caring, and happy. He also had the most dazzling collection of ski outfits I'd ever seen.

On Wednesday night, Mother Nature blessed us with a foot of fresh Utah powder, the best snow on earth. The next morning, Barry and I hit the slopes together. It was cold, still, and clear. Deep, virgin powder covered the trees and the runs. Every skier dreams about this kind of day.

As we rode Alta's Supreme lift, Barry told me he was taking home about one million dollars a year. He asked me, "If I hire you, how much do you think I can increase my income?"

I told him that I wasn't sure, since I didn't know that much about him or his business. "But," I said, "If we decide to work together, I'll not only help you increase your income, I'll also help you increase the quality of your life."

We watched two skiers carving flawless S-curves in the East Castle bowl. Then he said quietly, "Steve, you need to understand that I'm very bottom-line oriented."

I explained that, over the previous five years, I'd instituted business-development strategies that automatically increased quality of life. I said, "I can't separate financial success from quality of life. My strategies work synergistically to build a profitable business that supports a wonderful life."

There was a long pause while we watched a skier gliding gracefully through the powder, then catching some air off a small cliff. We both let out an appreciative *aaaah*. Then Barry adjusted his goggles, turned to me, and said, "Okay, Steve, as long as this quality-of-life stuff doesn't stop me from making more money, I'll hire you."

That decision changed his life.

As he interviewed his favorite clients to better understand how he could enhance his "value proposition," Barry's beliefs about his role in their lives started to shift. He began to discover and understand his clients' long-suppressed intrinsic desires, dreams, and aspirations. Many of them wanted help clarifying what made them happy and what gave their lives meaning. He told me that he realized, "They're all financially successful, but none of them have ever had any happiness training."

Hmmm. Sound familiar?

Barry has since become the most successful investment advisor I've ever worked with. He adapted brilliantly to his new role as a "life coach who specializes in money." He started helping his clients answer many of the questions you'll encounter in this book. The deeper listening bonded him with them and revealed a higher purpose for his work. He changed his business model so he could spend more time with his clients. He outsourced time-consuming administrative processes, built a solid team, and created a foundation of recurring revenue. His stress went down, his happiness and life satisfaction went up.

One day, he realized he was experiencing more "psychic income" from helping clients than from his possessions. When the lease on his Porsche expired, he returned it to the dealership. Slowly but surely, Barry evolved from a broker striving to earn more money to an advisor striving to help his clients flourish.

Then something he never expected happened.

Barry's best clients started becoming marketing apostles, recommending their family, friends, and colleagues to him so he could help them enhance the quality of their lives. With my guidance, Barry started hosting Endorphin Events for his clients and encouraged them to bring friends.

Referrals and new accounts came in faster and easier. His business exploded! He told me he had learned the secret to wealth and happiness: "The more you help other people define and get what they want, the more you'll get what you want. I help my clients and they help me. It's win-win for everyone."

About six years after we'd started working together, Barry called one day to thank me for what we'd done together. He gave me a quick report of his new and improved life: He's home every afternoon when his kids return from school, works out ten to twenty hours every week, and is in peak physical condition. He takes more vacations, skis more than ever, and has reconnected with an old passion, magic.

"It's not about the money."

I asked him how he had time for all of these activities. He responded, "I'm probably working half as many hours as I did in the past." Since he hadn't mentioned it, I asked him about his personal income. He proudly reported, "It's grown from one million to over two-and-a-half million dollars a year! And it's continuing to accelerate."

When I asked him if he thought his quality of life, his vacations, fun activities, and shorter work hours were interfering with his income, he laughed.

"Steve, it's not about the money. It's about quality of life. Mine is fantastic and it's getting better every day." Barry's transformation was complete.

I'm sharing his story with you because it illustrates a key point. Before we met, Barry, like Toby, was prepared to sacrifice his quality of life to earn more money. He thought that putting up with stress was necessary to achieve success. But that strategy wouldn't have worked any better for him than it did for Toby.

Now, Barry's healthier, wealthier, and happier than ever and is a role model for others. He's living a wonderful life!

* * *

The good news is you don't have to be rich to flourish. A slightly above-average income is all you need. If you were able to afford to buy this book, you probably have all the money you need to create a life you love!

But this book is about having it all. No matter how happy and successful you are now, you can evolve to a higher level of flourishing. Just follow the step-by-step process in this book. Every story, fact, suggestion, and exercise will enhance your positivity and bring you closer to a flourishing life!

Oh, and if you're wondering what happened to Toby, the stress eventually forced him to sell his business. People either change because of stress-caused breakdowns, like Toby, or through deep insights, like Barry. Stress is painful, but insights, like the ones you'll gain in the pages ahead, can eliminate stress and help you live your best possible life.

ENDORPHIN EVENT #1
How Much Money Do You "Need" to Be Happy?

Each chapter in this book ends with a thirty- to ninety-minute activity you can do by yourself or with others. (Don't let your family and friends be "endorphin orphans"; consider starting a monthly Endorphin Society meeting.)

Summarize this chapter for your guests by going through the pages and using the subheads and graphics to share the key points. Then brainstorm on the following topics.

1. How has your perception of the relationship between money and quality of life changed after reading this chapter?
2. Appreciate how good your life is by comparing yourself to others who are less fortunate. Discuss the things that you're grateful for in your life.
3. Based on the information in this chapter, estimate how much income you need to earn to eliminate all financial stress and feel optimistic about your future. This is the gross income that will allow you to pay all your taxes and living expenses, invest for a financially independent retirement, and have plenty of money for emergencies, opportunities, fun, and adventure.
4. How much income and/or net worth do you need to feel successful—as you define it?
5. If you suddenly had so much money that you could never run out, what would you probably do with your life? Make a prioritized list.
6. Which of the things you listed in #5 above can you do, experience, or accomplish with your current income and resources?
7. What will you do differently in the future, based on your insights from this chapter?

2

The Purpose of Positive Emotions

I say, follow your bliss and don't be afraid, and doors will open where you didn't know there were going to be doors.
—Joseph Campbell

One day, before attending a meeting in a seedy redevelopment area of downtown Los Angeles, I ventured across the street to buy a cup of coffee. The mean streets of "Hell-A" were bustling with pimps, prostitutes, druggies, alcoholics, hustlers, stockbrokers, and business people. As I absentmindedly jangled the coins in my pocket while waiting for a green light, I noticed a huge, filthy, homeless "outdoorsman" walking straight toward me.

My shoulders instinctively hunched forward as I looked away. Soon the behemoth was hovering over me, panting with fetid breath. Trapped by the people waiting for the light to change, I repeatedly pushed the WALK button, and a voice in my head screamed, *When the light turns green, RUN!*

My stomach clenched as I waited anxiously. My wife and I support many charities, but I have a cardinal rule never to give money to street beggars. I dreaded his reaction when I said, "No." I prayed he'd disappear.

But that's not how it went down.

"Sir," he said forcefully, thrusting his upturned palm at me. Our eyes met, his red and watery, mine dilated by fear. His face lit up in a gap-toothed grin as he cheerfully inquired, "Can you spare a thousand dollars?"

Belly laughing at his patently absurd request, my fear turned to delight, and a wave of relief washed over me. Without thinking, I rewarded him for cheering up my morning.

"No, but here's seventy-five cents!" I handed him my spare change.

Laughter is one of the best ways to loosen people up. When my emotional state changed from negative to positive, my behavior changed from stingy to generous, and I instantly abandoned my long-held rules and well-planned strategy. My behavior changed instantly when my emotional state changed.

Understanding Human Emotions

Mental processes are the foundation of human nature. And emotions are the key motivators and regulators of our mental processes. Tellingly, the Latin root for *emotion* means, "to move." No aspect of human life is more important to flourishing than your emotional state. Your feelings color every moment of your life and have a powerful impact on your thinking, behavior, health, wealth, and overall happiness.

All humans share the same basic emotions, and most of us easily recognize these seven emotions in peoples' faces: anger, contempt, disgust, fear, joy, sadness, and surprise. Other common emotions include amusement, contentment, embarrassment, elation, excitement, guilt, interest, love, pride, relief, satisfaction, shame, and sensory pleasure.

Our emotions subconsciously anticipate, evaluate, and instantly respond to changes in our outer environment or inner thoughts. When triggered, emotions automatically shift and coordinate the way we think, perceive the world, communicate, and behave—they also alter our outer, physical features, such as body language and vocal tone, along with our inner physiology, such as blood pressure and heart rate. Then they urge us to take immediate action to avoid threats or pursue opportunities.

What of logic? What role does it play in how we feel and act? Certainly, our thoughts and beliefs play a huge role in our emotional state. And they moderate and direct our emotional drives.

Through their belief systems, customs, and laws, different cultures suppress or encourage the expression of different emotions. Modern, technological societies generally discourage people from paying attention to their emotions. This is too bad, because emotions are powerful "inner guides" if you know how and when to listen to them.

So, emotions combine with logical processes and learned values and beliefs to shape your behavior. To flourish, you must understand and "harness" these natural mental processes.

We Have Three Brains in One

A typical adult brain weighs about three pounds and consists of approximately eighty-six billion jellylike, pinkish-grey neurons, or brain cells. Although it represents only about three percent of your body weight, your brain uses more than twenty-five percent of your energy—even when you're sleeping. With over five hundred trillion interconnections, your brain is one of the most complex structure in the universe.

Today's high-tech imaging technologies, especially functional magnetic resonance imaging (fMRI), are helping neurobiologists develop new theories about the true nature and purpose of our emotions and logic, and our brain's architecture.

While conducting research at the National Institute of Mental

Health way back in the 1970s, neuroscientist Paul MacLean realized that the human brain could actually be thought of as three brains in one. He discovered that your three "mini-brains" can be separated like the sections of an orange, and function like "three interconnected biological computers."

However, rather than resembling a state-of-the-art computer system, your brain resembles a ramshackle old network that was added on to over the years by successive generations of managers. Each new mini-brain wrapped around and integrated with the lower brain center(s), adding a distinct information-processing capability

The original structures and functions remain, because they still serve their purpose. But each addition was much more sophisticated than the earlier structure(s). Each new bio-computer added a different type of intelligence that addressed key limitations of the previous one(s). Each successive mini-brain dramatically increased our species' ability to adapt, survive, and reproduce.

The three mini-brains are 1) your "survival-focused: reptilian brain, 2) your "emotional" mammalian brain, and 3) your "thinking" hominid brain.

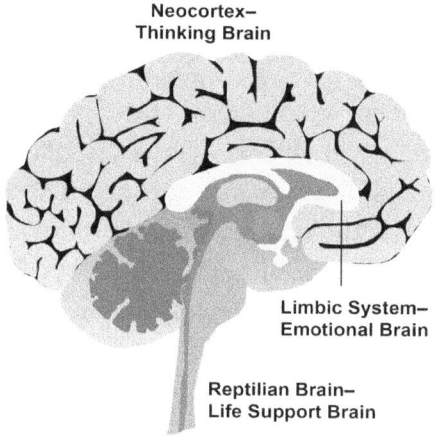

Figure 2.1. Three Brains in One

THE PURPOSE OF POSITIVE EMOTIONS

In healthy humans, all three mini-brains work together in a synergistic balance of feelings, thoughts, drives, and behaviors. But each one has the primary responsibility for a specific cognitive function involved in acquiring, storing, and assessing stimuli, and then generating appropriate responses.

Your "Survival-Focused" Reptilian Brain

Also known as the "hindbrain," the reptilian brain is the oldest, most primal information-processing system in humans. It first appeared in our ancestors about 450 million years ago. Your reptilian brain is located at the base of your skull, where it sits on top of your spinal column. This structure is almost exactly the same as the entire brain of ancient dinosaurs and modern reptiles.

The reptilian mini-brain is the center of all *reflexive and instinctive functions*. It has one mission: to keep you alive. *It's hardwired with life supporting bio-programs* that motivate one of two basic behaviors; approach or avoidance It's primarily responsible for instinctive behaviors such as feeding, elimination, social, and sexual dominance, and reproduction. It's also responsible for involuntary bodily functions such as heartbeat, breathing, digestion, etc.

Your reptilian brain's instinctive reactions to threats or opportunities are selfish, rigid, obsessive, compulsive, ritualistic, status-oriented, and paranoid. This mini-brain can be conditioned to behave habitually, but it can't learn to "connect the dots" to adapt to new situations.

Since this primitive brain can't learn from experience, it repeats the same set of hard-wired behaviors over and over again, regardless of the results. That's why you can't train a snake.

Your "Emotional" Mammalian Brain

Also known as the limbic system, the mammalian brain wraps around and sits on top of your reptilian brain. It's *the brain's emotional center and communications hub,* having extensive connections with your other two brains. The first version of this brain appeared in early mammals about 150 million years ago.

The limbic system greatly enhances your chances of surviving and reproducing because it learns from experience, emotionally tagging important ones for future reference. When it encounters a similar threat (negative emotional tag) or opportunity (positive emotional tag), it uses hindsight, gained from past experiences, to respond more appropriately than your reptilian brain.

This brain includes the pleasure centers and reward system that motivate you to pursue opportunities and resources. It also contains the amygdale, our brain's fear center that identifies threats and triggers the distress response.

Networks of neurons in your limbic system enable you to experience and express your emotions. They generate subtle and complex emotions such as hope and elation. In addition, it process more primal ones generated by your reptilian brain including fear, anger, jealousy, anxiety, rage, hedonic pleasure, sadness, and surprise.

Most importantly, circuits in your limbic system generate the pro-social emotions of attachment, empathy, connection, bonding, and parental love. They motivate mammals to care for their young instead of eating them like reptiles do. This brain is responsible for social cohesion in many species of mammals, including humans.

The mammalian brain also plays a key role in intentional behaviors like focusing attention, fighting, playing, courtship, learning, and remembering. Dogs are trainable because they have a well-developed limbic systems.

Your "Thinking" Hominid Brain

Your neocortex, the hominid brain, is the newest and largest of the three brains. When you look at a brain in a jar, you see the pinkish-grey neocortex, the outermost layer that makes up almost eighty percent of the brain's mass.

Early versions of this mini-brain appeared in our ancestors about 2.5 million years ago. It then went through a few million years of rapid evolution until it emerged in its current form only about 100,000 years ago. Humans share this brain structure with higher

THE PURPOSE OF POSITIVE EMOTIONS

mammals, such as great apes, dolphins, and whales.

The neocortex is your brain's command and control center. Like a CEO, it coordinates the activities of all three mini brains and is responsible for focusing attention, goal setting and achievement, decision-making, planning, initiating action, monitoring progress, and adjusting behavior.

It thinks logically and intentionally, acquires languages, and learns math. It's the center of consciousness, self-reflection, reason, intuition, inspiration, science, and culture. It's responsible for civilizations and modern, technological societies. According to MacLean, the neocortex "contains our model of reality."

This brain is highly interconnected with the two lower brains, especially the limbic system. In synergistic cooperation with that mini-brain, it learns, remembers, solves problems, and innovates new and better ways of doing things. MacLean calls the neocortex "the mother of invention and the father of abstract thought."

This brain added a spectacular new dimension to human intelligence; foresight, the ability to envision the future. The rich interplay between your neocortex and limbic system empowers you to dream of new possibilities, imagine better futures, set goals, make plans, and take action to turn your vision into reality. Your neocortex empowers you to go beyond surviving; it empowers you to flourish.

Because it can foresee potential consequences of your actions, your neocortex often tries to inhibit or moderate your selfish, short-term emotional and instinctive urges. When someone admonishes you to, "Stop and think about it," they're asking you to use your hominid brain.

Conventional thinking says your neocortex's role is to help satisfy the survival needs your two lower brains. A more empowering way of thinking is that the two lower brains exist to support the intuitions and visions of your higher brain.

Throughout each day, dominance constantly shifts between your three brains, depending on your emotional state. When you're experiencing positive emotions, your neocortex and limbic system actively communicate to perform higher brain functions like intuition, self-reflection, problem solving, or visualizing a design. In this higher state of consciousness, your mind, body, and soul work together synergistically to maximize your intelligence, creativity, and resourcefulness.

But when you experience negative emotions, your hominid brain instantly shuts down, blood drains out of it, and your survival oriented lower brains take control of your behavior.

Criticism, fear, and other forms of negativity also cause you to downshift to your lower brain functions. You upshift to your higher brain functions only when you experience positive emotions. That's why praise, appreciation, empathetic listening, and other forms of positivity unlock your brain's higher potential.

Now you understand the connection between positive emotions and higher thought processes that empower you to flourish.

The Purpose of Negative Emotions

A few years ago, I went hiking in the forest surrounding a conference I was attending. When my friends and I checked in with the camp manager to get directions, he warned us to take plenty of water and "watch out for rattlesnakes."

We set off into the dense pine forest with a watchful eye. When we came to a fallen log blocking our path, the hiker in front of me started to step over it. As she looked down to where her foot was about to land, she froze and let out a scream. Springing backward into my chest, she knocked us both to the ground. *Whoomp!*

"Snake! Snake!" She shrieked as we rolled away from the danger. Then, as she stood up and peered over the log, her face broke into a big grin, and she tried to stifle her cry of, "Arrgghhh!"

"I'm so sorry." She apologized as we dusted off our pants. "It wasn't a snake; it's only a stick."

Naturally, I kidded her for reacting so dramatically to a piece of wood. But I knew that knocking me on my butt wasn't a conscious decision. In fact, her neocortex wasn't even aware of the "snake" until she was out of harm's way. Her primal, reptilian brain had instantly

THE PURPOSE OF POSITIVE EMOTIONS

taken control and catapulted her away from the "threat" before her hominid brain was consciously aware of it. No higher-level, logical thinking had been required.

When her emotional brain assessed the stick as a possible threat, it triggered the powerful negative emotion of fear and a classic distress response. In a split second, a cascade of physiological changes prepared her to survive a physical threat. Adrenaline and cortisol flooded into her blood stream to boost her energy. Her breathing and heart rates accelerated while blood from her digestive tract and neocortex was shunted into her arms and legs.

Strong negative emotions allowed her reptilian brain to hijack her thinking processes, instantly narrowing her options to one of only three possible behaviors: fight, flee, or freeze. Without consciously thinking, she'd reflexively sprung away from possible mortal danger.

My companion's response to the "snake" was a classic example of the purpose of negative emotions.

Negative emotions, such as fear, anger, and disgust, prompt specific actions that evolved though natural selection to help you survive threats. They motivate you to avoid dangers, thoughts, behaviors, and people that threaten your survival or cause you pain. They also signal you to stop doing whatever you're doing.

Neuropsychologist Rick Hanson says, "Because the human brain evolved during a time when danger was everywhere, it has a built-in negativity bias." Only the hyper vigilant survived.

Negative emotions play a key role in survival. But they also shut you down and cause you to think win-lose. So don't let your negativity bias pull you down. To flourish, you must minimize negative emotions and learn from them without suppressing or indulging them.

Indulging and expressing negative emotions, such as anger, makes them stronger. And when you're enraged, the person you're most likely to hurt is yourself. Although "venting" anger and rage has been a popular recommendation in the past, you'll learn better ways to deal with negative emotions in the pages ahead.

So pay attention to your negative emotions. They'll help you avoid pain, frustration, danger, and disappointments. But focus your thoughts and efforts on minimizing the frequency and intensity of negative emotions and maximizing the frequency of positive emotions.

The Purpose of Positive Emotions

Late in 1998, Barbara Fredrickson published a landmark scientific paper, "What Good Are Positive Emotions?" Back then, the prevailing theories all had a major problem: a substantial number of emotions didn't fit the theories (or the theories didn't fit the emotions).

After reviewing many previous studies, especially those by Alice Isen of Cornell University, Fredrickson formulated a new theory that elegantly explained *all* emotions. Her insights led Martin Seligman to call her the "genius of the positive psychology movement."

Previously, scientific theories had dumped all emotions into the same pot. Fredrickson's paper presented a well-documented case for separating emotions into two distinct types: 1) the obvious and dramatic negative ones and 2) the more subtle and fleeting positive ones.

Fredrickson proved that avoidance-oriented negative emotions evolved first. Their purpose is to instantly fire up your bodily systems to help you avoid or survive physical threats. This is what happened when the hiker in front of me thought she saw a snake.

Fredrickson's biggest contribution was her discovery that approach-oriented positive emotions evolved to help us flourish. She showed that they motivate us to learn, grow, adapt, and acquire resources. They also encourage us to continue what we're doing (don't stop), or to do it again. In addition, they signal that we're secure and that there are no threats, so we can let our guard down and relax.

One more key purpose; positive emotions alert us to opportunities for meaningful personal growth.

You experience positive emotions when you perceive an opportunity. They alert you with a promise of future pleasure, motivating you to explore and, if appropriate, pursue the opportunity. When you satisfy a need, want, or aspiration, you're rewarded with more positive feelings.

THE PURPOSE OF POSITIVE EMOTIONS

Emotions Help Us Survive and Flourish

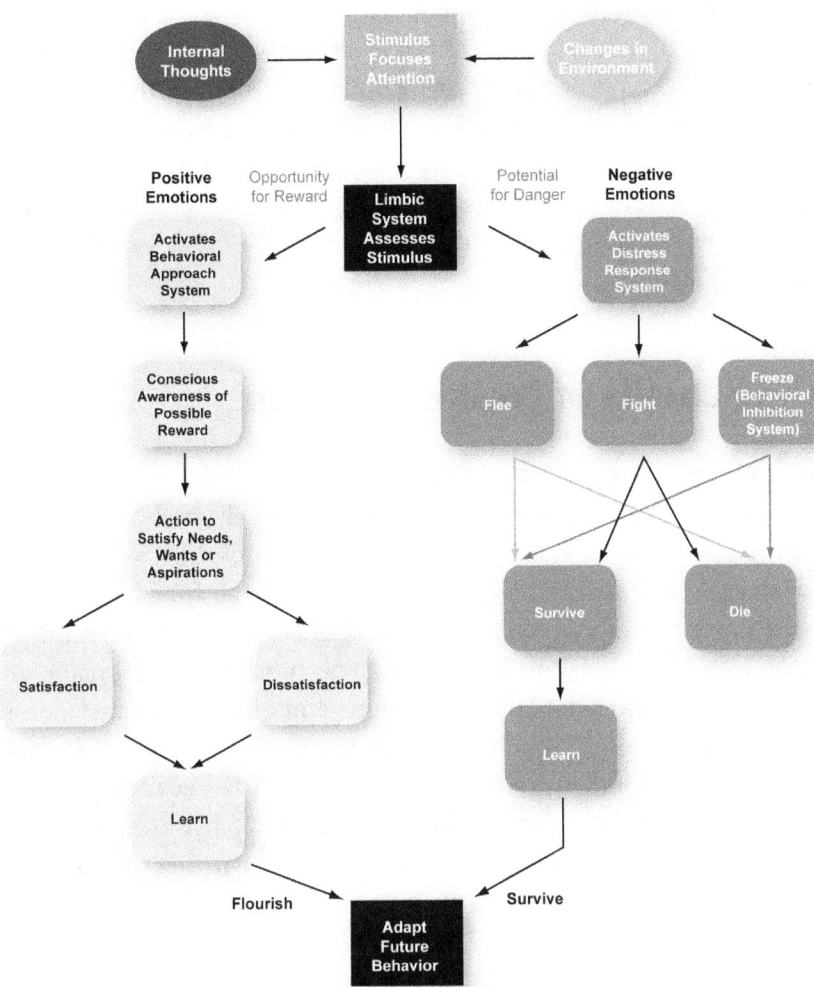

Figure 2.2. Human Emotional Responses

Picture our ancient ancestors sitting around a campfire after a successful hunt and feast. Everyone is fat and happy. They're safe at home, with family and friends and a full belly, enjoying shared celebrations. The hunters have accomplished a critically important task, and the flood of positive feelings reward them for their effort and motivates them to want to repeat the experience, soon.

So, at one end of the spectrum, positive emotions signal opportunity for some type of reward, which revs you up. On the other end, they signal safety and satisfaction which calms you down.

Although they're more fleeting and subtle than negative emotions, positive emotions such as amusement, awe, gratitude, hope, interest, inspiration, joy, love, pride, and serenity are the foundation for human flourishing.

The Benefits of Positive Emotions

Positive emotions dramatically enhance your mental processes, changing the way you perceive the world and your behavior. When you're feeling good, you're more optimistic and generous. You see the world as safer and the glass as half-full. If you're applying for a job, you'll be rated more favorably. You'll be more cooperative, helpful, and charitable with others. Happy states make you more trusting, loving, and responsive, supporting a richer social life and greater life satisfaction.

And there's more good news. Happier people are strikingly more decisive, self-confident, and outgoing. They have better coping abilities and are less likely to get upset over minor criticisms or problems. They also have greater self-control, which makes them more patient and persistent. Those are some of the intangible benefits of staying in the Endorphin Zone.

Amazingly, all of the intangible benefits lead directly to substantial *tangible* benefits, including more:

- productivity and better work quality;
- achievement, income, and wealth;
- openness to new ideas and adaptability to new ways of doing things;
- comfort with uncertainty;

- deferment of immediate gratification and achievement of longer-term rewards;
- creativity, innovation, and successful problem solving;
- effective decision making
- resilience, persistence, and tenacity;
- satisfying and longer marriages;
- social support and feelings of closeness with friends;
- physical activity and engagement;
- physical health and vitality; and
- years of life.

One of Fredrickson's most profound insights had to do with the long-term benefits of positive emotions. Unlike negative emotions, which severely constrain our thinking and behavior, Fredrickson found that positive emotions "broaden people's ideas about possible actions, opening up awareness to a wider range of thoughts and actions than is typical." In short, feeling good promotes questioning, thinking, and acting in new ways. And even though positive emotions and the changes they evoke are fleeting, their benefits accumulate over a lifetime.

This increased "novel and unscripted behavior"—new ways of thinking and acting—empowers you to acquire and build mental, psychological, social, physical, financial, and material resources.

How do they do that? Here are some of Fredrickson's key insights about the long-term benefits of positive emotions.

Learning, Knowledge, and Memory

Positive emotions, such as interest and curiosity, urge you to become deeply engaged in learning and problem solving. They broaden your attention and thinking by motivating you to explore and investigate interesting people, novel objects, new ideas, or unfamiliar situations. Then they narrow and sharpen your attention as you focus in on a new area of interest.

Exploring and investigating places, things, and ideas enables you to develop more accurate and complete "mental models" of your world. In the process, you acquire new knowledge, resources, skills, relationships, and experiences. This greater understanding results in more integrated and flexible ways of solving problems and adapting to new situations. You can bank your new mental resources and use them in future times of need or opportunity.

Interest and curiosity aren't the only positive emotions that enhance your knowledge; all positive feelings help you learn and recall information. In fact, just thinking happy thoughts can significantly improve your learning and memory.

In one study, before taking a test, subjects contemplated a past positive experience for a little less than a minute. The happy memory put them in positive mood, which switched on their higher brain functions. The result? They achieved higher tests scores than they had achieved in a neutral state. Putting yourself in a positive mood is a foolproof way to increase your intelligence and mental performance.

Resilience

In psychology, the term *resilience* refers to the ability to bounce back after setbacks. Resilience shields you from debilitating depression when you're overwhelmed by life's challenges; it's a key component of mental health and is closely linked with optimism and hope. Happy people recover more quickly from breakdowns and cope better with chronic stressors.

Positive states allow you to step back from your current situation and consider it from different perspectives. This empowers you to reframe events in a more positive light, which changes your emotional response.

Amazingly, scientists have discovered that you can store up and bank your resilience. Then you can draw on your reserves when you need to overcome future challenges. So the best way to increase your ability to bounce back and overcome obstacles is to increase your level of positivity—now.

THE PURPOSE OF POSITIVE EMOTIONS

Health, Vitality, and Energy

Joy, excitement, enthusiasm, zest, and related positive emotions all make us feel playful and energetic. Fredrickson's team found that joy and playfulness build a variety of physical, social, and psychological resources. And it's widely known that physical activity fosters positive emotions—so it's a bit of a chicken and egg. Does the emotion make you want to "jump for joy," or does the movement itself lift your spirits?

In this physical-emotional loop, the benefits are big. Aerobic exercise, sports, and play help you build your muscles and maintain your cardiovascular system. For youngsters, many games enhance hand-eye coordination.

Some games flex your problem-solving skills, while team sports teach you how to work together. The fun physical experiences of chasing, touching, and even tackling each other, strengthens your body and builds relationships.

Relationships

Positive emotions urge us to start new relationships and encourage us to strengthen existing ones. Happy people are more charismatic and attractive to others. This is significant because positive relationships are one of your most important resources. In stressful times, family, friends, and colleagues give you emotional support. In good times, they share information, lend you resources, and provide advice.

Since they're "contagious," positive emotions reverberate through groups of people. For instance, a person who is feeling good is more likely to commit a kind act or help someone else. That person in turn is likely to help another in an upward spiral of positive emotions and win-win relationships. This leads to more healthy, peaceful, cohesive, and prosperous societies.

Creativity and Problem Solving

Positive emotions open your mind to more creative, resourceful, and visionary ways of thinking. While negative emotions trigger narrow, tunnel-vision thinking, positive emotions foster wide-angle, global thinking. They empower you to see clearly and think effectively, opening you to new possibilities, new relationships, and new connections between thoughts and ideas.

When you experience positive emotions, you process information in more holistic and flexible ways. This makes happy people better at problem solving, innovating, and adapting to new situations.

On standard creativity tests, the happiest participants consistently outperform the unhappy folks. In one study, participants were given a challenging problem to solve. When researchers boosted their emotional state by having them watch a comedy film, seventy-five percent of them were able to solve the problem. But only thirteen percent of the subjects in the control group, who didn't watch the comedy, were able to solve it.

Income

Numerous studies show that happy, optimistic people earn more money than their less happy peers do. (Remember Barry from the beginning of this book?) And happiness leads to higher income; higher income doesn't lead to happiness.

In 1976, a study of college students included questions about their happiness. Researchers then re-interviewed the alums at age thirty-seven. As they approached midlife, the happiest of them were earning significantly more money than their less happy peers.

Happy people earn higher incomes because they're more energetic, productive, cooperative, innovative, and adaptable. They're also more likely to get a good education, find suitable work, be healthy, and be promoted faster. Finally, they're more confident, competent, and self-controlled, so the quality of their work is higher.

Happier people are diligent workers and make positive contributions to their company, society and the world. All of these beneficial behaviors and ways of thinking empower happy people to acquire more wealth.

Wealth

Imagine that ten people live on an island and fish every day, all day long, for food. They catch just enough fish to feed themselves. Then, one of them invents a net. Using this new technology, two islanders can catch enough fish to feed all ten people.

Because they no longer need to spend all their time fishing, the eight other people can now develop specialized skills to produce a greater variety and quantity of goods. One builds houses, another makes clothes, a third becomes a healer, a fourth grows a garden, a fifth becomes an artist, etc.

The upshot is that the new technology (the fishing net) allows this small group of people to produce more goods and services than they could before—more than they need to consume each day. Since they produce more, they can save for the future. In other words, they accumulate wealth. Throughout history, each new technological era has dramatically increased humankind's productivity and our ability to manage and harvest nature's wealth, and to create human-made wealth.

So, if technology is the key to productivity and, thus, wealth, what's the key to technology? The answer is research and innovation. What motivates and empowers us to research, innovate, overcome challenges, and create new and better technologies? The answer, as you've learned, is positive emotions!

Positive emotions are the spark behind all innovation. In fact, it's impossible to think creatively unless we're in a positive state. Negative emotions restrict blood flow to our neo-cortex causing our higher thinking and problem-solving functions to shut down.

As you've learned, wealth isn't the key to happiness. But, because they're the drivers behind all productivity-enhancing inventions, *positive emotions are the foundation for all wealth creation in advanced societies.*

This is a stunning revelation that has many implications, both for individuals and entire societies: more happiness will lead to more discoveries, innovations, productivity, and wealth.

You can see why Fredrickson says, "Simply experiencing positive emotions, our ancestors would have naturally accrued more personal resources." This is exactly what happened in America. A small country founded on the pursuit of happiness quickly became the world's wealthiest nation.

The good news is that you can nurture, enhance, and permanently increase your happiness and life satisfaction. And those positive thoughts and emotions will help you live a fuller, richer more satisfying life—on the upward spiral of human flourishing. But getting there will take time, effort, and persistence. That's why *committing to flourishing is the first step to living your best possible life.*

The Purpose of Human Emotions	
Positive Emotions	**Negative Emotions**
Help us thrive over time	Help us survive immediate threats
Motivate us to *approach opportunities*	Motivate us to *avoid threats*
Signal growth opportunities	Signal potential danger
Trigger relaxation and eustress response	Trigger distress response
Release dopamine, endorphins, serotonin, etc., into the nervous system	Release the stress hormones adrenaline and cortisol into the blood stream
Primarily trigger psychological and behavioral changes to acquire resources	Primarily trigger physiological changes to survive a physical threat
Broaden thinking and acting to new and innovative ways of satisfying needs and wants	Narrow thinking and acting to flight, fight, or freeze
Create long-term health benefits	Create depression, disease, and early death
Lead to an upward spiral of flourishing	Lead to a downward spiral of languishing

Figure 2.3. Positive Versus Negative Emotions

Although positive emotions empower us to adapt, build resources and flourish, they also have another, more sublime purpose. They empower us to transcend ordinary states of consciousness and connect deeply with nature and the divine.

Positive Moments, Peak Experiences, and Transcendence

Hiking deep into the Upper Amazon, I was on my way to photograph a waterfall considered sacred by the local people, the Naparona. It was a bright, sunny day, but deep in the ravine under the dense jungle canopy, it was dark and wet. About one hundred feet above me, at the top of the cliff, an enormous variety of trees reached another 150 feet toward the sun.

As my companions and I rounded a bend, the narrow canyon opened up, a ray of sunlight shot through several hundred feet of darkness to the stream bed in front of me. Pausing to rest, I watched the light dancing on the water.

Right in front of me, an iridescent green butterfly circled in the sun's ray. All around her was deep shadow, but she glowed in the brilliant sunlight. On a whim, I plunged my hand into the light and playfully commanded, "Come to papa." Amazingly, that exquisite little creature flew over and landed on my finger.

I pulled my hand closer to my face for a better look. As I peered into her big, black eyes, she leisurely flapped her wings. The green, teal, and aqua patterns shimmered brightly in the sunlight, enchanting me.

As I savored the experience, a feeling of connection with the butterfly, the rainforest, and nature came over me. I closed my eyes and luxuriated in the sounds of the jungle and the nearby waterfall, the birds calling, and the insects chirping. Silently, I thanked the butterfly for this enchanting experience. Then she flew off into the jungle.

The waterfall was spectacular, but my encounter with the green butterfly was one of the most memorable endorphin moments of my life!

Peak experiences like this are characterized by a profound sense of selfless wonder, awe, extreme joy, and universal love and unity. During these mystical moments, we feel an ecstatic state of merging into or connecting with a larger presence.

The intensity of peak experiences ranges along a continuum from mild euphoria to ecstatic, life-transforming, spiritual epiphanies, eliciting thoughts and feelings that are qualitatively different from ordinary states of consciousness.

In these non-ordinary states of consciousness, people forget their physical needs and become absorbed in the ecstasy of the moment. These deeply spiritual moments of "oneness" can change the trajectory of the experiencer's life. In some cases, they've changed the course of history.

Many spiritual transcenders are awestruck and at a loss for words to communicate their mystical experiences, often describing them with unusual terms, such as "oceanic bliss." During these experiences, religious people believe they're connecting with their god or gods. Non-religious people interpret these feelings as a connection with nature or some other "higher power."

People in these extraordinary, spiritual states experience a mixture of eight positive emotions:

- awe (wonder, amazement),
- compassion (empathy, care),
- forgiveness (renouncing anger or resentment),
- hope (optimism, encouragement),
- gratitude (appreciation, thankfulness),
- joy (gladness, happiness),
- love (attachment, connection, closeness), and
- trust (faith).

People who experience these ethereal states consistently report a diminished sense of self and a profound sense of oneness with everyone and everything in the universe. The most common situations that evoke transcendence are praying and communing with nature. So,

THE PURPOSE OF POSITIVE EMOTIONS

if you crave intense positive emotional/spiritual experiences, spend more time praying and in nature.

But don't get hung up on pursuing extremely rare and intense positive states such as spiritual ecstasy. They're notoriously difficult to evoke on purpose. And, it's more beneficial to experience many milder endorphin moments, throughout every day. For optimizing the quality of your life, the frequency of positive emotions is more important than the intensity.

Before we go on, take a moment to determine where you are currently on the spectrum of human emotions.

The Spectrum of Human Emotions					
Negative Emotions			**Positive Emotions**		
Psycho Zone	Medicated Zone	Cocktail Zone	Relaxation Zone	Comfort Zone	Endorphin Zone
Aggressive Angry Anxious Catatonic Contemptuous Disgusted Enraged Fearful Horrified Miserable Suffering Suicidal Tormented Violent	Agitated Annoyed Depressed Disappointed Disheartened Distressed Doubtful Envious Exasperated Flat Helpless Insecure Irritated Pained Remorseful Sad Shamed Zoned Out	Aimless Bored Embarrassed Frustrated Guilty Harried Overcommitted Powerless Purposeless Nervous Time pressured Tense Stressed	Calm Entertained Happy Relaxed Relieved Secure Serene	Affectionate Amused Comfortable Compassionate Connected Content Empathetic Fun Hopeful Meaningful Pleasant Satisfied	Accomplished Awed Cheerful Competent Curious Delighted Ecstatic Empowered Engaged Euphoric Excited Fulfilled Grateful Independent Inspired Interested Joyful Laughing Loved Optimistic Proud Purposeful Spiritual Surprised Transcendent Zestful
Very Negative		Slightly Negative	Slightly Positive		Very Positive
-10 -9 -8 -7 -6 -5 -4		-3 -2 -1	0 +1 +2 +3	+4 5 +6	7 8 +9 +10
Circle the number that indicates where are <u>you</u> most of the time, on this *spectrum?*					

Figure 2.4. The Spectrum of Human Emotions

Circle the number from -10 to +10 that describes your overall life, right now. That's your starting point. Now, ask yourself a very important question, *What percentage of my time do I spend in the Positive Zones?*

The Happiness Tipping Point

More happiness is generally better. But how much is enough—and is there such a thing as being too happy?

Fredrickson and her colleague, Marcial Losada, knew that experiencing more positive emotions than negative ones leads us on an upward spiral of flourishing. But they didn't know how much was enough.

Losada, a mathematician and organizational-development consultant, believed he could figure out the "exact positivity ratio that would distinguish those who flourished from those who didn't." With his statistical skills and her research skills, Losada and Fredrickson soon calculated a positivity tipping point.

They concluded that, on average, humans must experience a minimum of about three positive emotional episodes for every negative one. Above this tipping point, we grow, adapt, and flourish. Below it, we languish. The ideal positivity ratio is about five to one.

Fredrickson likens the unique tipping point of each individual to the freezing point of water. Above thirty-two degrees Fahrenheit, water is liquid, flowing, flexible, and dynamic. But, just one degree colder, below the tipping point, and water turns to ice: solid, rigid, and immobile.

I call Fredrickson's "positivity zone" the *Endorphin Zone*.

Although other scientists have challenged Fredrickson and Losada's methodology and ability to quantify the exact tipping point for every person in every situation, their conclusions provide a useful reference point.

Sadly, Fredrickson's research discovered that four out of five Americans don't achieve the minimum three-to-one positivity threshold. Clearly, the world needs more positivity.

Still, you don't need to aim for full-time positive emotions. Once the positivity ratio is greater than twelve to one, the benefits start to flatten out. Besides, the right amount of challenge and stress actually helps you flourish, as long as it's not overwhelming. No negative feedback indicates you aren't trying and failing at new things. That means you aren't stretching, learning, or growing.

You experience greater success and happiness in the long run if you step outside your comfort zone, embrace challenges and use them to become smarter, better, and stronger.

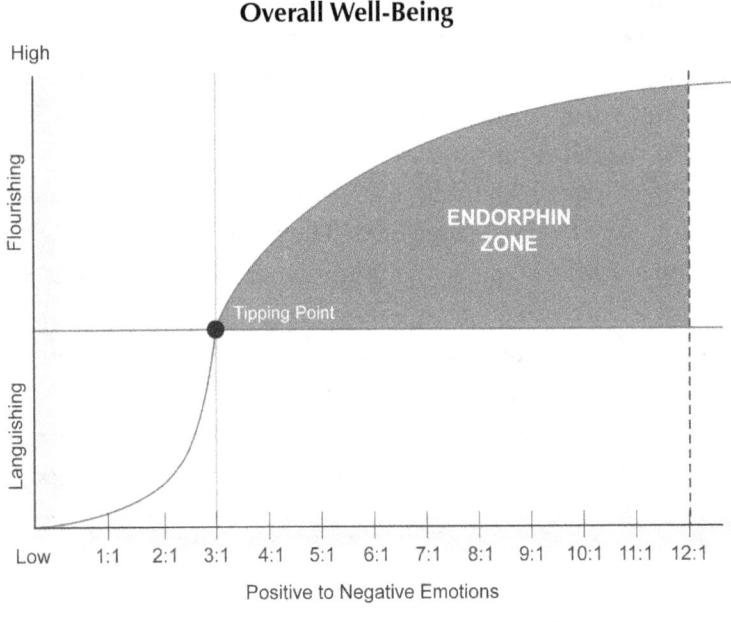

When we're experiencing between three and eleven positive experiences for every negative one, we flourish. This means we need to be experiencing positive emotions between seventy-five percent (3:1) and ninety-two percent (11:1) of the time. You can determine your current positivity ratio on Fredrickson's website, PositivityRatio.com.

* * *

A key premise of psychology is that humans are hardwired to express our "human-ness" by actively striving to become our authentic, natural selves. To flourish, each of us must constantly grow and evolve, to achieve more of our potential and to become our best possible selves. Fortunately, one of the greatest benefits of positive emotions is they signal opportunities for personal growth and psychological integration.

Positive emotions automatically direct our attention and mental energy to personal areas that are ripe for change. Fredrickson says, "Instead of solving problems of immediate survival . . . positive emotions solve problems concerning personal development and growth." Pursuing positive emotions is one of the most powerful things you can do to enhance your health, wealth, and happiness!

Fredrickson discovered that positive emotions are far more powerful than most of us ever imagined. They don't just feel good in the moment; they fundamentally transform you for the better, making you more optimistic, creative, energetic, resilient, and socially connected. Broadening your thinking empowers you to adapt to new situations, pursue new opportunities, and to acquire resources.

Charles Darwin said, "It is not the strongest of the species that survives, nor the most intelligent, it is the one that is most adaptable to change." We live in a rapidly changing world that requires us to constantly adapt and evolve just to keep up. Staying in the Endorphin Zone, your happiest, most resourceful state, is the key to flourishing in any environment.

ENDORPHIN EVENT #2
Discuss What Makes You Happy and Satisfied

Summarize this chapter for your guests by going through the pages and using the subheads and graphics to share the key points. Then brainstorm on the following topics.

1. Recall specific times when positive emotions attracted you to an opportunity to acquire resources, build relationships, or to evolve and grow. Discuss what happened, how you felt, and the tangible results.
2. Recall and share endorphin moments and peak experiences with each other. These are moments of intense happiness, joy, or transcendence. Where were you? What were you doing? How did you feel? What insights did you get from these positive experiences?
3. What are you happy about right now? What are you satisfied with right now?
4. Make a short "endorphin report" describing your positive moments yesterday and what triggered them. What did it feel like? What sensory memories do you have? (Sights, sounds, touches, smells, tastes?)
5. What puts you in a positive state each day? Make a list of endorphin-enhancing activities.
6. What is your current positivity ratio on positivity.com?
7. What percentage of the time are you in the Endorphin Zone?
8. How can you increase your positivity ratio, spend more time in the Endorphin Zone, and enjoy more peak experiences?
9. What will you do differently in the future, based on your insights from this chapter?

3

Endorphins Each Day Keep the Doctors Away

> *A cheerful heart is good medicine.*
> *But a crushed spirit dries up the bones.*
> —**Proverbs 17:22**

After my parents divorced, I spent most summer vacations with my dad's new family. One afternoon, I was reading in the den when I heard his Mercedes coming up the gravel driveway. When he came in, Dad went straight to the liquor cabinet.

He clinked ice cubes into a highball glass, filled it with vodka, and, without sitting down, chugged it. He filled and drained the glass three more times. Then, without a word, he lurched into the living room and collapsed on the couch.

In a few minutes, he was snoring.

Dad must have had a really bad day, I thought. Now, though, I realize he wasn't just having a bad day: my dad suffered from chronic stress almost every day of his adult life.

That kind of long-term stress takes its toll. In his mid-forties, Dad got rheumatoid arthritis, an autoimmune disease. By forty-seven, his condition was so severe he had to warm up his joints with heat lamps before he could get out of bed each morning. He eventually became disabled and had to sell his orthodontics practice. For five years, he lived in constant pain. Then, a few weeks shy of his fifty-third birthday, he died of a heart attack.

If you want to live a long and healthy life, you must minimize your stress.

The Perils of Too Much Stress

In 1936, Hungarian-born scientist, Hans Selye, first introduced the terms *stress* and *distress response*. He defined stress as the body's response to any demands made upon it, whether pleasant or unpleasant.

When negative emotions such as fear trigger the distress response, the stress hormones adrenaline (epinephrine) and cortisol are released into your blood system. These chemical messengers increase your breathing and heart rate, muscle tension, and strength. The purpose of this "flight or fight" response is to prepare your body to survive a *physical* threat.

But, modern humans have more *psychological* threats, than physical ones. Uncertainty and lack of control are two common psychological stressors. Boredom—a combination of apathy, monotony, and disengagement—is also a high-stress condition.

How you respond to stressors depends on 1) your beliefs, 2) your current emotional state, 3) your assessment of the stressor's meaning to you, and, 4) your perceived ability to cope with it. This means that two people who are exposed to the same stressor could have completely different reactions to it. The greater your psychological and material resources, the easier it is to cope with stress.

Your beliefs play a huge role in how you handle stress. Some beliefs can literally kill. Walter P. Cannon (Selye's teacher and a Harvard physiologist) identified people who developed a massive stress response and died simply because they believed a powerful witch doctor had cast a voodoo death spell on them. They believed themselves to death. After decades of studying it, Cannon concluded that distress plays a major role in almost all illnesses.

Say Yes to Eustress

In contrast to the distress response, Selye also identified *eustress*, which is triggered by positive emotions and meaningful challenges. Both distress and eustress activate the sympathetic nervous system, which prepares you for action, but eustress produces a much milder response. People experiencing eustress are fired up, exuding charisma and enthusiasm.

Eustress elevates your mood, sharpens your attention, and makes you focused and alert. It motivates and excites you, preparing your mind and body to perform better. Afterward, your body returns quickly to a healthy, low-stress state.

The nervous energy you feel before a competition or a performance is eustress. So is the thrill you get from a roller coaster ride, or the flutters you experience when you're around someone you find attractive. You also experience eustress when you get a promotion, buy a home, or win a prize. Eustress energizes you, promoting learning, peak performance, and personal growth.

For example, eustress motivates you to study for a test. Stressing your cardiovascular system and muscles with exercise makes them stronger, which is a kind of physical eustress. Children who experience mild stress do better as adults than those who grow up without stress.

Scientists at Northwestern University say, "Sustained stress is definitely not good for you, but it appears that an occasional burst of stress, or low levels of stress, can be very protective."

In the sweet spot between deep relaxation and high anxiety, you'll find the perfect amount of stimulation and challenge: eustress. Eustress, moderate alertness, and relaxation are all emotional states that characterize the Endorphin Zone.

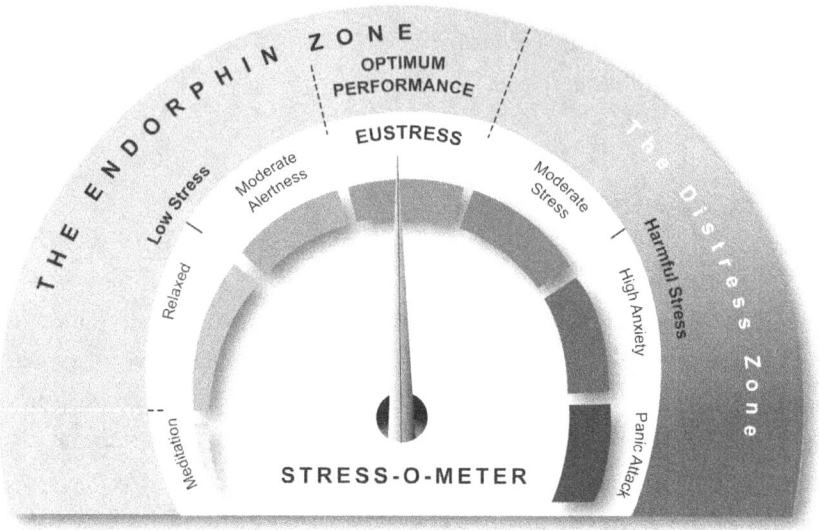

Figure 3.1. The Stress-O-Meter

Use the Stress-O-Meter to evaluate your own life. Ask yourself,

Where am I right now on this Stress-O-Meter?
More generally, what's my overall life score on the Stress-O-Meter?
Where would I like to be most of the time?
What percentage of my waking hours am I currently in the Endorphin Zone? The Eustress Zone? The Distress Zone?
What percentage of my waking hours do I want to be in the Endorphin Zone?

Endorphinomics is about minimizing the stressors in your life—and spending the majority of your time in the Endorphin Zone. But, modern societies can make this simple goal difficult to achieve.

Modern Culture Is Stressful

The Yagua Indians live far from civilization, deep in Peru's rainforest. Sociologists recently queried them about their level of stress, and were surprised when the Indians couldn't understand their question. It turns out that the Yagua had no word for stress in their language—because they rarely experienced it.

People in hunting-gathering societies, like the Yagua and our ancient ancestors, probably encountered (survived) only a few heart-stopping, life-threatening situations in their entire lives. When they did experience a distress response, they would have fought to the death, or escaped. Fighting and running both burned off (metabolized) the toxic stress hormones and quickly returned their bodies to a normal state. So chronic stress, a big problem in modern societies, is almost unheard of in traditional, hunting-gathering communities.

Many people in industrialized societies endure more than one serious distress response every day. They often suffer constant, damaging stress for decades because most of the modern stressors are psychological, not physical. They tend to be based on social or mental "threats" instead of wild beasts and inhospitable environments.

One of the worst types of psychological stress happens when you feel responsible for a problem but don't have the power (or authority) to fix it. This is what makes middle management, and the nightly news, so stressful.

A survey by the World Health Organization referred to chronic stress as a worldwide epidemic. The worst part is we can't run away, fight it out, or even work it off. We have to suffer through toxic bosses, traffic jams, financial challenges, family problems, business deadlines, information overload, constant uncertainty, and change. Stress for most people living in modern, industrialized societies is inescapable. So we rarely get back to a healthy, low-stress baseline.

Just dealing with the stresses of modern life marinates our tissues, organs, and brains in toxic stress hormones. This "structural stress" is taking a huge toll on our health—and on our nation's wealth.

Chronic Stress Destroys Your Health and Well-Being

Ancient Greek physicians first wrote about the connection between negative emotions and the onset of diseases. Throughout history, we've suspected deep connections between our emotions and our health. Summing up a bit of folk wisdom, the great American writer John Steinbeck observed, "A sad heart will kill you quicker, far quicker, than a germ."

Until recently, researchers weren't able to identify the biological processes that converted emotional and physical stressors into bodily disease, but we now know that every emotion, thought, experience, and belief affects the body.

Today medical researchers can measure the destructive impact of stress on cells, tissues, organs, and physiological systems. They've proven that negative thoughts and emotions, and the distress response they evoke can cause real and measurable damage to our physical and mental health.

For instance, T. H. Holmes created the Social Readjustment Rating Scale (http://www.mindtools.com/pages/article/newTCS_82.htm), which rates stressors on a scale of 1 to 100 and helps measure cumulative distress. Getting a driving ticket rated a 12, while the death of a spouse rated the highest score of 100. Holmes documented that people who experienced more than 250 points of stress during any two-year period were at extreme risk of developing a life-threatening illness.

Holmes' research focused on single stressful events, but many people suffer from ongoing stress. Chronic stress on the body is like friction in a car's engine: over time, it wears out the engine's parts, and the higher the friction, the faster the parts wear out. The more stress your body experiences, the faster its parts wear out, too.

Here are some of the main health problems caused by excessive negative emotions and the stress response they trigger.

Unmitigated stress makes you fat.

Stress is a major contributor to America's obesity epidemic. Many people overeat when they're stressed, because eating is pleasant and calming, temporarily lifting our mood. But constant overeating makes us gain weight. This is a serious problem because people who are forty percent overweight are twice as likely to die prematurely as a person of healthy weight.

Chronic stress also changes the way your body metabolizes fats and carbohydrates. This causes an inner tube of extra pounds to form around the waist. People who keep packing on the pounds are at great risk of developing metabolic syndrome. This dangerous condition increases the chances of coming down with type-two diabetes.

Obesity is linked to all kinds of health problems, including cancer, gallstones, gall bladder disease, osteoarthritis, gout, sleep apnea, and angina. Weight gain also puts a heavier load on our joints, lungs, and cardiovascular system.

Chronic stress damages your cardiovascular system.

Under constant stress, a cardiovascular system becomes overworked and under maintained, leading directly to cardiovascular disease including strokes and heart attacks. Each year, about 1.5 million Americans suffer heart attacks. The majority of them are caused or worsened by chronic stress.

Americans aren't the only ones suffering from stress-induced heart attacks. Jussi Vahtera and Mika Kivimäki conducted a landmark health study of Finnish municipal employees who survived a downsizing. The "lucky" workers who kept their jobs had to take on greater workloads and, of course, more stress.

Over the following seven years, the researchers tracked the employees' health to quantify stress-related cardiovascular damage. In the divisions with the most downsizing, and thus the most stress, workers experienced twice the rate of deaths from cardiovascular disease as the general public. Their stress-filled jobs literally worked them to death.

Chronic stress is killing people all over the world in both rich and poor countries. In a recent study of eleven thousand heart attack victims spanning fifty-two countries, the year before they had a heart attack, the victims had been under significantly more stress than people in the control group.

These are only two surveys among hundreds that all point to stress as the main cause of most cardiovascular disease. That's significant because heart attacks are America's leading cause of death, and strokes are the fourth biggest killer.

Unrelenting stress wears you out.

Prolonged periods of stress interfere with normal maintenance our bodies need and otherwise would perform regularly. When you perceive that your environment is safe, your cells, organs, and biological systems direct energy toward growth and repair. But when you're exposed to stressors, your cells stop normal repair and maintenance functions and reallocate all their resources to surviving the threat.

That's one reason children under great stress grow more slowly than children who aren't. When adults are under great stress, the growth of bones, muscles and the metabolism of fat are all hindered. The stress response also bombards cells, tissues, and organs with toxic hormones, such as cortisol.

In this weakened condition, cells and tissues become vulnerable to breakdowns and invasions by pathogens and disease, including autoimmune diseases like lupus, chronic fatigue, and rheumatoid arthritis. All these cell-level health problems are compounded because stress weakens the immune system.

Stress increases your chances of sickness and disease.

Stress lowers your defenses against all kinds of infections, viruses, and diseases.

Richard J. Davidson, a neuroscientist, is a leader in the fascinating new field psychoneuroimmunology (PNI), the study of the links between our thoughts, emotions, and health. In 2003, he and his team conducted a landmark study documenting the effects of emotions on the immune system. They changed volunteers' emotional state by asking them to recount either an incidence of "intense happiness or joy" or an event that evoked "intense sadness, fear, or anger."

Immediately after writing about their emotionally charged experiences, the participants were given a flu vaccination. Six months later, the researchers conducted tests to determine how the participants' immune systems had reacted to the vaccine, and the results were dramatic.

The subjects who were in a happy mood when they were vaccinated had much higher levels of flu antibodies than the sad group. This helped prove that positive emotions enhance the immune system's ability to resist viruses and negative emotions reduce those abilities. Davidson's experiment provided some of the strongest proof that thoughts and emotions do have a direct and measurable impact on the efficacy of our immune systems.

Look at some of the illness, ailments, conditions, and diseases that stress causes or aggravates:

- asthma
- cancer
- cardiac arrhythmia
- Crohn's disease
- colitis
- compulsive eating
- constipation

- depression
- diarrhea
- digestive difficulties
- eczema
- erectile dysfunction
- excessive colds and flu
- gum disease
- hair loss in women
- heart and cardiovascular disease
- high cholesterol
- impaired memory
- increased rates of infection and complications after surgery
- longer recovery time
- infertility
- insomnia
- insulin resistance
- irritable bowel syndrome,
- lower sexual drive
- migraine headaches
- multiple sclerosis
- obesity
- osteoporosis
- panic attacks
- rheumatoid arthritis
- skin problems
- slow wound healing
- ulcers

Unrelenting stress over a long period causes your body to lose its ability to "calm down" naturally. That's when you're in danger of going over the cliff health wise. As chronic stress breaks down one after another of the body's defenses and life support systems, this leads to a downward spiral of disease, depression, and early death.

Overwhelming stress depresses you.

Each year, almost twenty million Americans suffer from major depression. Chronic stress is the most common cause of Major Depressive Disorder (MDD). Over the past several decades, rates of depression have risen dramatically and it is afflicting more people at younger ages. It's the primary complaint that drives people to mental health professionals.

Major depression has grown to be America's fourth most common cause of disability. If growth rates continue, it will soon be the second most common disabling disease.

When you're under stress, blood flow to your neocortex shuts down. Prolonged and severe stress causes the whole brain to overload and burn out. If the stress doesn't stop, it eventually shuts down all regeneration of brain cells and the growth of new connections between neurons. If you aren't replacing dying neurons, your brain physically shrinks in size.

All these physical changes make it hard to think straight. People suffering from these conditions have difficulty concentrating, solving problems, and remembering things. They feel helpless, isolated, and out of control. Severely depressed people say things like, "Nothing feels good," and "I feel empty, without feelings or hope." They lose interest in pleasurable activities, including sex.

Mild depression is a common emotional state. But don't confuse occasional sadness, boredom, or disappointment with major depression. This dreadful condition dooms a person to crying, withdrawing from life, and staying in bed for weeks at a time. And every year depression is the principal instigator of more than thirty thousand suicides.

I should mention that this book isn't meant to heal severely depressed people. If anyone you know has the described symptoms, get competent counseling immediately. It may save their life.

Stress can bankrupt you.

Sixty to ninety percent of all doctor visits in America involve stress-related complaints. Yale University estimates that eighty-five percent of serious illnesses are caused by stress. And the health problems these people suffer are costing more than we can afford.

America spends more money per person on healthcare than any other nation. Today, one of every six dollars of our economy (GDP) goes to healthcare. These massive costs are expected to double in the next ten to twelve years. That's depressingly expensive and it's bankrupting our country.

It's also destroying financial security at the individual level: medical expenses are now the leading cause of personal bankruptcy in America. Often, people who become ill due to stress must take time off from work to deal with their problems. This causes them to lose income and, sometimes, their health insurance when they need it most.

Another unhappy reality is that the health and financial problems that stress causes makes us . . . even more stressed and depressed!

Don't Manage Stress—Minimize It!

Many stress-management techniques have been developed to mitigate the modern stress epidemic. The most popular ones are relaxation practices, including meditation, and cognitive approaches, such as reframing events to see them more positively. Of course, some people exercise to burn off the toxic stress hormones.

All these techniques work to relax us. But a big problem with all stress-management techniques is that, before we can employ them, much of the damage has already occurred. And if we're chronically stressed, relaxation techniques offer only temporary relief.

Stressed people may turn to illicit drugs that further destroy their health and positivity. But, even if getting wasted suppresses the emotional pain, the physical damage continues. Using drugs or alcohol to mask stress and depression only makes things worse.

It's much better to avoid excessive stress than to try to manage or limit the damage after it's happened. *Endorphinomics* focuses on minimizing or eliminating stress—not coping with it.

If you or someone you love is experiencing prolonged, severe stress, you need to stop it as soon as possible. The pages ahead will show you how.

Positive Emotions Vanquish Stress

A couple of years ago, just before I was about to go to my company Christmas party, I got a terrible shock. My best friend, Bruce, called to tell me he'd been diagnosed with terminal cancer. My stomach tightened and my face scrunched in emotional pain. I told Brooke, my wife, "I can't go to our party tonight. I'm too sad." I just wanted to stay home and cry.

She left me alone for a while. Then she gently put her hand on my shoulder and said, "All of your employees will be there with their dates. Bruce would want you to go." I finally agreed.

When we arrived, everyone was having a great time, so I faked a happy face. To avoid spoiling the holiday spirit, I didn't tell anyone the sad news. Before long, I was engaged in animated conversation, laughing and enjoying the company of my team.

To my surprise, I soon felt much better. I was relaxed, energized, and entertained. I hadn't forgotten the bad news; it just wasn't dominating my thoughts and feelings any more. The positive vibes at the party displaced my deep sadness over the impending loss of my best friend. Obviously, one happy event didn't heal the pain in my heart, but it helped me get through a tough evening.

The Relaxation Response

I didn't realize it at the time, but the shift I experienced at my Christmas party is well documented by scientists. I now know I benefited from the "undoing" effect of the "relaxation response"—the antidote to the distress response.

When you feel stressed or depressed, the best cure isn't to ruminate on your problems; it's to do something fun! Positive emotions activate the parasympathetic nervous system, which calms us down after we've been revved up. Our muscles relax, our breathing slows, our blood pressure and heart rate drop. We feel calm, serene, and content.

Everything we do that evokes the relaxation response or avoids the distress response enhances our health. To vanquish stress, consciously avoid stressors and replace them with positive thoughts, activities, and experiences.

What's more, positive emotions don't just relax us; they also trigger the release of endorphins and other "happy molecules" into our bodies and brains.

The Endorphin Epiphany

Endorphins played a central role in scientific understanding of how the mind, body, and emotions communicate and interact in perfect harmony.

Our nervous systems use both electrical and chemical signals to transmit information. To facilitate this communication, they produce more than one hundred types of peptide molecules called "neurotransmitters." When they're released, each of these messenger molecules bonds to specific receptor sites on specific neurons—much like a key fits into a lock. This process transmits over 100,000 chemical messages in our nervous system—every second.

Researchers had long suspected that opiate-based drugs, such as heroin and morphine, mimicked natural molecules that bond to specific receptor sites in our brains. In 1973, they finally discovered opiate receptors in our brains. A few years later, they identified two neuropeptides that bind perfectly with these receptors. They named these feel-good molecules "endorphins," short for endogenous morphine (morphine from within).

Soon, researchers made another landmark discovery. Opiate receptors aren't just in the brain and spinal column. Endorphins and other messenger molecules bond to receptor sites *throughout the entire nervous system*—brain, spinal cord, and peripheral neurons. They also bond to receptors in the stomach, intestines, and heart. Most important, researchers discovered these receptors in the endocrine (glandular) system, which controls the release of hormones.

Scientists concluded that chemical messengers enable all the cells in our minds and bodies to instantaneously communicate with each other. So, by discovering that endorphins bonded with receptors throughout our bodies, researchers learned how our minds and bodies communicate and work in complete harmony with our emotions. They proved that our mind and body are one! And they soon discovered many amazing benefits of endorphins.

The Role of Endorphins

Endorphins are naturally occurring painkillers and tranquilizers. Their pain-blocking properties evolved as a survival mechanism. If you're injured during a life-threatening situation, endorphins enable you to continue fighting, or to escape, without being incapacitated by pain. If endorphins are triggered when you're not in pain, you experience a calm, content feeling of euphoria.

When you're distressed, endorphins are released into your brain's emotional center, which lessens anxiety. By reducing cortisol and other stress hormones in the blood, endorphins create a sense of well-being and elevated mood, soothing and lifting you out of depression.

You experience endorphins when you fall in love, have an orgasm (an endorphin surge of up to five times normal), watch an awesome sunset, have a transcendent or spiritual experience, undergo acupuncture, get massaged, or eat dark chocolate and hot chili peppers. Women also experience them during childbirth.

Strenuous exercise is a well-known way to release endorphins. In fact, after an eight-mile race, trained runners have up to 3.5 times more endorphins than normal. Any time you feel calm, peaceful, serene, or pleasant, endorphins are cascading through your mind and body, evoking the perfect "natural high."

This is the Endorphin Effect: euphoric neuromodulators serve as natural pain blockers and mood enhancers. Some types are up to fifty times stronger than morphine, the strongest manufactured painkiller. Endorphins modify your feelings of pain or pleasure rather than actually transmitting the pain signals. They alert us to opportunities to build resources and for personal growth. These happy messengers help motivate and enable learning, memory, and social bonding.

Because of their critical role in stopping pain, reducing the effects of stress, and evoking the feelings of joy and euphoria, I use the term *Endorphin Effect* as a metaphor for positive emotions, the relaxation response they evoke, and all the happy messenger molecules associated with them.

The good news is that, no matter how much we experience them, we can't become addicted to endorphins. That's because they don't stay in our bodies long enough for us to form a tolerance or dependency. As soon as they cascade through our minds and bodies with their soothing message, endorphins are rapidly metabolized and reabsorbed. That's why we need a constant "flow" of positive emotions throughout each day.

Fortunately, once we experience their serene and euphoric pleasures, we pursue the Endorphin Effect again and again. That's why people get hooked on exercise. The more endorphins we get, the harder we'll work to get even more. This creates a virtuous upward spiral of health, happiness, and positivity.

Health Benefits of Positive Emotions

Simply being happy—at work and at play—triggers specific relaxation responses that bolster our immune systems and protect us against cardiovascular disease, diabetes, and other stress-related illnesses.

They can even help us avoid the common cold.

We can get inoculated against the flu. But there's nothing we can do to stop the most frequent human infection, the common cold. Or is there? Sheldon Cohen and his colleagues conducted a study of common colds and happiness. After assessing each participant's level of three positive emotions—vigor, well-being, and calm—the volunteers received a squirt of rhinovirus up the nose. (Yuck!) This nasty little germ causes most colds.

Participants who had higher levels of positive emotions experienced fewer infections and experienced less severe cold symptoms, which lasted for a shorter period of time. The negative emotion group got sick more often and suffered more and longer from the cold's symptoms.

Positivity banishes coughs, sniffles, sore throats, and runny noses!

Positive emotions heal the damages of negative emotions.

In addition to being antidotes for negative emotions, positive emotions actually repair physical damage to blood vessels caused by the distress response. In 1998, Barbara Fredrickson and a colleague developed an experiment that proved it.

First, the researchers stressed volunteers by telling them they would have to present an off-the cuff speech immediately after the experiment. That triggered a distress response, which increased their blood pressure and heart rates. Then each volunteer watched one of four different short film clips. Two clips evoked positive emotions, one evoked amusement, and the other contentment. The third film elicited three negative emotions: fear, sadness, and anxiety. The fourth film was the control and evoked no emotions at all.

After stressing the volunteers and having them watch one of the films, Fredrickson's team measured the amount of time it took the subject's heart rate, blood pressure, and other physical indicators of stress to normalize. The subjects who watched the two feel-good films returned to normal faster than the subjects who watched the neutral film. Participants who watched the stress-inducing film took the longest time to recover.

By reversing the physical effects of stress, positive emotions help us heal our spirits and even our hearts. Positive emotions measurably and predictably reverse harmful cardiovascular effects brought on by negative emotions. They reduce blood pressure and toxic stress hormones. They also clean out the toxic sludge that causes most cardiovascular disease and promote healing of the delicate lining of blood vessels.

Fredrickson refers to these beneficial effects of positive emotions as the "undoing effect." Her research revealed a key reason happy people experience fewer heart attacks.

Positive emotions reduce heart attacks.

Today, Lee Berk is one of the world's top experts in the growing field of psychoneuroimmunology. One of Berk's key studies involved diabetics who had survived a heart attack. In addition to conventional treatment, patients in Berk's group watched thirty minutes of humorous videos at least five times a week. This positive intervention had an amazing result.

At the end of the year, for every twelve participants who watched the humorous videos, only one suffered another heart attack. But in the control group, which didn't watch the humorous movies, five times as many people suffered a second heart attack. Wow! That's a good reason to watch a comedy tonight.

The results of his research inspired Berk to joke, "If we could invent a pill that actually did for us what laughter does, we would be winning a Nobel Prize."

Here's more good news from an even longer-term study: Laura Kubzansky, a health psychologist at Harvard's School of Public Health, tracked 1,300 men for ten years. She found that heart-disease rates among men who called themselves "optimists" were half the rate for men who didn't refer to themselves that way. "It [optimism] was a much bigger effect than we expected," Kubzansky said. In fact, being optimistic made as big of an impact on longevity as not smoking.

Reams of studies over decades have proved that positive emotions, including optimism, humor, contentedness, hope, love, trust, and faith, have a clear, dramatic, and measurable impact on our heart's health.

Positive emotions increase longevity.

A large and growing number of studies have directly linked happiness with longer lives. Here's a small sampling of some of the research.

In the Arnhem Elderly Study, researchers in Holland studied 999 elderly men and women from 1991 to 2001. During that time, 397 of the subjects died. However, a high level of optimism was by far the best predictor of staying alive. In fact, a positive outlook reduced an individual's risk of death by fifty percent during the time of the study. Significantly, the more optimistic a person was the more likely they were to be alive at the end of the study.

Another long-term study has become a classic in the field of positive psychology. In the 1930s, several hundred young Catholic nuns wrote short, personal essays about their lives. They described key events from childhood, including the spiritual experiences and religious influences that led them to enter the convent. In 1986, David Snowden and his colleagues analyzed the content of the nun's writings by counting emotional words. The results were astounding.

The nuns who expressed the most positive emotions in their essays lived up to ten years longer than those who expressed the fewest positive emotions.

Because of all the health benefits of positive emotions, a happy optimist can reasonably expect to live at least ten years longer than a grumpy pessimist.

You can see from this sampling of long-term studies that positive emotions and the Endorphin Effect they trigger have massive health benefits and extend life expectancy. Sometimes, they can even work miracles.

Laughter Is the Best Medicine

In his classic book *Anatomy of an Illness,* Norman Cousins wrote about his struggle to cure himself of ankylosing spondylitis, a degenerative form of arthritis. This autoimmune disease was slowly and painfully destroying the connective tissues in his body. He once said he felt like he was, "being pulled apart by his joints."

Cousins became bedridden and was so weak that he could barely raise his fingers. He was in such agony that his doctors prescribed twenty-six aspirins a day, sleeping pills, and codeine. The experts told him he was doomed to permanent paralysis, giving him a one-in-five hundred chance of complete recovery.

But Cousins believed in the healing power of love, hope, humor, and laughter. As Groucho Marx once said, "A clown is like an aspirin, only he works twice as fast." So Cousins worked closely with his doctor and experimented with his own theories about health, healing, and positivity. Over time he discovered that, a daily ten-minute dose of bellyaching laughter provided a few hours of pain-free sleep. His unconventional treatments included watching slapstick Marx Brother's films, reading funny stories, and humming.

All these activities enhanced his emotional state, got his endorphins flowing, and evoked the relaxation response. After a few months of his "humor treatments," Cousins was able to stop taking any painkillers. Eventually, he completely recovered from his "incurable" illness.

After the publication of *Anatomy of an Illness* in 1979, Cousins, a journalist, endured blistering criticism from the medical community. At the time, most of them didn't believe there was *any* connection between emotions and health. But he was soon offered a job as an adjunct professor at the prestigious UCLA School of Medicine. In that role, he became one of the world's leading advocates for scientific research into emotions and their impact on our health.

Scientists now know that mirthful laughter lowers blood pressure, reduces stress hormones in the blood, and enhances immune system functions. It also triggers the release of endorphins, which reduces pain and produces a general state of well-being.

A good belly laugh uses all of your muscles and is equivalent to about fifteen minutes of exercise. These benefits have earned laughter the nickname "internal jogging."

* * *

You could fill a small library with the research that connects positive emotions and the relaxation response with health. Today, the medical community has accepted the fact that our minds, bodies, and emotions are integrated into one holistic system. They know that love, serenity and optimism, and anxiety, alienation, and hopelessness change our body's chemical and physical makeup—for better or worse.

Commenting on a study that she co-authored on the connection between positive emotions and health, Oxford-educated psychology professor Jane Wardle said, "This research suggests we should aim to maximize the happiness of the population."

That's a brilliant idea and the subject of the next section of this book.

ENDORPHIN EVENT #3

Plan to Reduce Your Stress and Enhance Your Health

Summarize this chapter for your guests by going through the pages and using the subheads and graphics to share the key points. Then brainstorm on the following topics.

1. What generates eustress, the perfect level of challenge that brings out the best in you and inspires you to learn, grow, and flourish?
2. What are your favorite ways to relax? What healthy ways do you have for de-stressing after becoming dis-stressed? What new ways to relax do you want to try?
3. What activities or people will help you burn off stress?
4. What stressors are you looking forward to getting behind you? What will it feel like when you eliminate them? How can you start to reduce or minimize them?
5. What would have to happen for your life to be ninety percent stress-free?
6. What or who makes you laugh? How can you laugh more in your life?
7. What will you do differently in the future, based on your insights from this chapter?

SUMMARY:
Commit to Flourishing

Congratulations! You've completed the first section of this book. Let's review what you've learned so far.

Chapter 1. Money is a good servant, but a bad master. You also learned that wealth doesn't create happiness; happiness creates wealth. The single-minded pursuit of wealth is a prescription for stress and unhappiness. If you want to be happy, healthy, and wealthy, seek balance and overall quality of life. You can have it all if you commit to it, as Barry did.

Chapter 2. Following your bliss will empower you to build resources to support a better future. Positive emotions inspire you to adapt, evolve, and prosper. They also broaden and build our thoughts and resources. If you want the Endorphin Effect, you must experience more than three positive emotional events for every negative one. But a small amount of negative feedback is healthy. It fosters learning, growth, and adaptation in an ever-changing world.

Chapter 3. Stress leads directly to many avoidable ailments. Positive emotions optimize your health and maximize your longevity. Your health is a key resource that will enhance your wealth and your quality of life. (You can't be healthy, wealthy, and happy if you're dead, can you?) So say good-bye to stress, doctors, and hospitals, and yes to feeling all right, all the time.

Scientists believe that human beings evolved to their current form between 40,000 and 100,000 years ago on the plains of East Africa. We're perfectly adapted to survive and flourish in the savannah. But we now live in a completely different environment that we aren't well adapted to. That "fish out of water" situation is highly stressful.

Barbara Fredrickson discovered that only one out of five Americans are flourishing, experiencing a preponderance of positive emotions.

The other four out of five Americans are languishing, mentally and physically. This means that literally millions of Americas, and billions of people around the globe, would benefit from happiness and flourishing training.

That's what this book is about. The information and exercises in the chapters ahead will show you how to live a healthy, wealthy, happy and virtually stress-free life—a life you love—in the modern world.

By reading this far you've already started your transformation. You've created new neurological connections in your brain. You've started on the path to the Endorphin Zone.

STEP TWO

Discover Your Flourishing Self

4

Optimize Your Personal Operating System

The mind is everything. What we think we become.
—**Buddha**

Before Norman Cousins could heal himself with "humor therapy," he needed to cross a critical psychological barrier: he had to believe it would work. Medical researchers have since established that beliefs can, indeed, sicken or heal people. But beliefs influence far more than health. Scientists in Vancouver found that some beliefs can also make you smarter.

After subliminally influencing female students' beliefs, researchers gave them a math test. One group of young women was primed to believe that differences in math abilities between men and women were based on experience and were, therefore, changeable. A second group was primed to believe the differences were genetically based and, therefore, they'd never be very good at math.

The students who were primed to believe they could improve their math scores consistently scored about fifty percent higher than the students who were led to believe they were destined to do poorly in math. The researchers could predictably raise or lower students' test scores by influencing their beliefs with a few paragraphs of text before the test. Most significantly, the improvements occurred instantly, with no additional studying or effort.

This type of self-fulfilling prophesy happens constantly and in every domain of our lives. If we think we can, we can, and if we think we can't, we can't. That's why optimizing your beliefs, assumptions and mental models is essential if you want to flourish.

Think what would happen if you chose to adopt the most empowering attitudes, beliefs, and mental models in every domain of your life. Not if you started believing a bunch of made-up nonsense, but if you were to consciously adopt evidence-based beliefs that are known to enhance health, wealth, and happiness. That's what you'll learn in this chapter.

So let's start by looking at your personal operating system, which is comprised of your

1. aspirations,
2. beliefs, and
3. habits.

Your goal is to optimize each of these components so they generate behavior that makes you happy and satisfied. Let's start by learning what determines these important feelings.

What Determines How Happy We Are

The default emotional state for healthy humans is mildly positive. But some people are naturally cheerful and others are cheerless. Why the difference?

Scientists know that our default emotional state—our natural positivity ratio—is inherited from our parents. This genetically derived

OPTIMIZE YOUR PERSONAL OPERATING SYSTEM

happiness set point is responsible for about half of our emotional state at any given time. The other half is determined by a combination of our objective life circumstances and our intentional thoughts and behaviors.

In the 1970s, David Lykken conducted landmark studies of four thousand fraternal and identical twins born in Minnesota. After comparing their happiness, Lykken and his colleagues discovered that our objective life circumstances, such as our home, possessions, wealth and income, play a surprisingly small role in our happiness.

Through statistical analysis, Lykken determined that our life circumstances, whether luxurious or Spartan, are responsible for only about ten percent of our emotional state. Take two identical twins, separate them at birth, and raise one in the lap of luxury and privilege. Raise the other twin in very modest circumstances, but with all their basic needs taken care of. Lykken's team discovered that, on average, these two twins were very similar in their level of happiness and life satisfaction. Their objective life circumstances made little difference in their positivity.

The scientists also proved that the most effective way to enhance positivity is to upgrade intentional thoughts and behaviors. That's because your aspirations, beliefs, habits, and intentional behaviors are responsible for about forty percent of your emotional state.

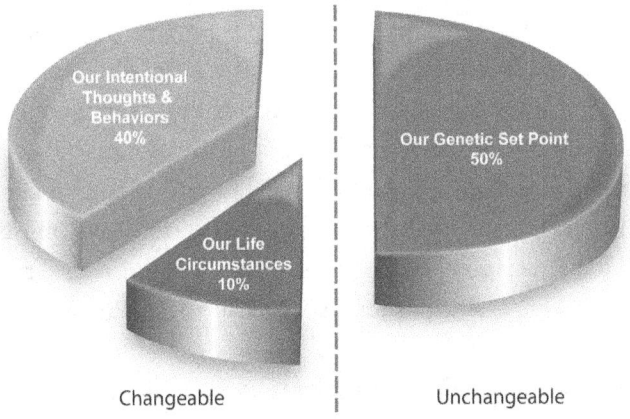

Figure 4.1. What Determines Our Emotional State?

Upgrading your personal operating system—to generate more empowering thoughts and behaviors—is the fastest, surest, and easiest way to enhance your quality of life. It's where you have both control and leverage, and it's four times more effective than upgrading your life circumstances. What's more, the results are instantaneous.

When Brooke and I moved from the rural foothills outside Sacramento to Los Angeles, initially she was fearful that she'd get lost in the big city. I explained that I believed there was no such thing as getting lost: "There's just the long way and the short way of getting somewhere." That empowering belief instantly reduced Brooke's anxiety and increased her sense of confidence.

Satisfying Universal Human "Needs"

In addition to our in-born drives and behaviors, after birth, our parents and culture teach us what to value, what to think, and how to behave. We also learn from our direct experiences. In the process of growing up, each of us acquires a unique personal operating system (OS). The more accurately our OS represents the real world, the more successful we'll be at satisfying our "human needs."

But, what needs should we strive to satisfy?

The underlying motivators behind all human behavior are our 1) biological needs, 2) emotional desires, and 3) psycho/spiritual aspirations. For you to survive and flourish, your OS must generate behaviors that satisfy these three universal human motivations.

If your OS is flawed, you'll be frustrated. But, when your OS empowers you to successfully engage with your environment you're rewarded with pleasure, positive emotions, satisfaction and resources—you flourish. These rewards encourage you to repeat your behavior in the future.

To better understand what it means to flourish, let's look at each of the three types of human motivations.

Biological Needs

As living organisms, we have biological needs that we must satisfy: respiration (air), nourishment (food and water), physical safety (from predators, enemies, diseases, and natural disasters, as well as protection from the elements), elimination, sleep, and reproduction (sex). Yes, sex is a biological need. No, you won't die if you don't get laid, but our species will die if we don't reproduce. The instinctive programs that drive us to satisfy our biological needs are hard-wired into our survival-obsessed reptilian brain, and it's a good thing they are: If we can't fulfill our biological needs, we will die.

That's why needs are always more demanding and urgent than desires and aspirations.

Once you're safe and have enough resources to satisfy your biological needs, you can focus on satisfying your desires and pursuing your aspirations.

Emotional Desires

Humans are profoundly driven by emotional desires, feelings and cravings, which originate primarily in our mammalian brain. Recently, scientists have identified a small set of universal emotional desires that make the biggest contribution to our subjective well-being. If you're unable to satisfy them, you'll feel frustrated, stressed, angry, and depressed. Satisfying them is the foundation for flourishing.

What universal human desires should you strive to satisfy?

In the late 1990s, Kennon Sheldon and his colleagues conducted research to discover which emotions, when satisfied, cause humans to flourish, "the same way that proper fertilization promotes the growth of plants." He also wanted to know if any commonly pursued desires failed to satisfy.

After reviewing the work of other psychologists, Sheldon's team identified ten potential universal psychological "needs." Then they developed a survey to determine how much each "need," when satisfied, contributed to happiness and satisfaction. They asked participants what contributed most to their satisfying experiences, and what their unsatisfying experiences lacked.

The team discovered that only four intrinsically rewarding emotions contributed the lion's share of our happiness and satisfaction during positive experiences, and two other emotions played a minor role:

1. security (physical, emotional, financial),
2. autonomy (freedom),
3. competence (successfully expressing strengths),
4. connection (love and friendship),
5. self-esteem (confidence, positive self-opinion and respect), and
6. pleasure (hedonic, aesthetic, intellectual, amusement).

Significantly, the unsatisfying experiences all lacked the first four positive emotions. The study also revealed that pleasure adds to positive experiences. But only a little bit. And security is extremely important, but only if we don't have it. Let's look at each of these six universally satisfying emotional desires.

1. Security (Not Having It Creates a Big Problem)

Physical safety is a biological need, but feeling secure about your personal safety, finances, or relationships is an emotional desire. Human beings crave predictability and stability, and their absence causes stress.

If you already feel secure, you don't strive for it or appreciate it. But feelings of insecurity are stressful. In other words, being secure doesn't increase your happiness, but feeling insecure makes you unhappy. That's why feeling physically and emotionally secure is an essential element of positive experiences.

2. Autonomy

To fully enjoy an experience or relationship, you must feel that it's freely chosen, without external rewards or pressure, and that you're intrinsically committed to it. When you're free to choose your own path in life, you feel most alive, happy, and in control, the master of your own destiny. If you do things out of fear, intimidation, or coercion, your stress goes up, and your happiness and satisfaction plummets.

Ultimately, you're the only one who knows what will make you happy. So follow your inner guides, your positive emotions, on your journey to the Endorphin Zone. Don't let others distract you with rewards or coercion. Following your inner voice is essential if you want to grow and flourish.

3. Competence

When you're expressing your personal power, doing things you're good at, and achieving important goals, you feel competent. When you feel competent, it makes you optimistic about your future. That's because you're confident that you can satisfy your needs and desires through your own efforts.

When you apply your competencies or skills over time, you experience the positive state of accomplishment, the thoughts, and feelings of success. If you can't satisfy your basic needs and wants, you feel inept, dependent, frustrated and stressed (and probably hungry).

You can't fake competence. You have to earn it. Building and maintaining your knowledge and skills is essential for feeling competent—and for achieving objective well-being.

4. Connection

People are social animals. That means you're hardwired to desire affection, respect, intimate conversations, appreciation, and understanding from people you care about. You want someone to love and someone to love you. Feeling autonomous and competent empowers you to interact in win-win relationships with others. Feeling disconnected, alone and alienated leads to stress and depression.

Connecting with others, in work and play, is one of the great joys of life. It's impossible to flourish as a hermit. People reach their highest potential for success and happiness when they care about and interact positively with others.

People also have a natural desire to be affiliated with one or more groups. Establishing and maintaining win-win relationships is the foundation for individual and communal flourishing.

5. Self-Esteem (The Payoff)

Sheldon's team discovered that the single most *gratifying* state for Americans is self-esteem, a combination of positive feelings and positive self-assessments. But you can't satisfy your desire for self-esteem directly. That's because you experience it only when you've satisfied your other key emotional desires. If you're unable to satisfy your biological needs or the four key emotional desires, your self-esteem plummets.

When you feel secure, autonomous, competent, and connected, your self-esteem automatically goes up. There aren't any shortcuts to this pinnacle of positivity. Like competence, you have to earn high self-esteem.

People with high esteem are optimistic about their ability to satisfy their wants and needs, support their loved ones, and contribute to their community. They're confident in their beliefs and secure enough to change their minds when it makes sense. This makes them coachable and comfortable asking for help. They're also great mentors, coaches, and leaders.

6. Pleasure (Not Really All That Important)

Pleasure is one, highly-touted component of a good life. Many pleasurable activities involve satisfying survival needs such as eating, drinking, mating, and hunting and gathering (bar hopping and shopping?). Pleasure is a paradox. You're hardwired to seek it, it feels good in the moment, and it's sometimes memorable. But this sought-after emotion only contributes a small amount to your positivity and its absence doesn't diminish it.

Pleasures make us happy while we're experiencing them, but unlike other positive emotions, they contribute almost nothing to our life satisfaction.

So remember you're naturally programmed to pursue pleasurable experiences and feelings and often find them hard to resist. But pursue them in moderation. They can distract you from lasting satisfaction and fulfillment. And, if you pursue them too enthusiastically, they might get you into trouble.

When you satisfy all six key intrinsic desires during an event or experience—security, autonomy, competence, connection, pleasure, and self-esteem—you'll feel happy and satisfied. These universal human desires will guide you on the upward spiral of flourishing. But not all of our emotional desires will lead us to the Endorphin Zone.

The Least Satisfying Emotional Desires

Sheldon's team discovered that four popular emotional desires contribute almost nothing to our happiness and life satisfaction, unless we're desperately poor.

These low payoff desires aren't inborn; they're extrinsic, not intrinsic like our six key desires. We learn these motivations from our parents, peers, culture, environment, and media.

The least satisfying emotional desires include

- high income,
- wealth,
- possessions,
- luxury/comfort,
- fame/status, and
- power, influence, and control over others.

Extrinsically motivated people often try to achieve happiness and satisfaction by pursuing fame, fortune, and power. But the happiest and most satisfied people achieve high income and wealth by pursuing the six most satisfying emotional desires.

Our Aspirations

Aspirations are divine discomforts that pull you toward your destiny. The word *aspire* comes from a Latin root word that means to breathe, as in "to breathe life into." Psycho/spiritual aspirations are powerful emotional yearnings that you want to breathe life into. They define your hopes for a better life and a better world.

Aspirations are motivated by both our hard-wired neuro circuits and our acquired values and beliefs. They're higher order motivations that are generated during complex interactions between our hominid brain (head) and our mammalian brain (heart). Aspirations are a key component of our personal operating system and a primary motivator of personal growth.

Unlike our subconscious needs and desires, we're often consciously aware of our aspirations. You process and experience them in the "desktop of your brain," your pre-frontal cortex, just above and behind your eyes.

They're motivated by our innate desires, but our culture, upbringing, values, and beliefs determine the specific aspirations we pursue.

Here are a dozen aspirations of flourishing people:

1. psychological growth, evolution, and adaptation;
2. fulfilling your potential;
3. ethics and morality;
4. learning and understanding;
5. personal integration and authenticity;
6. helping others to adapt, evolve, and succeed;
7. beauty, aesthetics, and harmony;
8. balance and synergy in life;
9. spirituality, transcendence, and connection with a higher power;
10. meaning and purpose;
11. peak experiences and positive moments,
12. discovering and fulfilling a higher purpose.

Not everyone has aspirations. And not everyone who has aspirations pursues them. But identifying and pursuing aspirations has many benefits. Aspiring to values such as authenticity, compassion, contribution, peace, sustainability, and spirituality can give meaning, purpose, and direction to our lives. It nurtures our heads, hearts, and spirits.

Unlike your needs and desires that motivate you only when you experience a deficit, aspirations motivate you all the time. For instance, hunger motivates you to seek and consume food. Once you satisfy your hunger, your motivation to eat vanishes, until you become hungry again. But pursuing aspirations increases your motivation instead of satiating it. This increased motivation leads you on an endless cycle of personal growth, psychological integration, and spiritual connection.

People who pursue their aspirations enjoy more peak experiences and positive moments. They experience higher, more sublime and lasting feelings of satisfaction than those who don't strive to fulfill their potential.

If you don't have any aspirations, you won't suffer or die. But you'll never truly flourish.

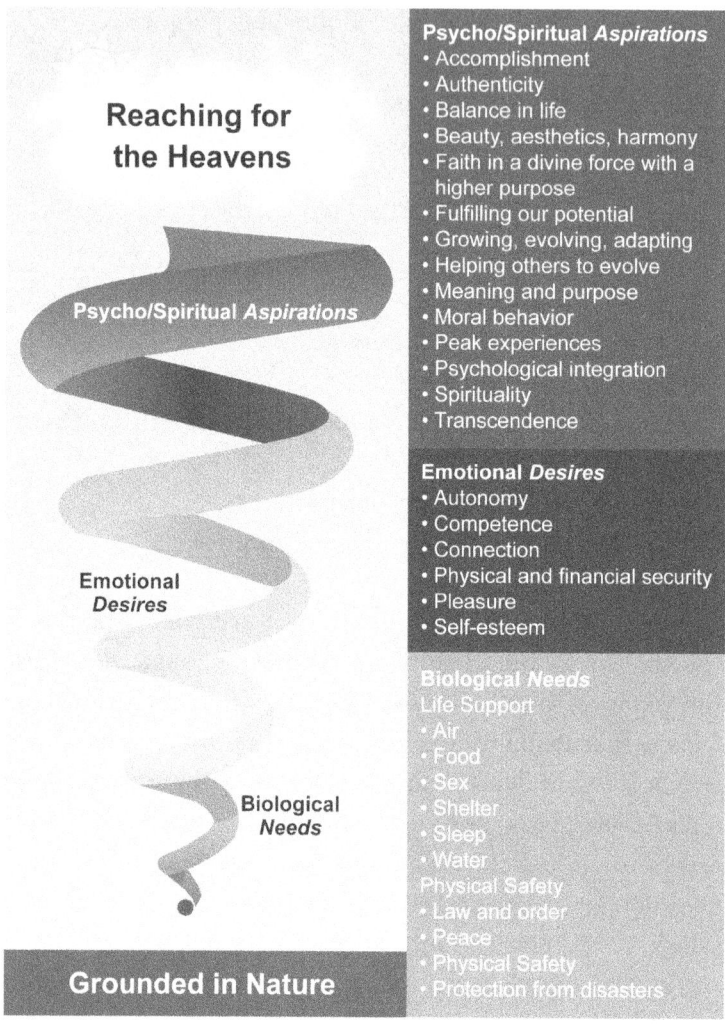

Figure 4.2. The Upward Spiral of Human Flourishing.

Maslow believed that human needs operate as a hierarchy, that we strive to achieve our aspirations for self actualization only after we've satisfied our needs and wants. But it's not this linear (unless our lower needs aren't being met). Most of us multitask to satisfy many of our needs, desires, and aspirations at the same time.

Imagine going out to lunch and then to a museum with your lover. Afterward you come home and have a romantic, sexy time. That one event would satisfy your need for sustenance, and your desire for connection and pleasure. It would also fulfill your aspirations for aesthetics. What a satisfying event!

Our Beliefs

As the Roman Emperor Marcus Aurelius said, "Our life is what our thoughts make it." Some of your beliefs add to your positivity, and some of them detract from it.

Your beliefs are based on your knowledge, life experience, and upbringing. They encompass everything you know, or think you know. They color and filter everything you perceive and interpret about yourself, others, your world, and the future. Beliefs help you understand how the world works and what the rules are. They shape your aspirations, your expectations, and your hopes for the future. Your values, a special type of belief, establish relative importance and priorities.

Most beliefs are established in the subconscious by experiences with parents, media, religion, education, peers, and significant life events. By the time people reach their early twenties, their personal "operating system" and the neurological pathways that support it are firmly in place. Then they spend the rest of their lives defending their beliefs. The subconscious mind seeks information to reinforce its mental models and filters out information that challenges them. Diarist Anaïs Nin nailed it when she wrote, "We don't see things as they are. We see things as we are."

Defending your beliefs is normal and healthy—to a point. It helps you maintain stability in your life. If you changed your beliefs every time someone or something challenged them, you'd be so confused and directionless you wouldn't be able to function. But, if you don't replace limiting beliefs with more empowering ones, you can't grow, adapt, and flourish.

The famous nineteenth-century philosopher and psychologist, William James, observed, "The greatest discovery of my generation is that a human being can alter his life by altering his attitudes of mind. As you think, so shall you be."

Change your beliefs and you'll change your life. Consciously embracing empowering beliefs will create a solid foundation for a flourishing life.

Beliefs that Will Help You Flourish

Each of us has many different beliefs. So it's beyond the scope of this book to list all the empowering ones. But here's a short list of beliefs that scientists know lead to personal growth, high self-esteem, and flourishing individuals and communities.

You are responsible for your life.

One of the most disempowering beliefs is that you're a victim. That belief leaves you powerless to change things to make them better. Victims believe their quality of life is dependent on the action of others, or on factors beyond their control. Blaming others for your situation and unhappiness won't make you more successful or happier. That belief sabotages your feelings of autonomy and competence.

To flourish, you must believe and act as if you are entirely responsible for your life. Then you must take intentional actions to increase your positivity ratio.

Even if you don't have any control over your situation, you can control how you interpret and respond to it. Believing that you're responsible means never blaming others for your emotional state or your life circumstances. To be happy and successful, you must become the master of your thoughts, your emotions, and your life.

The glass is always half-full.

In the early 1900s, two shoe salesmen were sent to Africa to assess the potential market for their wares. One wrote back, "Situation hopeless. No one wears shoes here." The other wrote, "Fantastic opportunity. No one has any shoes yet."

Optimism is one of the most common traits of successful, happy people. They believe they can make a positive difference in their lives and the world. Because of this, they're more likely to take action and persist in the face of adversity.

Pessimists often give up quickly on important life goals. They're worried about the future but have difficulty taking action to make their lives better. They often become angry and withdrawn as they age. Both pessimism and optimism are powerful self-fulfilling prophesies. Fortunately, pessimism isn't hard-wired. It's learned after birth.

Martin Seligman wrote an important book called *Learned Optimism* in which he explained techniques that pessimists can use to become more optimistic. If you have trouble seeing the glass as half-full, read this book.

Focus on what you want, not what you don't want.

My grandfather, Ernie, was healthy and vital until midway through his ninety-sixth year. On his ninety-seventh birthday, I asked him, "Grandpa, how have you managed to live such a long and healthy life?" Since he was a vegetarian, I assumed that was his secret. But it wasn't.

"The most important thing," he said, "is that I never became an old fogey."

I had heard that term before but wasn't sure what he meant. So I asked him.

He told me this analogy. "If you touch a hot stove and get burned, you learn instantly not to touch a hot stove again. If you fall in love with someone and get dumped, you'll be reluctant to get emotionally involved again."

He explained that these are natural learning processes that help us avoid physical and emotional pain. No one has to tell you to avoid things that hurt you. It's part of human nature. But if you go through life focused on avoiding things, he said, your options narrow and you shut down.

"Eventually, you become afraid to leave the house. You watch TV and read the obituaries all day, avoiding life and waiting for death. That's what I call an 'old fogey.'"

Then he told me something I'll never forget.

"The secret to living a long and happy life is to focus on what you do want, not on what you don't want."

He was so right! If you focus on avoiding things you don't want, you'll constantly be thinking negative thoughts. That focus will put you in a negative mood. But if you focus on what you do want, you'll constantly be thinking positive thoughts. That will enhance your emotional state.

Another problem is that if you don't know what you want, stress is likely to drive you away from one bad situation, to a worse situation. So, whenever that feeling in your gut or that voice in your head says, "I don't want —————— (fill in the blank)," use that thought or feeling as a cue to trigger an empowering question: "What *do* I want?" Then focus on and take action to get what you want.

Be grateful.

Our minds are fantastic problem solvers. They naturally focus on problems, failures, uncompleted tasks, and disappointments and try to fix whatever's "wrong." They also have a negativity bias that causes them to pay more attention to threats and bad news than to opportunities and good news. And we tend to compare ourselves with people who are better off than we are. All of these natural thought processes reduce our positivity.

The solution is to *consciously appreciate the things that are going right in your life.* Psychologist Sonya Lyubomirsky reports that grateful people are "happier, more energetic, and more hopeful" than average. They're also more helpful, empathetic, spiritually oriented, forgiving, and less materialistic than ungrateful people.

Out of all the scientific "interventions" developed by positive psychologists, counting your blessings is undoubtedly the fastest, easiest, and most rewarding one. So, to increase your happiness and life satisfaction, keep a journal of the good things you experience every day. Review and savor the most compelling ones at least weekly. You'll immediately feel happier.

Learn from flourishing people.

The United States ranks first in happiness among nations with populations greater than 150 million people. It's also in the top ten percent of the happiest nations overall. Decades of social surveys of Americans' beliefs and behaviors provide us with a snapshot of the happiest and most satisfied Americans, those who are flourishing.

Flourishing Americans are optimists and believe they can provide for themselves and their families. Their optimism and positivity inspire them to be *proactive* and *resilient* during adversity.

They *believe in* the democratic, market-based system they live in, and they see America as a land of opportunity. They are grateful to live in such a safe, prosperous, and free country. Flourishing Americans are goal-oriented and believe that focus and hard work will lead to a brighter future for themselves and their families.

They believe in contributing their fair share to the benefit of their community and hold strong religious, faith-based, or spiritual beliefs.

Their positive behaviors reinforce their positive beliefs. Flourishing Americans are *more likely to be married*, have *more friends*, attend *religious or spiritual ceremonies more often*, and *give a higher percentage of their incomes to charities*. These behaviors have been proven to enhance happiness and life satisfaction.

All these positive beliefs and behaviors make them feel more *secure, autonomous, competent, and connected* which increases their *self-esteem*. This high level of positivity empowers them to grow and evolve, throughout their lives, so they never become an old fogey.

In wealthy, industrialized democracies, many people languish amidst opportunity because they have suboptimal belief systems. If your destination is the Endorphin Zone, embrace the most empowering beliefs. They will lead you on an upward spiral of flourishing.

Your Habits

When the whistle blew, two workers put down their tools and grabbed their lunch boxes. As he looked at his sandwich, Mike lamented, "Darn, ham and cheese again." To which his friend responded, "You complain about your lunch every day. Why don't you ask your wife to make something else?

Angrily, Mike replied, "You leave my wife out of this! I make my own lunches."

Habits can keep you in unsatisfying ruts when you aren't aware of their impact on your life. That's because close to half of your actions each day are habitual, requiring almost no conscious thought or awareness. The good news is that habitual behaviors free you to focus on tasks that are more important. The bad news is that behaviors that are engrained in your neural circuits are difficult to change, or even to recognize.

Most new behavior starts with conscious thought and effort. As you repeat a behavior over and over again, new neurological circuits grow. Repeated behavior eventually becomes encoded deep within our reptilian brain. Once that happens, you can repeat the behavior with little or no conscious thought from our hominoid brain. It's become a conditioned habit.

If you develop good habits, you'll flourish. But bad habits can destroy your health, wealth, and happiness. Fortunately, once you become aware of your habits, you can change or eliminate them.

According to Charles Duhigg, the author of *The Power of Habit: Why We Do What We Do,* every habit has three components:

1. The cue triggers the behavior.
2. The routine, or habit, runs its course.
3. Finally, at the end for the routine, there is the reward (or payoff).

The key to changing a habit is to understand the cues and rewards that drive it. Common cues are time of day, a specific place, person, emotion, or a set of ritualized behaviors, like getting dressed in the morning. Other common cues are boredom, low blood sugar, and hunger. Rewards can be positive emotions, food, sweets, companionship, or other pleasures.

We often acquire habits without much conscious thought, since the reward subconsciously encourages us to do the behavior over and over until it becomes a conditioned habit. Then we continue doing them even when they no longer add to our quality of life and keep us from growing.

Replacing negative habits with positive ones is an important step in your journey to the Endorphin Zone. In the final chapter, I'll reveal a powerful technique for replacing disempowering thoughts, behaviors, and habits with empowering ones. For now, make a list of your empowering habits. Then identify any habits you want to change, and their cues and rewards.

* * *

Before May 6, 1954, no human had ever run a mile in under four minutes. Many doctors believed we lacked the heart and lung capacity for such a feat. But Roger Bannister, a lanky British medical student, believed he could break the four-minute barrier.

Bannister applied his knowledge of physiology to create a scientific but highly unconventional training program. He developed a habit of training every day during his lunch hour. For years, he made slow, steady progress toward his goal. Finally, he had his opportunity at Oxford in 1954.

Even though windy and rainy weather made his chances of success almost nil, Bannister decided to go for it. When the starter's pistol fired, he launched out of his blocks. He ran the first three laps in a little over three minutes, leaving just fifty-nine seconds for his final lap.

In the last bend, fifty yards from the finish line, Bannister kicked in a Herculean burst of effort. He was totally exhausted, but felt that "the moment of a lifetime had come." When he broke the finish-line tape, the crowd exploded in pandemonium.

This plucky, twenty-five-year-old amateur had officially accomplished the "impossible" and set a new world record, finishing a mile in 03:59.4! With one of his highest aspirations fulfilled, Bannister said, "No words could be invented for such supreme happiness."

Bannister's breakthrough made headlines around the world. *Sports Illustrated* called it one of the greatest athletic breakthroughs of the twentieth century. He became a national hero. But the most important result of his achievement was the impact it had on other people.

When they learned of Bannister's breakthrough, runners around the world instantly upgraded their beliefs about what was possible and adopted Bannister's training habits and techniques, now aspiring to sub-four-minute miles themselves

Within one year, thirty-seven other runners broke the four-minute barrier. In the following year, three hundred runners broke it! Today, running a four-minute mile is routine for serious competitors.

One person's aspirations, beliefs, habits, and accomplishments can expand human boundaries and empower others to achieve more of their potential.

That's what can happen when you optimize your personal operating system!

ENDORPHIN EVENT #4
Identify Your Empowering Beliefs

Summarize this chapter for your guests by going through the pages and using the subheads and graphics to share the key points. Then brainstorm on the following topics.

1. On a scale of one to ten, with ten being "incredibly well," how are your current beliefs working for you?
2. Where did your beliefs come from? Did you choose them because they empower you to live your best possible life? Or did you acquire them, without thinking about it, from your family, friends, popular culture, the media, etc.?
3. What are you optimistic about for the future? What new behaviors or thoughts would increase your optimism?
4. Which of your aspirations, beliefs, and habits contribute the most to your success and happiness? Which ones do you want to change or upgrade?
5. Which disempowering beliefs do you want to change so you can adapt, and evolve to your higher potential?
6. What new empowering beliefs have you gained by reading this far?
7. What will you do differently in the future, based on your insights from this chapter?

Define Your Personal Powers

> *Know thyself.*
> **–Ancient Greek aphorism**

Participants in the Experience Sampling Method (ESM) study wore pagers that beeped randomly ten times a day. After each beep, they completed a short questionnaire recording where they were, what they were doing, how they were feeling, and the level of skill they were using.

With this technique, research psychologist Mihaly Csikszentmihalyi ("ME-high Chick-sent-ME-high") created the first moment-by-moment record of people's activities and circumstances and their accompanying emotions. After three decades of sampling over eight thousand people worldwide, he probably knows more about moment-by-moment happiness than anyone on Earth.

Not long ago, I enjoyed a lunch with Professor Mike (which is what Dr. Csikszentmihalyi's students call him), while he shared some of his insights about happiness, engagement, and the good life.

"Imagine you have a stressful day at work. When you come home, you play with your kids, your grandkids, or even your dog. After fifteen minutes of laughing and goofing around, you feel happy and relaxed."

I nodded, visualizing my excited dog, Kiwi, when I come home. Then he said something that changed my thinking about happiness.

"Once you've discovered an activity that reduces your stress and makes you feel happy—why not do it for *thirty* minutes every day instead of fifteen? That will double the amount of time you experience positive emotions!"

He cocked his head and raised his bushy eyebrows at me. For a moment, his impish smile, white beard, and twinkling blue eyes reminding me of Santa Claus.

Then he gave me this gift of wisdom.

"The key to a good life is to discover what lights you up, engages you, and makes you happy, then do it more often."

A major *aha!* flashed through my mind. *Why not arrange your whole day to reduce stress and increase your happiness?* An epiphany hit me: *Why not arrange your whole life to minimize stress and maximize your happiness?* That conversation planted the seed for Endorphinomics.

The Seven Endorphin Domains

Your personal operating system, covered in the last chapter, is the first of seven interconnected Endorphin Domains that determine the quality of your life. Your operating system is the most important one because it's the foundation for success and happiness, or frustration and stress, in the other six domains.

Four of your Endorphin Domains are internal, and three are external, existing in the world outside of you. The internal ones are 1) your personal operating system, 2) your powers, 3) your passions, and 4) your purpose. The external ones are 5) positive people, 6) positive places, 7) financial sustainability. Each domain is comprised of three key elements, components, or sub domains.

DEFINE YOUR PERSONAL POWERS

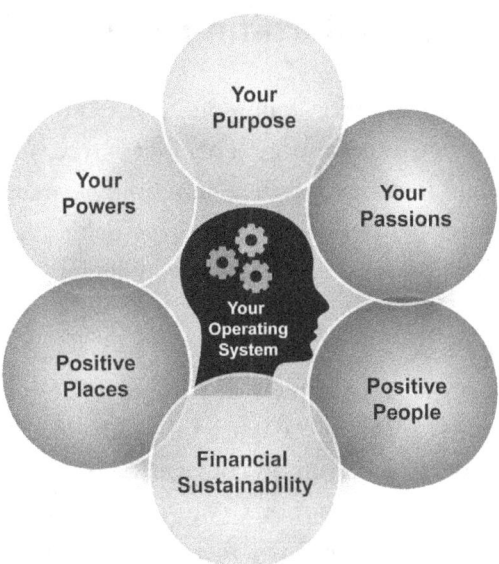

Figure 5.1. The Seven Endorphin Domains

Internal	External
The Seven Endorphin Domains & their Sub Domains	

1) **Your Operating System**
  a) Aspirations
  b) Beliefs
  c) Habits
	5) **Positive People**
	  a) Soul Mates
	  b) Family & Friends
	  c) Mentors

2) **Your Powers**
  a) Unique Abilities
  b) Character Strengths
  c) Health & Vitality
	6) **Positive Places**
	  a) Region & Community
	  b) Neighborhood & Home
	  c) Favorite Places

3) **Your Purpose**
  a) Transformative Events
  b) Values
  c) Role Models
	7) **Financial Sustainability**
	  a) Positive Cash Flow
	  b) Building Resources
	  c) Financial Independence

4) **Your Passions**
  a) Key Interests
  b) Favorite Activities
  c) Worthy Causes	

Exhibit 5.2. The Twenty-One Subdomains

Discover Your Endorphin Data and Dreams

Two sources of information will guide you to your best possible life and help you avoid miswanting. The first is the science of human flourishing. That includes positive psychology, neuroscience, social science, and other fields. Scientists in these fields are uncovering universal values, beliefs, desires, aspirations, behaviors and circumstances that lead—across all cultures—to flourishing individuals and peaceful, thriving societies.

Their work provides a framework for enhancing personal well-being. But you must fill in the details for yourself. That's where your second source of information on your ideal life comes in. That source is you—specifically your emotions, your inner guides.

You know immediately how you feel in any present situation. But you can't accurately predict how you'll feel in future situations. So guessing what will make you happy in the future often leads to "miswanting."

Although you can't know exactly how you'll feel in future situations, you're excellent at remembering how you felt in past situations, especially during emotionally charged experiences. So, to know what will evoke positive emotions in the future, simply identify what evoked them in the past, in each of the six remaining Endorphin Domains. I call this historical information your "Endorphin Data."

In addition to your Endorphin Data, you need to identify your "Endorphin Dreams." These are things you want to experience, accomplish, or become in the future. You yearn for them and believe they'll make you happy, but you haven't tried them yet. It's best to test drive your Endorphin Dreams before you commit to them.

In the pages ahead I'll provide information, questions and exercises that will help you identify your Endorphin Data and Dreams, in each of the remaining Endorphin Domains. You don't have to answer all of the questions, just the ones you intuitively feel a desire to answer. You can answer additional questions later, on your second and third read of this book.

Defining your Endorphin Data and Dreams is an ongoing process. It takes time and introspection to know what made you happy and successful in the past and will help you flourish in the future.

Your Personal Powers

Your personal powers are comprised of your

1. unique abilities,
2. character strengths, and
3. health and vitality.

After completing the exercises in this section, you'll be able to confidently answer the question, "What are you naturally good at that you really love to do?" In chapter 10, I'll explain how this information can help you identify the ideal work, for you.

Long ago, the Buddha counseled, "Your work is to discover your work and then with all your heart to give yourself to it." The more you develop and express your personal powers, the more you'll accomplish and the more you'll flourish.

Your operating system is your most important Endorphin Domain, and your personal powers is probably the second most important one. Sonya Lyubomirsky and two colleagues came to this conclusion after analyzing 225 different studies on happiness. The reasons are obvious.

When we express our personal powers through work, we earn money to pay for our needs and desires and to pursue our aspirations. Satisfying these universal human "needs" evokes key positive emotions including, competence, autonomy, and engagement.

Health, wealth, and happiness naturally follow when we cultivate and express our personal powers. Professor Mike says, "People feel best when doing what they do best."

That brings us to a problem that reduces many people's success and happiness: unsatisfying work. According to Marcus Buckingham, the co-author of *Now, Discover Your Strengths,* only about one in six American workers express their personal powers daily at work. And the Gallup organization reports that about seven in ten workers are "not engaged" or are "actively disengaged" at work.

It seems like most Americans could use help finding engaging, rewarding, and fulfilling work.

The ideal work environment empowers you to develop and express your powers: It doesn't require you to use any of your weaknesses. You're able to pursue your passions and fulfill your purpose while achieving meaningful goals with positive people, in positive places, and it would all be sustainable. You experience the joy of work every day, all day.

This brings us to one of the most important concepts in positive psychology.

Get Into the Flow

"The best moments usually occur if a person's body or mind is stretched to its limits in a voluntary effort to accomplish something difficult and worthwhile." That's according to Professor Mike, who literally wrote the book on the subject, *Flow.*

When we concentrate our attention and efforts on overcoming difficult but surmountable challenges, it often evokes an intensely absorbing, gratifying, and enjoyable feeling. Athletes call it "the zone." Professor Mike named it "flow," and defined it as a non-ordinary state of consciousness. It happens both at work and at play, especially when you're engaged in creative activities.

Like eustress, flow is an optimal state of psychological arousal. But, unlike eustress, flow occurs only when your skills are perfectly matched to the challenge at hand. When challenges are greater than your skills, you become frustrated. Flow happens between boredom and anxiety—the perfect amount of stimulation and concentration. You're intensely absorbed with your task, often feeling like you're on autopilot; you lose your self-awareness and any sense of time.

To experience flow, you must have clear rules and objectives, and immediate feedback, so you can adapt your behavior to achieve your goal. During a flow experience, the world seems to fade away. Professor Mike says people experiencing flow feel "strong, alert, in effortless control, unselfconscious, and at the peak of their abilities."

Imagine yourself skiing the deep powder in Utah. It's the first run of the day. The sun is shining, the sky is blue, and the snow is perfect. You bounce rhythmically between turns and effortlessly sink into the next one as you carve perfect S's in the snow.

You're intensely absorbed; nothing else matters to you. Although you've taken ski lessons for years and consciously struggled to improve, today you're skiing challenging terrain with no conscious effort. You're feeling powerful, on the edge. You're skiing at the top end of your ability. You're in the flow and don't ever want it to end.

During flow states, all your attention is focused on the task in front of you, leaving no cognitive bandwidth for experiencing emotions. But, immediately afterward, you usually feel intense joy, elation, competence, accomplishment, contentment, satisfaction, and even exhilaration. *Optimal experience* is the term that Professor Mike uses to describe flow's intensely rewarding feelings.

Flow leads to better skills and bigger accomplishments. To avoid boredom as you improve your skills, you must constantly take on greater challenges and set higher goals. This is what motivates people to climb mountains, play music, golf, paint, ski, design buildings, build businesses, and engage in many other challenging activities.

Work that creates flow can provide some of the most enjoyable moments—true endorphin moments. When your work evokes flow, extrinsic rewards such as money and status become secondary to the sheer joy of work.

Flow usually occurs only after we achieve mastery in a field. The more you develop your raw talents, the more flow and accomplishment you'll enjoy. Identifying your unique talents and abilities is the first step to expressing them through flow-generating work.

Your Unique Abilities

In high school, I took a jewelry course: attended every class, learned the basic skills, and worked hard at creating aesthetically pleasing pieces. With all my effort, I created only amateurish work. But Liz, another jewelry student, created masterpieces.

It was her first jewelry class, too, but Liz crafted dazzling pieces of intense beauty. She had an innate talent for transforming lumps of silver and inexpensive gemstones into highly desirable *objets d'art*. Liz had natural talent that flowed through her into her jewelry.

Like Liz, each one of us has unique raw talents that we inherited from our parents. They come in two forms, physical talents such as athletics or dance, and mental talents such as IQ and social intelligence. Our inborn talents determine which subjects we learn the fastest and have potential to excel in, but our interests usually determine which specific knowledge and skills we pursue.

Although natural talents are important, they're just the foundation. By developing your natural talents and interests into skills, you can transform them into unique abilities.

Researcher Anders Ericsson and his colleagues discovered that it takes about ten thousand hours of practice to achieve mastery-level ability—in almost any skill. Since almost no one practices forty hours a week, we typically don't achieve our full potential until after ten years of concentrated effort.

Mastery occurs through the process of brain plasticity as learning and practice lay down robust neurological pathways. It requires natural talent and many years of focused effort and practice. So it's critical to have a strong interest in the talents and skills you decide to develop.

Here's a process that will help you identify your unique natural talents.

Identify Your Peak Successes

Most of your raw talents expressed themselves when you were young. That's because they're core traits. When I was nine years old,

I had a paper route and doubled the number of subscribers in the first year. This was a spontaneous and untrained expression of my natural entrepreneurial talent. I bought magic tricks with the money I earned and entertained my friends at birthday parties. This was an early expression of my talent for public speaking.

If you think back, you'll discover natural talents and interests that you've expressed in the past, so start making a list of your previous peak success experiences. These are events, projects, or activities that you were personally responsible for that meet the following criteria. (Note: bookmark or dog-ear this page, because you'll want to refer to these criteria during the Endorphin Event suggested at the end of this chapter.)

1. *You experienced positive emotions* while you were doing them (interest, fun, pleasure, joy, competence, engagement, confidence, flow, etc.). You'd love to do them more in the future.
2. *You intuitively knew* what to do and learned quickly with little training or instruction (used your natural talents).
3. *You did it easily and competently,* compared to others (received awards, accolades, bonuses, promotions, etc.).
4. *You feel satisfied* when you think about these successful experiences (proud, content, fulfilled, a sense of having made a positive contribution, accomplishment, self-esteem, etc.).

Can you remember a specific time when you experienced a peak success that fits these four criteria? What were you doing? How did you feel? How do you feel now, as you think about it? Make a list of ten to twenty peak success experiences that fit these criteria. Start with the earliest ones you can remember. Include a mixture of personal and work successes from different chapters of your life.

Name each peak success. For instance, "started a garden," or "raised two happy and successful children," or "won a Nobel peace prize." They don't have to be about winning awards or competitive contests. List the things you did well in the past that you'd love to do more of in the future, because they made you feel happy at the time and satisfied now.

Identify Your Natural Talents and Learned Skills

Once you identify meaningful past successes the next step to identify the specific talents, knowledge and skills that enabled you to accomplish each one. For each experience, write down four things:

1. Name each past success.
2. What was the activity, event, project, etc. that you successfully accomplished? (Write one or two sentences.)
3. What natural talents, and learned knowledge and skills, did you use to achieve each success? Identify each small step of each success and what you did to make it happen. Did you plan, call, write, research, sell, produce, influence, manage, innovate, fix, solve, or build anything? (Write one to three paragraphs.)
4. What specific, tangible outcomes did your efforts achieve? This could include sales, production, awards, achievements, problems solved, accolades, promotions, new products developed, etc. (Write one or two sentences highlighting your most significant results.)

In your responses, paint word pictures and use active verbs so you can see yourself doing the things that led to your successes. Use these success stories to identify your: 1) natural talents, 2) learned knowledge, and 3) acquired skills.

To see a sample description of a peak success, go to EndorphinZone.com.

It's best to do this exercise over a couple of days or even weeks. When you give yourself an assignment, your subconscious mind will start searching your memory banks. Slowly, your past peak successes and the talents and abilities you used will bubble up into your conscious thoughts. Be prepared to record your personal insights when they occur.

Ask Others for Help

If trying to identify your past successes makes your brain hurt, you're not alone. Our extrinsically oriented culture doesn't encourage us to note or value our intrinsic rewards. If it wasn't an organized competition and we didn't win a prize, we typically don't think of a past experience as a "real" success. Plus, it's hard to see ourselves objectively.

So another effective strategy is to ask your family, friends, and colleagues for help identifying your unique talents and abilities. Simply ask five to ten people who know you well, "What do you think my natural talents and unique abilities are?" Their thoughts and observations will help you verify or refine your conclusions.

You can elaborate:

> *"I need your help. I'm trying to identify and better understand my unique talents and abilities so I can discover how to make a bigger contribution to ——————— [your field, or the world]. Would you be willing to write one or two paragraphs describing my greatest strengths and skills, as you see them? I'm interested in the things that you think I naturally do easily and well."*

Don't be surprised if your family and friends identify unique powers that you hadn't yet recognized in yourself. We're often blind to our natural talents because they come so easily to us. We tend to think that everyone can do what we can do. But each one of us has unique raw talents and learned abilities.

Combine your family and friends' insights with your own. Are your natural talents working with people? Organizing, analyzing, and processing information? Or, are you gifted at working with your hands, tools, objects, and things?

Once you've identified your natural talents and unique abilities, you'll probably want to match them to specific work interests and income opportunities. I recommend you take an online interest inventory such as the Campbell Interest and Skills Inventory (CISS®) at http://psychcorp.pearsonassessments.com. There is a nominal cost for the service, about $20. But the reports are excellent and will match your talents, interests, and skills to specific fields and occupations.

Review the report and highlight the fields and job descriptions that light you up. What are your strongest work interests and skills? Which ones do you want to explore? Which ones are the best match for your natural talents, unique abilities, and interests?

Now, you have good information on your work strengths from three sources, yourself, people who know you well, and an objective assessment of the best work for you. *Synthesize all this information into concise success stories that telegraph your strongest talents, knowledge, and skills.*

Make it easy for others to quickly understand your personal powers. Use active words (verbs) that describe what you did to make each success happen, i.e. built, sold, managed, wrote, created, analyzed, designed, solved, researched, etc. End each story with the positive results of your actions: you at your best.

What About Your Weaknesses?

When I was going through career counseling, after I finally got all my peak successes and unique abilities down on paper, my counselor gave me an assignment to list my weaknesses. I showed up at my next counseling session expecting to discuss how I could improve them.

"Did you bring your list of weaknesses?" my counselor asked as I sat down.

I pulled out a page full of things that I didn't do easily or well, feeling a bit disheartened by its length.

"Excellent," he said as he briefly scanned the page. Then he crumpled it into a wad and hurled it into the trash.

"What are you doing?" I howled as I shot upright in my chair.

He told me that researchers at Harvard had discovered that our weaknesses don't change much over our lifetime, but our strengths are almost infinitely expandable. Then he said, "Steve, your weaknesses aren't going to help you get where you want to go. Besides, even if you improved them dramatically, you'd still only be mediocre in those areas."

We both laughed, knowing he was speaking the truth.

Each of us has unique talents and interests. Focus on identifying and developing yours to their fullest potential. Then use them as often as possible. As best as you can, avoid situations that force you to use your weaknesses.

Your Character Strengths

More than 2300 years ago, Aristotle introduced an important dimension to the concept of flourishing—character strengths. He believed that the single-minded pursuit of hedonic pleasures and selfish interests stunted personal growth and harmed communities. His path to flourishing was through virtuous behaviors in the service of others.

Character strengths, the outward behavioral expressions of our inner values, are also called "values in action." Positive character strengths lead to flourishing individuals and healthy societies. That's because they encourage virtuous behavior and discourage us from doing things that feel good in the moment but could lead to problems in the future.

But we don't always have to wait for the payoffs, since virtuous behaviors also make us happier in the present. Michael F. Steger and his colleagues at Colorado State University asked students to complete logs of their daily activities and their emotional state. The researchers found that ". . . the more virtue-building activities people engaged in, the happier they said they were, both on the day in question and on the following day."

What's more, the students' reported that pleasurable activities like drinking alcohol or taking a walk didn't contribute to their happiness.

Your virtuous character strengths complement your unique abilities. You may have in-demand skills, but if you're chronically late, rude, lazy, argumentative, drunk, and smelly, you won't thrive. Here's what you need to know about these important personal powers.

After three years of research, Martin Seligman and his colleague, Chris Peterson, identified six core virtues encompassing twenty-four character strengths that are universally valued across most of the world's cultures. The six virtues are wisdom and knowledge, courage, humanity, justice, temperance, and transcendence.

The 24 Character Strengths

Wisdom and Knowledge. Cognitive strengths that involve acquiring information and knowledge and turning them into actionable insights:

1. Creativity (artistic, originality, ingenuity, problem solving, innovation)
2. Curiosity (interest, novelty seeking, adventure, exploring, open to new ideas and experiences)
3. Judgment (critical thinking, withholding conclusions until you know the facts, willing to consider all sides impartially, willing to change your mind in light of evidence)
4. Love of learning (formal and informal studies to master a subject, adding systematically to what you already know)
5. Perspective (wisdom, providing sensible counsel)

Courage. *Emotional strengths that give you the will to take action to accomplish goals, even in the face of perceived or real obstacles:*

6. Bravery (valor, physical and moral courage, standing up to threats and challenges)
7. Perseverance (persistence, industriousness, following through to completion in spite of obstacles)
8. Honesty (authenticity, integrity, genuine and sincere)
9. Zest (vitality, enthusiasm, vigor, energy)

Humanity. *Relationship strengths, including giving care, serving others, teaching, coaching and engaging with people:*

10. Love (the ability to love and be loved, valuing sharing and caring, romantic, familial, and brotherly relationships)
11. Kindness (generosity, nurturance, care, compassion, altruism, "niceness")
12. Social Intelligence (emotional and interpersonal intelligence, aware of your own and others' feelings and motives)

Justice. *Civic strengths that create flourishing communities, strong democracies and a better world:*

13. Teamwork (citizenship, social responsibility, loyalty, contributing your fair share)
14. Fairness (equality, fair chance, treat everyone the same)
15. Leadership (organizing groups and getting them to accomplish things, consensus building, communicating a shared vision, making the group feel special)

Temperance. *Willpower that gives us the ability to avoid excesses:*

16. Forgiveness (accepting others' faults and shortcomings, not seeking revenge, mercy)
17. Humility (modesty, not bragging, feeling equal and not superior to others)
18. Prudence (wisely cautious, avoiding painful mistakes, evaluating the future impact of current actions or decisions)
19. Self-regulation (self-control of appetites, emotions, and behaviors)

Transcendence. *Strengths that can connect you with your interpretation of the divine and provide meaning in your life:*

20. Appreciation of Beauty and Excellence (awe, wonder, elevation, valuing aesthetics and excellence in the world)
21. Gratitude (being thankful for the good things in your life, counting your blessings)
22. Hope (optimism, future-mindedness, believing you can create a better future)
23. Humor (playfulness, laughing, teasing, making people smile, spontaneous silliness, and jokes)
24. Spirituality (faith, purpose, coherent mental models about the purpose and meaning of life that provide comfort and guide behavior)

You may notice that many of these character strengths are also positive emotions. Also, there are undoubtedly more than twenty-four widely valued character strengths. Scientists are working to identify other ones to add to this list.

Discover your character strengths.

The simplest way to identify your character strengths is to prioritize this list. But the most accurate and effective way is to take an online survey. The VIA Institute on Character has a website that you can use to identify and rank your character strengths. (Simply complete the free *VIA Me!* survey at viacharacter.org/www/.)

When you finish, the website ranks the twenty-four character strengths from your strongest to weakest. Print a hard copy. For about $20.00, you can purchase the *VIA Me! Pathways* report, which has more detailed explanations of your results and each character strength.

After taking the VIA questionnaire, review your top five character strengths. These are your "signature" strengths, the ones that you value the most and express the most often. Your character strengths aren't as tangible as your knowledge and skills. Think of your unique abilities as tangible work skills and your character strengths as intangible work/life skills. In many work situations, they are more important than your skills. Good character takes decades to develop; many work skills can be learned in a few months.

How did your signature strengths contribute to your peak work successes? Now that you know what they are, weave your top five "signature character strengths" into your success stories.

The Most Satisfying Character Strengths

There's a direct correlation between high ranking on 21 of the character strengths and high life satisfaction. So commit to cultivating all of your character strengths, but pay special attention to the five most satisfying ones.

After surveying about four thousand people, Seligman and his colleagues realized that the happiest and most satisfied people consistently ranked high on these five character strengths:

1. gratitude,
2. optimism,
3. zest/vitality,
4. curiosity, and
5. love.

In addition to these five strengths, Chris Peterson, one of the leading researchers on character strengths, discovered that forgiveness is vitally important for flourishing. He calls it the "queen of all virtues" and laments it's "probably the hardest to come by." No matter what your signature character strengths are, everyone will benefit by cultivating all six of these universally valued virtues.

Your Health and Vitality

A study by the Pew Research Center concluded, "While there's a strong association between feeling healthy and happy, there's an even stronger association between feeling unhealthy and unhappy.... No other characteristic ... comes close to rivaling poor health as a predictor of unhappiness."

Unfortunately, American workers aren't very healthy, and that's dampening our positivity. According to a 2011 Gallop poll, six out of seven (86%) are either obese or have chronic health problems. Nearly half are dangerously overweight and suffer from one or more chronic (lifelong) health issues.

When you combine these findings with American's low positivity ratio and high levels of stress, you realize we're suffering from a costly stress/unhappiness/health pandemic. How can we reverse this huge and growing problem?

The Secret to Health and Vitality

During a recent check-up, my doctor noted that I'd gained some weight, and my cholesterol and blood pressure were a bit high. Her prescription, to bring all of my vital signs into healthy ranges was ... to exercise more. No pills, special diets, or amazing secrets. Just exercise more.

Physical activity plays a key role in health because it helps prevent and heal virtually all chronic diseases. And a lifestyle that doesn't include physical activity is a sure road to early decay, disease, and death.

Dr. Karim Kahn shocked the audience of the 2011 American College of Sports Medicine (ACSM) conference when he told them the risks of a sedentary lifestyle: "At epidemic proportions, smoking, diabetes and obesity are major public health concerns—yet low physical fitness kills more people than all these in combination!"

Unfortunately, a dangerously sedentary lifestyle is the norm in America and much of the industrialized world. As a result, not exercising is ruining our lives in many ways.

Why is exercise so important to your health and energy level?

Our bodies thrive when they're active. Our ancient ancestors hunted and gathered for four to six hours a day. They climbed trees, chased game, dug up roots and gathered nuts and berries. They probably walked, ran, and sprinted between eight and ten miles a day, working all their muscles hard, just surviving. Being in peak physical condition wasn't an option, it was a necessity.

For us modern humans, robust physical activity floods our minds and bodies with increased blood flow and fills every cell with nurturing, healing, regenerating molecules. It also releases endorphins, which strengthen our immune system.

Exercise also builds healthy hearts, muscular bodies, strong bones, and boosts sex drive. It reduces the risk of heart attacks, stroke, hypertension, Alzheimer's disease, arthritis, diabetes, and high-cholesterol.

Both aerobics and strength training rev up your metabolism. That causes you to burn more fat calories. So, even though you're burning more calories, exercise suppresses your appetite. As you become leaner, more muscular, and more vital, you become sexier and more attractive. That increases your confidence and self-esteem.

Happy people exercise more, which enhances mental and physical health and increases energy. The self-discipline required to stay fit creates a deep sense of pride, accomplishment, and optimism. That makes you more willing to take on bigger projects because you know you have the energy and discipline to succeed. My friend Humberto, a personal trainer, says, "Exercise makes us healthy, sexy, and energetic!" Who wouldn't want that?

Exercise also makes us more engaged, proactive, and productive. It enhances creativity and curiosity. Robust activity elevates your mood and alleviates depression better than the widely prescribed anti-depression drugs, such as Prozac. That's partially because exercise floods your brain with mood enhancing neurotransmitters, including endorphins and dopamine. Regular exercisers produce endorphins faster and in far greater amounts than sedentary people do.

On the other hand, not exercising is like taking a depressant every day!

All those reasons should convince you to exercise regularly. But there are other important benefits.

Exercise makes you smarter.

Robust physical activity that makes you sweat unleashes a cocktail of nourishing molecules in your brain. These neuropeptides foster the growth of new brain cells (neurogenesis) and facilitate the growth of new and more robust neural pathways in a process called "brain plasticity." The result is faster, deeper learning and improved memory and recall—a higher IQ.

Carl Cotman, director of the Institute of Brain Aging and Dementia at the University of California, Irvine says, "Exercise can improve anyone's mood and mental performance."

Good sleep is an important element of learning and mental health. Heart-pounding activities release serotonin, a neurotransmitter that moderates mood and helps you sleep deeper and longer, enabling the important REM (Rapid Eye Movement) cycles that process, sort, and integrate new experiences and information. After a good night's sleep, you actually remember information and perform new skills better. You awake feeling refreshed, energized, and eager to take on the challenges of the day.

In addition to all these amazing benefits of exercising, there's one more really big one.

Exercise enhances longevity.

Aerobic exercise slows and can even reverse aging. In the book *Younger Next Year,* Henry Lodge, a world-renowned anti-aging specialist, describes how exercise makes you younger.

"Some seventy percent of premature death and aging is lifestyle-related. Heart attacks, strokes, the common cancers, diabetes, most falls, fractures and serious injuries, and many more illnesses are primarily caused by the way we live." It turns out most of what we think of as normal aging is actually decay due to a sedentary lifestyle. The happy alternative to decay and depression is a life-long commitment to physical activity.

Lodge writes, "The keys to overriding the decay code are daily exercise, emotional commitment, reasonable nutrition, and a real engagement with living. But it starts with exercise. . . . Exercise is the master signal for growth."

Vigorous aerobic exercise cuts the risk of dying from a heart attack in half. But even walking your dog for twenty minutes a day makes a huge impact on your health, vitality, and longevity.

Develop your exercise program.

If you're serious about living a long, happy, and successful life, commit to robust physical activity almost every day.

To stay youthful for as long as possible after age sixty, Lodge recommends exercising enthusiastically for one hour, six days each week. This includes four days of aerobics and two days of weight training and stretching. Experts seem to agree on the minimal recommended amount of exercise is 30 minutes a day for five or six days a week. Anything less is suboptimal.

Start by determining your current health and fitness levels. Be sure to get a physical exam and the approval of your doctor before cranking up your activity. Then set realistic and achievable goals to optimize your health and vitality.

The simplest and least expensive way to get more exercise is make a list of the physical activities that you enjoy doing. Then *determine how you can integrate some or all of them into your daily or weekly routine, and schedule exercise dates with your friends and lovers.* Embrace activity, physical exertion, and sweat; don't avoid them.

In the summer, I ride my bike to work almost every day. I can easily get in thirty minutes of exercise by just going to work. I also swim laps after work and on weekends. In the winter, I work out on my elliptical trainer while watching music or educational DVDs. Brooke and I both like to garden, which often gives us a good work out. Even house cleaning, if done with the right attitude and music, can provide a boost in your heart rate and mood.

There are many great resources to help you set up a successful exercise program. If you have the time and money, hire a personal trainer or join a gym. Whatever you do, don't sit passively as your health and happiness slowly deteriorate. That's what old fogeys do. Wise happies exercise because they know it's powerful medicine that will optimize their quality of life.

John J. Ratey, of Harvard Medical School, muses, "If exercise came in pill form, it would be plastered across the front page, hailed as the blockbuster drug of the century."

Document Your Personal Powers

The final step in defining your powers is to identify which unique abilities, character strengths, and/or health and vitality contributed the most to your most fulfilling work successes. So prioritize the key personal powers that you identified in the exercises above. These are your *core competencies* that define your competitive advantage. No one else can be as good as you at being you.

Awareness and appreciation of your powers is the first step to expressing them more often. *Write a short story about three to five of your most significant successes and the unique powers that made them possible.* These stories will describe you at your best, when you're working in the Endorphin Zone.

Think what would happen if you constantly improved your personal powers and expressed them every day doing intrinsically rewarding work.

* * *

DEFINE YOUR PERSONAL POWERS

Years ago, Marissa was an administrative assistant in the investment industry. She had worked her way through college and always earned good grades. She'd graduated with a business degree, but she was more naturally gifted in dealing with people than data.

However, Marissa's job involved almost no people contact and forced her to do things she wasn't good at: clerical work and data analysis. It drained her energy, and even though she tried hard, her supervisor always found errors in her work.

Marissa had taken the first job offered to her out of college, without any understanding of her personal powers. As you can imagine, she was underpaid, under-appreciated, and unhappy. Because she wasn't doing a good job, her boss wouldn't give her a much-needed raise. Instead, he was considering letting her go. Worst of all, she felt incompetent and frustrated. She didn't experience any flow at work.

And then Marissa discovered the type of work that would allow her to flourish.

She went through the process I described above to define her personal powers. As her coach, I helped her determine where her natural talents, unique abilities, and character strengths would make the biggest contribution. Her youth and active lifestyle guaranteed health and vitality. Once Marissa knew what she was naturally good at and liked to do, she drafted a resume using her peak success stories to quickly communicate her core competencies to others.

Then she let all of her friends and contacts know she was looking for a new opportunity. A friend told her about a job opening in the city where she went to college and had many friends. She applied for and was immediately offered the position. When she compared it to her current situation, it was a much better fit for her talents, abilities, character strengths, and interests: she'd be working directly with people and would have minimal administrative duties.

She weighed the pros and cons of moving to another city and giving up her current position. Since the new job played to her strengths and minimized the use of her weaknesses, and she already had friends in the city, Marissa accepted the opportunity.

Besides the intrinsic rewards, Marissa's new job included a twenty percent raise, bonuses, and future equity. In this position, now she's more fully expressing her powers. She's also experiencing more autonomy, competence, connection, and self-esteem. By defining her powers and taking action on her insights, Marissa stepped into a new position where she could flourish.

By completing the exercises and questions in this chapter, you'll define the personal powers that you want to develop and express. Once you're clear on those, you can start identifying ways to express them more fully and more often, at work and in your personal life.

ENDORPHIN EVENT #5
Describe Your Personal Powers

Summarize this chapter for your guests by going through the pages and using the subheads and graphics to share the key points. Then brainstorm on the following topics.

1. Share the concept of *flow* and give some examples from your own life. Have everyone identify one or more activities that often put them into a flow state. Brainstorm and make plans to experience more flow in your work and play.
2. Explain the concept of character strengths and brainstorm to help each person identify a few of theirs.
3. Share the four criteria for a peak success experience with your group. (Refer to the page you bookmarked earlier.) Share one or two of your own peak successes that showcase your personal powers.
4. Have each participant identify one or more peak successes from their past.
5. Coach each other to define your top personal powers: your natural talents, unique abilities, character strengths, and elements of health and vitality that contributed to each peak success.
6. Help each other develop peak success stories that showcase your top personal powers and describe you at your best.
7. Brainstorm and make plans to integrate exercise into your routine.
8. Brainstorm and make plans to express your core competencies more often in new, profitable, and rewarding ways.
9. What will you do differently in the future, based on your insights from this chapter?

Discover Your Life's Purpose

> The best way to find yourself
> is to lose yourself in the service of others.
> —**Mohandas Gandhi**

From his humble beginnings as the son of an Alabama sharecropper, Millard Fuller became fabulously wealthy. His story is a testament to the power of purpose.

Fuller became a millionaire before he was thirty when a business he co-founded rocketed to success. He started the company with a single goal: to get rich. Unfortunately, Millard's obsession with money, and his long absences from home stressed his relationship with Linda, his wife. When the pain became unbearable, she fled with their two young children, agonizing over the prospect of divorce. Thanks to Fuller's single-minded pursuit of "more," he had become a "successful miserable person."

The breakdown forced Fuller to re-examine his priorities, leading to a cathartic breakthrough and the renewal of his religious faith. After clarifying his values, he defined a philosophy of life based on "sweat equity," living simply and the "theology of enough." To convince Linda that he loved her more than money, Fuller took a dramatic step: he sold his business and all his possessions. When he gave all the money to non-profit organizations, Linda knew he was sincere.

The Fullers reconciled and began searching for a shared mission. As they clarified what was important to them, their purpose came into focus: to build simple, inexpensive homes for families that couldn't afford conventional homes. They got right to work testing their innovative ideas.

Recycled and locally sourced materials, volunteer help, and zero-interest loans minimized the cost of construction and financing. Future homeowners learned basic construction skills, helped build their own homes, and then helped build homes for others, creating a shared sense of connection and community.

By 1976, having built homes for more than two thousand people in Africa, the Fullers had proven their concept. They held a meeting with their closest associates to share their progress. When their associates realized the implications of the Fullers' successes, they created a non-profit organization to support their mission. By the end of 2008, the organization, Habitat for Humanity International, had provided shelter for more than 1.5 million people in 92 countries around the world!

It all started when Millard and Linda discovered their life's purpose, a purpose that saved their marriage and transformed their lives, and then it enhanced the quality of life of millions of people around the world.

Because your purpose includes both emotional and logical components, clarifying and documenting it turbo-charges your life, infusing you with clarity, direction, and commitment. Your head and your heart work in synergy to achieve rapid progress towards meaningful goals.

Three pathways to discovering, or refining, your purpose are

1. insights from transformative experiences and events,
2. clarifying your values, and
3. observing or learning about role models.

Many people discover their purpose through a combination of these three methods.

No one can discover your purpose for you; you must do it yourself. The key is self-awareness, knowing what's important to you. By answering a series of questions, you'll define and prioritize your Endorphin Data. Then you'll synthesize that information into a short statement of the higher purpose, or mission, for your life. It's easy. I'll walk you through the steps.

The Power of Purpose

The formal study of purpose in life started with Viktor Frankl's reflections on his ordeal in Nazi death camps. In the midst of unspeakable horrors, the young Jewish doctor realized the only prisoners who survived had an unshakeable reason to live, a *purpose* for enduring the misery and hopelessness of their situation.

Specifics didn't seem to matter; personal *meaning* was what counted. While captive, Frankl felt destined to write a book about his experience. Incredibly, he survived the Holocaust, and as soon as he could, Frankl completed his book. Then, in a burst of inspiration, he dictated his entire second book in only nine days. That classic work, *Man's Search for Meaning*, launched the scientific study of purpose and meaning in life.

In modern, industrialized societies, having lost faith in the traditional answers to existential questions, more and more people are searching for meaning in their lives. Like Millard Fillmore, many default to a culturally endorsed purpose: to get rich. But, why work just for money when you can work for money and a higher purpose, a purpose that lifts your heart, your mind, and your spirit?

Discovering and striving for something more important than yourself is one of the most empowering and motivating things you can do. A meaningful purpose, or mission, unleashes your higher powers and inspires you to *go for it* to make your greatest contribution to the world.

A clear and meaningful purpose gives you something to live for and something worth dying for; it guides your decision-making when competing options vie for your finite resources. It empowers and motivates you to focus your time, energy, and money on the things you value most, inspiring you to persevere against difficult, long-term challenges because you know your work is too important to give up.

Although a sense of purpose can dramatically enhance positivity and help you flourish, many people live their entire lives without it. That's understandable, because the yearning for deeper meaning and contribution is a psycho/spiritual aspiration, a far subtler motivator than biological needs and emotional desires. Plenty of people stay focused on their personal needs and wants and never seriously consider loftier aspirations.

For many people, raising a family and working at a job they like provide ample direction, meaning, and fulfillment in their lives. In times of peace, security, and prosperity, the need for a higher purpose subsides. But in times of personal crisis, war, civil unrest or life transitions, such as retirement or losing a spouse, a meaningful purpose can literally save your life. If you're retired, or retiring soon, discovering your purpose will enhance and lengthen the remaining chapters of your life.

Patricia A. Boyle, a neuropsychologist and researcher with the Rush Memory and Aging Project, summarized the results of a study of 1,500 men and women: "Those who reported having purpose in life showed a thirty percent slower rate of cognitive decline than those who didn't.... [W]e think that people who are purposeful are actively pursuing goals, and by virtue of doing this, they are enhancing their brains."

In other words, a purpose will help you keep your "mental marbles" longer and give you a reason to stay fit and healthy, which enhances your longevity.

People who lack purpose never achieve their full potential, tending to live suboptimal lives, suffering from aimlessness and boredom. They lack fulfilling goals and meander through life, often in a precarious state of emptiness, despair, and depression. Viktor Frankl believed that purposeless people experience lives of "existential frustration," echoing what philosopher Thomas Carlyle said: "A person without a purpose is like a ship without a rudder."

A meaningful purpose will inspire you to accomplish great things, motivating you to grow and stretch beyond your comfort zone, guiding you to set and achieve what business expert Jim Collins called "big, hairy, audacious goals" (BHAGS) in the service of your higher calling.

Once you've discovered and defined it, your life purpose becomes the central theme of your identity, the bedrock foundation for your life priorities—the driving motivation behind all of your dreams, aspirations, and actions.

Our Purpose Is to Contribute

A meaningful purpose isn't just an abstract concept; it's a critical component of human civilization. Your purpose inspires you to transcend selfish interests and cooperate with others in the service of a cause that's more important than you alone. That's natural, because humans are hard-wired to collaborate with others. In fact, our ancient ancestors wouldn't have survived if they didn't cooperate, and the most cooperative groups would have had a competitive advantage over less cooperative groups.

Social scientist Jonathan Haidt believes we have evolved "to throw ourselves into noble enterprises, in the pursuit of noble goals, in the company of people we trust."

It's a good thing we're hard-wired to engage in win-win interactions with others, because when we cooperate, we create synergy: everyone gets more of what they need and want. Everyone flourishes. And we experience the most positivity when we're working in groups that are helping other groups. So discover your purpose, and then join a group of people who share it.

Look for Your Purpose in Transformative Events

A chance event or experience can cause you to instantly reevaluate your priorities and the trajectory of your life. These experiences can be direct, like Millard Fuller's breakdown, or indirect, like watching someone else deal with an incurable disease. Shared traumatic events, like the 9/11 jihadist attacks on the United States, can instantly cause millions of previously uninvolved people to band together for a shared purpose.

Not all transformational events or experiences are negative. Some are sublime. Positive experiences and events are an ideal way to discover your purpose. When Barry, the financial "coach" you read about earlier, realized helping people was more rewarding to him than making money (and that they weren't mutually exclusive), he discovered his higher purpose without drama or trauma. After reconnecting with his deeply held values, he developed a personal philosophy of life based on five Fs: family, faith, fitness, finances, and fun. Today, he uses that mental model to maintain balance and to stay focused on the things that matter most—on purpose.

Retreats, workshops, travel, and volunteering are other positive experiences that can lead you to discover your purpose. Still, my favorite transformational events are heart-opening spiritual experiences.

Spiritual Experiences

Throughout history, mystics, shamans, and others have sought to transcend ordinary reality, connect with the divine, and discover their life's' purpose through prayer, chanting, dancing, drumming, fasting, meditating, consuming psychotropic plants, conducting rituals; having sacred sex, undergoing sensory deprivation, and even breathing volcanic gasses (don't try this one at home).

During a vision quest, adolescent Native Americans spend days alone in the wilderness where they commune with the energies and forces of nature. Their goal is a spiritual experience, often in the form of a dream that reveals their purpose and destiny in life.

The spiritual path to discovering your purpose has often been claimed as the exclusive domain of religions. But religion is only one of many ways to connect with the divine, or have an experience of unity and oneness, or to pursue enlightenment. The trend today is more and more people are seeking personal and secular spiritual experiences without the doctrines and rituals of an organized religion.

George Valliant, an eminent professor of psychiatry at Harvard Medical School, has found that secular *peak experiences* (as described by Maslow) and transcendent *spiritual events* (as described by meditators, saints, and prophets) are virtually identical. People who have religious "spiritual experiences" use the same words to describe them as people describing secular "peak experiences." And the same regions of the brain light up no matter what the experiencers call it.

So you can experience transformational thoughts and feelings regardless of your religious or spiritual orientation, or non-orientation.

Emotionally powerful insights about your purpose can occur in a house of worship, in nature, while meditating or even daydreaming. Intense spiritual epiphanies often trigger life-transforming shifts in values and priorities that give you a profound sense of purpose and direction in your life.

Valuing spirituality and spiritual experiences, regardless of your specific beliefs and practices, produces measurable positive effects. In one poll, people with the highest commitment to spirituality were twice as likely to report they were "very happy" as those with the lowest spiritual commitment.

What have your key life experiences led you to believe, to do, and to become?

1. What past experiences have shaped your beliefs and philosophy of life? Have they caused you to reprioritize your values or helped clarify your purpose?

2. What are your beliefs about transcendent spiritual or religious experiences? Have you ever had one? List the key transcendent experiences you've had in the past. How would you describe them?
3. Where have most of your peak moments and insights occurred? What insights about your purpose have you gleaned from these rare glimpses into the infinite?

Since my most profound spiritual experiences have all occurred in pristine, natural places, an important component of my purpose is to protect and sustain healthy ecosystems and to preserve wilderness areas for future generations. My spiritual experiences caused me to feel more connected to nature and therefore value the environment more.

Let Your Faith Guide You

Like Millard Fuller, many people discover their purpose through religion or the socially endorsed tenets of their faith. Although from a scientific point of view, believing in supernatural beings, divine revelations, and an afterlife isn't logical, from a practical point of view, having faith in a god and a formal religion can be the ultimate source of purpose, meaning, and morality. For people in communities that value religion, it's one of the surest ways to flourish

Certainly, religions have been responsible for many wars, conflicts, and even genocide throughout the ages, but they have also made positive contributions to humanity. They are the primary organizing forces, the divine operating systems, of advanced civilizations, acting as "sacred glue" that binds strangers together with common morality, values, belief systems, and purpose.

In a special issue on "Mind, Body, and Happiness," *Time* magazine declared, "Hundreds of scholarly articles in academic publications on the relationship between religion and mental health indicate that it's good to believe." In one study, the Pew Organization found that forty-three percent of Americans who attend religious services at least weekly are "very happy," while only twenty-six percent of those who seldom or never attend services are likely to say they're "very happy."

Adhering to a formal religion has many benefits for individuals and societies. It fosters a sense of identity, direction, reassurance, optimism, and social connection; it reduces insecurity and anxiety by answering questions that science and reason can't. Shared beliefs provide a sense of grand design, sacred mystery, and divinely sanctioned purpose for many people's lives. Experiencing faith-based communal rituals is one of the most fulfilling of all human activities.

The more people integrate religious beliefs and activities into their lives, the happier they are, but only if their beliefs are in harmony with their society's prevailing values. Religion is particularly helpful during stressful times. Faith, combined with support from fellow believers, consoles people in times of difficulty, increasing their resilience and emotional security during setbacks, loneliness, depression, illness, divorce, or loss of a loved one.

Most religious doctrines encourage virtuous behaviors, such as altruism, charity, forgiveness, kindness, and volunteerism. This is why, in America, religious people volunteer at twice the rate of non-religious people, and frequent churchgoers contribute four times as much to all types of charities as non-attendees. All of these culturally endorsed behaviors increase your positivity ratio and help you flourish.

A major benefit of religions is they enhance self-control. Because believers have clearly delineated values, acceptable behaviors, and an omnipotent deity watching their every move, they're better at resisting their "base" impulses than nonbelievers. This makes them more likely than nonbelievers to eschew smoking, drugs, alcohol, and breaking the law.

So, even if the common belief in god(s) and religious doctrines is only an artifact of ancient cognitive processes, as some scientists believe, it pays to believe in something. Like all things in life, the stronger your commitment, the greater your rewards. Devout atheists are actually happier than lukewarm believers are, perhaps because they, too, have unshakable faith in something: their ability to observe, reason, and come to their own conclusions.

Reflecting the values and beliefs that underlie them, religions vary in their ability to satisfy universal human needs and desires. You can see the "fruit" of each religion in the societies their doctrines engender. Religions that undergird flourishing societies suppress the worst and bring out the best in human nature.

The Endorphin Church

If you're seeking a more rewarding religious/spiritual experience than the one you have now, use the sciences of human flourishing to identify your "endorphin church." The ideal religion would bring out the best in you. It would encompass all of the benefits of religions and none of the control, superstition, self-righteousness, conflicts, and violence that have historically plagued them.

The ideal deity would be loving, compassionate, and empowering, a role model for a "wise happy," perfectly balancing the head and the heart, male and female, the Benevolent Father in the heavens above us and the Nurturing Mother in the earth below us.

The doctrines of this belief system would be based on the science of human flourishing and ecological sustainability, perfectly aligning with human nature (psychology) and mother nature (the laws of physics and biology), evolving as researchers gain new knowledge and insights.

Your endorphin church's ceremonies would evoke positive spiritual emotions, such as awe, compassion, forgiveness, gratitude, joy, love, optimism, and trust. Church leaders would guide members in prayers and activities that help them imagine and create better lives for themselves and a more peaceful, ecologically sustainable world for all.

If you're religiously oriented, commit to a faith-based organization that resonates with you. Participate in shared religious activities often. The more the merrier.

But if formal religion isn't your thing, don't worry; you don't have to attend religious services, or even believe in a divine being, to benefit from the positive effects of the concept of god.

Azim Shariff induced research subjects to think about God by solving simple word puzzles. They rearranged random letters to spell words related to spiritual matters. This subconscious priming dramatically increased the subjects' cooperative behavior and generosity to strangers. Most surprisingly, thinking about God evoked positive thoughts and behaviors, even in people who don't believe that he or she exists.

Clarify What You Value

Your values are your criteria for what "ought to be," what is good, beneficial, beautiful, useful, desirable, and appropriate. They motivate you to encourage, or approach, what you believe is "good," and to discourage, or avoid, what you believe is "bad." Prioritizing your values will clarify what's most important to you, which will reveal your life's purpose.

Some values, such as *love*, are desired end states, while other values, such as *self-control*, are means to an end. All of your values have both a logical and an emotional dimension, making them especially powerful type of belief.

Since your value system prioritizes what's important and desirable to you, and what's right and wrong, it's the source of many of your attitudes, aspirations, goals, and intentional behavior.

You can determine what people value by observing how they spend their time and money. It's obvious that someone who hangs out in bars and drives a gas-guzzling Hummer has different values than someone who spends time with their family and drives a gas-sipping Prius.

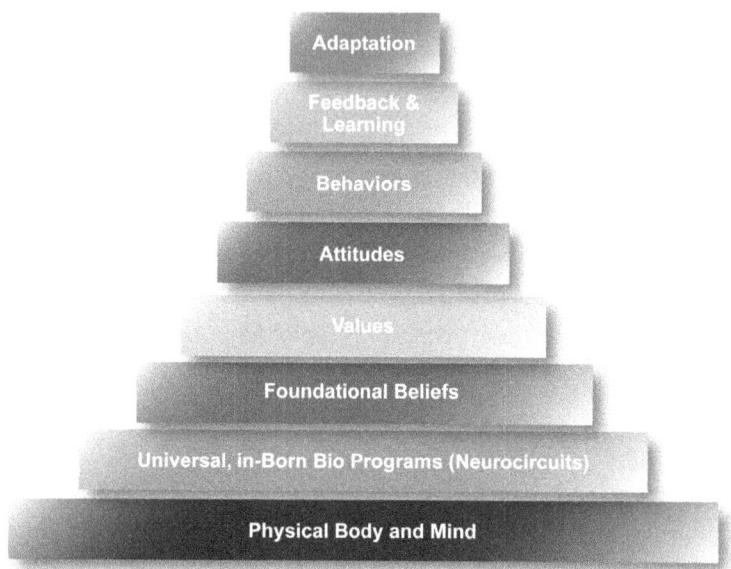

Figure 6.1. Values: An Important Component of Your Personal Operating System

Dysfunctional value systems lead to a downward spiral of languishing. These poor souls often suffer from *anhedonia*, the inability to experience positive emotions, and *anomie*, social alienation. They have trouble connecting with others because they lack common values and social norms. They also experience higher levels of apathy, hopelessness, cynicism, and physical illness.

Individuals with a poorly defined (amoral) or negative (immoral) values system can't distinguish right from wrong. Their lack of "boundaries," that restrict selfish, violent, or greedy behavior, makes them antisocial, deceptive, dishonest, and dangerous. Our prisons are full of criminals whose aberrant value systems and subsequent character weaknesses are the root cause of their troubles.

On the other hand, positive values are the basis for positive character strengths that promote virtuous behaviors that lead to an upward spiral of human flourishing.

Where Do Our Values Come From?

Your values are a product of both nurture and nature. The culture, your religious beliefs (if you're a believer), your peers, and your parents have all inculcated their values into your mind, with various levels of success. But your life experiences and natural intuition also influence which values you ultimately embrace.

A growing body of research shows that many intuitive judgments of right and wrong aren't learned from your culture or religion—they're hard-wired. All humans are born with neuro-circuits that automatically and predictable evoke moral feelings and behaviors in certain situations. These "moral intuitions" form the neurological foundations for many of our most deeply held ethical values.

The strongest evidence for moral intuitions and the values they engender come from research with infants and international studies. When presented with new and unfamiliar moral questions, people from a broad cross-section of cultures, religions, and value systems, including atheists and agnostics, all make identical ethical judgments.

When we're presented with an ethical dilemma, our moral intuitions instantly "know" what the "proper" position or answer should be. This is more than a simple gut reaction; it's an innate sense of right and wrong based on in-born rules, not learned ones. The theory is that these moral intuitions evolved to moderate our selfish urges, allowing us to live in harmony with communities of unrelated people.

So far, scientists have identified six universal, moral intuitions that moderate selfish, violent, and predatory instincts, listed below. Healthy humans naturally favor

1. care (versus harm),
2. fairness and justice (versus inequality and injustice),
3. liberty or freedom (versus oppression),
4. loyalty (versus betrayal),
5. respect for authority (versus subversion), and
6. sacredness or purity (versus degradation, taboos or contamination or indecency)

Our hard-wired moral intuitions define universal ethical values for all humanity. But traumatic life events, dangerous environments, radical ideologies, and brainwashing can completely override these benevolent tendencies in human nature, leading to conflict and violence.

Flourishing individuals and societies value universal moral intuitions and encourage the virtuous behaviors they engender.

Positive Values

One way to categorize values is by their motivation, either extrinsic or intrinsic. Valuing intrinsic rewards is generally more satisfying than valuing extrinsic rewards. But many extrinsic values help us flourish when pursued in moderation. Their tangible results are often culturally endorsed, encouraging you to fit in, be responsible, and contribute to society.

Extrinsic values, such as *work ethic* and *prosperity,* underlie much of the technological progress and material abundance in industrialized nations. Material abundance empowers you to easily satisfy your needs, allowing you to focus on satisfying your desires and aspirations. So, once again, strive for a happy balance between extrinsic and intrinsic values.

You can also categorize values by their impact on behavior.

Core values are typically motivated by our biological needs and emotional wants. They're important, but we act on them only when they're threatened. Since core values are universally valued, free societies create governments, laws, institutions, and businesses to satisfy them. *Signature values* underlie character strengths and, as you've learned, evoke automatic virtuous behavior.

At the heart of your life's purpose, *aspirational values* motivate you to take action to close the gap between the current situation and your ideal. We live to pursue our *aspirational values;* we will die for our *core values*. Patrick Henry expressed his commitment to a core value when he said: "Give me liberty, or give me death." Core and signature values define who you are; aspirational values guide you to who you are becoming.

Prioritize your values.

In the last chapter, you identified your signature values. Now it's time to identify your core and aspirational values, as well. Below you'll find sixty-six positive values, which includes all of the ones mentioned in the previous pages. That's because some signature values may also be core or aspirational values. I've clarified and expanded each of these master values with the words in parentheses.

Although I've organized the list by Endorphin domains, it's in random order, with no implied hierarchy. (Download a PDF of this list from my website, EndorphinZone.com.)

Prioritize them according to your own values system by rating each master value a 1, 2, or 3, where 1 means "very important," 2 means "somewhat important" and 3 means "not important" to you. Go fast and trust your gut. There are no right or wrong answers, only individual priorities. If a word inside the parentheses resonates with you, circle it. When you're through, follow the instructions below.

Index of Positive Human Values
The 66 Values that Enhance Individual and Communal Flourishing

1. Personal Operating System

Culturally Endorsed Values:

___Work Ethic (industriousness, productivity, staying busy, diligence)

___Self-Direction (entrepreneurial self-starter, independent thought and action, need little supervision, master of own destiny)

___Competition (winners and losers, no monopolies or cartels, free markets)

___Respect for Authority (hierarchy, honor, social order, institutions, status)

___Conformity (fit in, suppress impulses that might upset others or violate social norms, harmonious group functioning)

___Heroism (self-sacrifice for the good of the group)

___Tradition (respect for customs, values, and beliefs of one's culture or religion; support group solidarity and survival)

___Purity (chastity; respect for taboos, customs and sacred objects and places; devoutness, piety)

___Prosperity (abundance of money, wealth, and resources)

___Power (influence and control over money, people, and resources)

___Status (respect, social recognition, admiration)

___Image (looking good, being attractive, fashionable)

Personal Growth Values:

___Positive Emotions (autonomy, competence, connection, self-esteem, pleasure, security, etc.)

___Self-Actualization (meaningful growth, positive change, integration of different aspects of self into a synergistic, holistic, authentic state of being, fulfilling your potential, adapting, flourishing)

___Personal Responsibility (conscientiousness, accountability, reliability, do what you say you'll do, punctuality)

___Self-Expression (individualism, non-conformity, being yourself, expressing your opinions and experiences)

___Self-Esteem (self-respect, honor, confidence, dignity)

___Integrity (authenticity, free from inner conflict and incongruities, will stand up for things that matter)

2. Personal Powers

___Engagement (flow, immersion, absorption, effortlessness)
___Self-Control (self-regulation, willpower, discipline over impulses and urges, deferred gratification)
___Zest (vitality, enthusiasm, vigor, aliveness, energy)
___Health (physical and mental well-being; absence of stress, pain, and disease)
___Physical Fitness (proper exercise and diet, lean, flexible and muscular, active lifestyle)
___Competence (skills, mastery, specialized knowledge, abilities, talents, character strengths, self-sufficiency)
___Creativity (imagination, originality, ingenuity, innovation, inspiration, concepts and ideas, art, music, writing)
___Learning (acquiring new knowledge and developing skills, adding to and refining mental models, optimizing your personal operating system)
___Critical Thinking (listen to all sides, able to change mind in light of evidence, thorough and logical decisions)
___Wisdom (perspective, using insights to advise, coach, counsel and guide others)
___Accomplishment (successes and achievements, making a positive contribution, completing meaningful goals and projects)
___Honesty (truth, sincerity, open communication, moral courage)
___Perseverance (persistence, industriousness, finish what you start, overcome challenges, and obstacles)
___Valor (bravery, physical and moral courage, will fight to protect values and stand for what's right)
___Intelligence (learn quickly, able to transform knowledge into action, good problem solver and flexible thinker)

3. Passions

___Curiosity (interest, novelty seeking, exploration, openness to new experiences and ideas)
___Beauty (balance, aesthetics, form, design, symmetry, awe, wonder, elevation)
___Excellence (mastery, genius, brilliance, merit)
___Excitement (stimulation, novelty, thrills, risk, variety, adventure)
___Pleasure (sensory stimulation and gratification, intellectual stimulation, warmth, movement, luxury, aesthetics)
___Comfort (material abundance, leisure, low stress and mostly positive experiences)

4. Purpose

___Meaning (purpose, direction, belonging and committing to something more significant than yourself)
___Contribution (making a positive difference, supporting the community or greater good, give more than you take)
___Gratitude (appreciation, thankfulness, gratefulness)
___Spirituality (inner harmony, connection with the divine, oneness, transcending ordinary consciousness, profound sense of purpose and meaning)
___Religiousness (faith in a divine being; sacred text; doctrines and historical religious figures that provide purpose, comfort, and meaning)

5. Positive People

___Connection (empowering relationships, love, friendships, family, romance, intimacy, belonging to one or more groups)
___Kindness (generosity, empathy, benevolence, nurturance, compassion, niceness)

___Humor (playfulness, smiles, the lighter side of life, jokes, funny stories, and laughter)

___Social Intelligence (emotional and intrapersonal talents, empathy, and understanding others' states of mind)

___Helpfulness (concern for others, support, cooperation, benevolence, win-win, altruism)

___Forgiveness (mercy, second chances, accepting flaws and transgressions of others)

___Care (do not harm others, nonviolence, protecting human life and well-being, peace, charity, nurturance, altruism)

___Fairness (reciprocity, equality in rights and opportunities for all, honest dealing, justice)

___Humility/Modesty (not feeling superior to others, letting your accomplishments speak for themselves, treating everyone as equal to you)

___Loyalty (to family, community, worthy groups and nation, self-sacrifice for group, patriotism)

___Leadership (consensus building, inspiring others to act, positive role models)

___Teamwork (citizenship, social responsibility, contribution to shared goals, social harmony and cohesion, synergy)

6. Positive Places

___Inspiration (flash of insight, flow of ideas or artistic creation, motivated to create)

___Connection with Nature (sacred places; love of plants, animals, rocks, trees, clouds, stars, rain, waterfalls, sunsets and the outdoors)

___Democracy (representative government; one-person, one-vote; rule of law; property rights; free markets)

___Freedom (autonomy, sovereignty, freedom of speech, liberty, independence, self-rule, master of your life)

___National Security (secure borders; civil order; economic stability; low organized crime and corruption; free from fear of conquest, civil war, invasion, rebellion, or annihilation)

___Personal Security (physical safety, civil rights, property rights, low crime and violence, safe homes and communities)

7. Financial Sustainability

___Optimism (hope, faith, future-mindedness, believe you can create a better future)

___Prudence (wisely cautious in planning for the future, thinking through the potential results of actions or thoughts, saving for a rainy day)

___Financial Fitness (money in the bank, predictable income, spend less then you take home, insurance, control personal finances and investments, preserve resources for future generations)

___Ecological Sustainability (food security, clean air, water, and land; healthy and diverse ecosystem, conserve resources, leave the Earth a better place for future generations)

Now, put a checkmark beside the most important values that you're currently satisfied with. These are your core values. Then circle the most important values that you want to pursue, experience, or manifest. These are your aspirational values.

Next, prioritize your top ten core and aspirational values. Focus on the top five in each category. Complete this exercise by writing a brief statement that explains what's important about each of your top ten values, to you.

When you're through, answer these questions:
Am I living in alignment with my most important values?
Does my work, life, and behavior support my top values?
Am I acting in alignment with my most important values?
How can I align my work and my life more closely with my top values?

Identifying and prioritizing this Endorphin Data will empower you to intentionally focus your time, energy, and resources on the things you value most.

Your top aspirational values are key components of your purpose.

Look for Your Purpose in Role Models

Many individuals discover their purpose by observing or learning about other people, including role models and heroes. This pathway to discovering purpose is typically based on the virtuous behavior of saints, transformational leaders, and cultural heroes. Role models can inspire you to become a better person and to behave more virtuously, and in so doing, reveal your life's purpose.

When you're inspired by people who've made positive contributions to humanity, you experience the positive emotion of elevation. Jonathan Haidt, one of the first scientists to study this "self-transcendent" emotion, defines elevation as the warm, fuzzy feeling you get when you see acts of moral beauty.

When you see or learn about someone doing something good, kind, courageous or compassionate, you feel emotionally uplifted. Elevation causes an expansion of your chest and an especially warm, pleasant, or "tingling" sensation emanating from your heart.

Positive role models inspire you to become a better person, to contribute more to the world. They can fill you with hope, optimism, love, and moral inspiration. You'll find elevating role models in real life and fiction, in history and current times, in unsung heroes and famous leaders, in politics, and in your religion or spiritual pursuits.

Make a list of the role models who have influenced your life. What aspects of their life do you want to emulate or inspire you? What values do they communicate with their actions and words?

Define Your Purpose

Now, combine your Endorphin Data from your life experiences, core and aspirational values and positive role models to answer these questions:

What purposes, values, or aspirations call to me, what do I yearn for?
What values, character strengths, or accomplishments do I appreciate in the people, stories, or historical figures that inspire me?
What general direction does my Endorphin Data point to as a meaningful purpose for my life?

Discuss your thoughts, insights, and purpose with someone you respect who shares your values and worldview.

Synthesize Your Endorphin Data into Your Purpose

Imagine you're very old. You've lived a long, happy, and fulfilling life. You've made a meaningful contribution to the world. Now, your doctor has told you that you only have thirty days to live. Looking back at your life, what are the key contributions that you want to be remembered for? Who sees you as their hero?

If you haven't discovered your purpose in your life experiences, your faith, or role models, you'll find it in your top aspirational (or core) values. Your goal is to synthesize this information into one sentence that explains how you will to contribute to the greater good.

DISCOVER YOUR LIFE'S PURPOSE

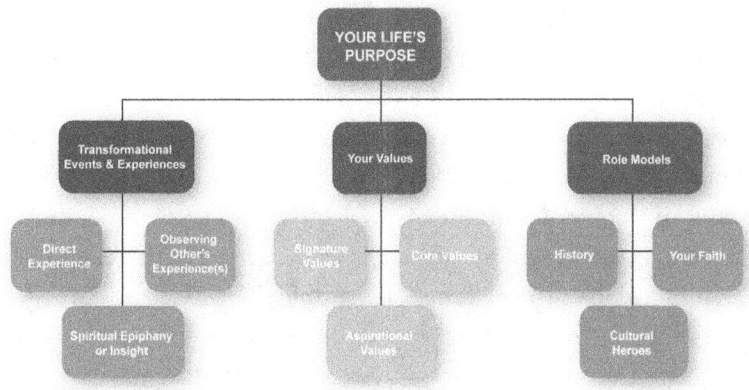

Figure 6.2. Your Life's Purpose

Here's an example. My top aspirational values are *connection, inspiration, imagination, creativity, joy,* and *sustainability.* Here is my one-sentence purpose statement:

I inspire people to imagine and create more success and happiness in their lives, and a more peaceful, sustainable world for all.

Work on your own purpose statement until it lights you up whenever you read it or share it with others. *Express what you aspire to accomplish, stand for, cure, fix, or create.* When your head and your heart agree on your purpose, you'll feel energy and joy in your entire being.

Don't get discouraged if your purpose doesn't come to you immediately. You're already living it, just not consciously, yet. Do the suggested exercises and then let your subconscious mind go to work on the "problem." Your purpose will reveal itself at the perfect time.

Discovering and committing to a meaningful purpose unlocks your potential to make a huge contribution to the world. When people with a shared purpose work together, they can overcome great obstacles and sometimes even transform the world!

* * *

America's founding fathers didn't create the world's most successful political system by accident. They did it on purpose. Although they came from different countries and religious traditions, they all shared a sacred belief in a loving, compassionate god who endowed every human being with certain inalienable rights.

Many of their values were shaped by the philosophers and thinkers of the Enlightenment and their experiences with religious wars and tyrannical European kings, exemplified by King George. They set out with a shared purpose to design a new type of political system, one that would enhance the well-being of citizens, not subjugate them. They researched every system of government that ever existed to discover the formula for success.

They wanted to create a government that not only provided freedom, peace, and prosperity for Americans, but that would be a role model for all of humanity. Their shared purpose resulted in two amazing documents, the Declaration of Independence and the Constitution of the United States. Then they committed their lives, their fortunes, and their sacred honor to protecting the values they espoused.

While striving to fulfill their purpose, America's founders used their resources and their personal powers to defeat the most powerful army the world had ever known. Their experiment in democracy resulted in the most prosperous, free, and innovative society in history. Their shared purpose ignited the flame of liberty that spread around the world.

America's founders are long gone. But they'll always be remembered for their contribution to humanity: creating a government of the people, by the people, and for the people, a government focused on human flourishing.

ENDORPHIN EVENT #6
How Do You Want To Be Remembered?

Summarize this chapter for your guests by going through the pages and using the subheads and graphics to share the key points. Then brainstorm on the following topics.

1. Share and discuss the transformative events or experiences that have shaped your life. How have they affected you? In what direction do they call you?
2. Share and discuss your top aspirational and core values. Share what's important about them with each other. What causes or projects do they steer you toward?
3. What role models have influenced your life? What values, behaviors, or accomplishments of theirs do you want to emulate?
4. Share your life purpose and the values, beliefs, and experiences that influenced you to select it.
5. Brainstorm ideas for better aligning your life and your work with your purpose. How can you use your personal powers in the service of your purpose?
6. Discuss and explore what you want to be remembered for after you're gone. What key contributions do you want to be highlighted at your eulogy, and your funeral?
7. What will you do differently in the future, based on your insights from this chapter?

7

Pursue Your Passions in Positive Places

> *Only passion, great passion can set a life on fire.*
> —**Anonymous**

Her first meal in the small French village of Rouen transformed Julia Child's life. That's the moment she found her passion. In her autobiography, *My Life in France*, Julia described her lunch of oysters, wine, sole meunière, and salad as "an opening up of the soul and spirit . . . the most exciting moment in my life."

From that moment on, she dedicated herself to her new passion, French food. Following her bliss started Julia on the path to the Endorphin Zone, inspiring her to gush, "I felt myself opening up like a flower."

Her love for French cuisine, organizing skills, and engaging writing style made Julia Child a best-selling author. But her TV shows, joyful spirit, and fluty voice established her as an American icon. Julia continued to work until her late eighties. She died at ninety-one. Near the end, she said, "In this line of work . . . you keep right on till you're through. Retired people are boring."

Your Passions

Any interest or activity you love and value, and that you devote your time, money, and attention to pursue is a *passion*. You choose to pursue your passions instead of other activities because they're so intrinsically rewarding, holding your attention like nothing else. Your passions light you up and generate positive energy in your life. They help define who you are, and they shape who you're becoming.

You'll experience many of your most powerful endorphin moments while pursuing them, feeling engaged, energized, and fully alive—exuberant! Your passions guide you in the direction of meaningful growth and self-actualization. Sometimes, they evoke the deeply gratifying state of accomplishment.

This Endorphin Domain, your passions, includes

1. key interests,
2. favorite activities, and
3. worthy causes.

Define Your Key Interests

Interest—simply being curious and eager to know more—is one of the most common positive emotions. It's also a character strength. It includes curiosity, attraction, and fascination. These positive emotions alert you to potential opportunities and inspire you to approach, explore, inquire, learn, and grow.

Here, *key interests* refer to things that catch your *intellectual* fancy: they include information, ideas, theories, and concepts. They're the primary motivators of personal growth. We often experience "aha!" moments while engaging in them.

What do you want to learn more about? Do you find history or politics fascinating? Are you interested in gardening? Cooking?

Is psychology your thing? Veterinary medicine? Music? Extreme sports? Anything that captures your imagination and sparks your curiosity counts.

Make a prioritized list of your key interests. Next, list a few *new* areas that you want to learn more about, something you haven't yet explored. Follow your interests, and they will lead you to greater understanding and insights about yourself and your world. If you intensely study any subject for five years, you'll become an expert; in ten years, you can become world-class in your "field of interest."

Document Your Favorite Activities

As people grow older, busy routines and responsibilities often disconnect them from activities enjoyed in youth. The indigenous Shuar people of the Upper Amazon have a solution for this common problem: parents teach their kids how to work, and kids teach their parents how to play.

The dads take their sons hunting and fishing, while the moms teach their daughters how to tend the garden, gather resources, and prepare food. The whole family shares work and play, with not much distinction between the two. We can all benefit from more "play time."

Your favorite activities amuse, challenge, engage, exhilarate, and energize you. This subdomain of passion includes enjoyable and gratifying pursuits of all kinds, including physical activities, such as sports, as well as hobbies, like cooking, traveling, and gardening, along with socializing, religious or spiritual activities, romance (including sex), and helping others. It also includes leisure activities, such as reading, getting massaged and watching movies.

Pleasurable activities are in this subdomain because they represent one component of the good life. There are two types, the more physical, hedonic ones, and more mental, aesthetic ones. Psychologists refer to the thrills, delight, mirth, fun, ecstasy, exuberance, and comfort of hedonic pleasures as "raw feels."

Hedonic pleasures usually occur when we're satisfying our survival needs, such as eating, drinking, and making love. Aesthetic pleasures are more ethereal. We experience them when we watch a glorious sunset, visit a museum, read a moving novel, or listen to beautiful music.

Enjoy your pleasures, but spread them out, mix them up, and take them in small doses.

Here's why you can't flourish by only pursuing pleasure. Recall that pleasure is but a small factor in life satisfaction. Pleasure fades instantly once the external stimulus ceases. And if it continues, we quickly become habituated, so we need bigger and bigger doses to get the same positive feelings. (Except for sex—more on this important subject is coming up.)

Also, pleasure is all about self, and not about contributing to others. Finally, although pleasures feel good in the moment, they don't broaden your thinking or build resources like other positive emotions.

Passive leisure activities can be enjoyable, but they aren't gratifying. You experience the deeply engaging flow state only when you're actively immersed in challenging activities, such as making music, painting, or hiking. And you experience the gratifying sense of accomplishment only *after* you've played the song, finished the painting, or climbed the mountain. Because they require more thought, skill, and engagement than passive pleasures, engaging in active passions is more rewarding than engaging in passive ones.

Doing difficult and even unpleasant activities that you're passionate about evokes much more positivity—the warm glow of accomplishment—than activities that are easy and pleasurable. Efforts that challenge you make you feel competent and proud.

What's more, pleasurable and gratifying activities and experiences generate more happiness and life satisfaction than buying stuff. A once-in-a-lifetime vacation will generate longer-lasting positivity than buying an expensive toy.

Researchers have discovered one more benefit of valuing experiences over possessions. Psychologist Leaf Van Boven says, "When you are known as being experiential, you become a more likable person than when you are known as a materialistic person." So focus on experiencing and being, instead of having.

Finally, engaging in your favorite activities is a powerful antidote for negative emotions and mild depression.

However, one popular activity is almost guaranteed to *reduce* your positivity.

Turn screen time into passion time.

Electronic devices can be relaxing, engaging, and addicting, But they don't satisfy our key desires for autonomy, connection, competence, or self-esteem—and they don't bring you any real pleasure or gratification. In fact, Professor Mike's research shows that the normal state while watching TV is slightly, hypnotically depressed.

When social scientists reviewed the most important media studies written over the previous three decades, a staggering eighty percent of the studies came to the same conclusions: heavy electronic media exposure increases the chances you'll get fat, smoke tobacco, abuse drugs, drink excessively, engage in risky sex, underperform in school, have trouble paying attention, and find it difficult to finish projects. Watching TV tends to make people more violent, materialistic, and socially isolated! Here's why.

Savvy media folks have learned how to exploit our built-in "orienting response" to mesmerize us and sell us more stuff. Fast-action cutting from scene to scene, like the ones in action films, commercials, music videos, and other TV programming grab and hold our attention by triggering our "what's that?" reflex.

This is part of our brain's early warning system. Unexpected or novel noises, movement, or other changes get our instant and full attention until we confirm they're not a threat. By triggering our orienting response continuously, TV programs lull us into a mild state of passivity and attention, a perfect, receptive state for advertisers. This is what makes TV such a powerful "idiot box." No thinking or acting is required; it's totally passive.

The most distressing electronic media is the (bad) news, which paints a depressing picture of a world that's much more violent, dangerous, and dysfunctional than reality. Filling your mind with problems that you can't fix raises your blood pressure and makes you feel helplessly depressed. Don't allow concentrated negativity to bombard your consciousness. The less (bad) news and other toxic media you "consume," especially on TV, the happier and more optimistic you'll be.

My recommendation? Be more selective in what you watch on a screen, if you watch anything at all. One family I know "cut the cable" and relies strictly on streaming options. This allows them to be more aware of what they're choosing to watch (no channel flipping—they have to actively seek out something they want to see). It's also limited the advertising that used to bombard their son when he was allowed to watch TV. Their selective media strategy has drastically reduced the "I wants" in their household.

So, if you're spending a lot of your precious time in front of a screen, start coming up with better alternatives. Not only will it reduce or eliminate your exposure to anti-happiness programming, it will also free you up to engage in this amazing gift called life.

What do you like to do when you feel like getting some exercise, expressing your creativity, relaxing, or just having fun? Think back through the different chapters of your life. What endorphin moments or peak experiences come to mind in each chapter? What were you doing when they occurred? Which ones were most relaxing and pleasurable? Which ones generated positive memories and a sense of accomplishment that are still with you today?

Make a prioritized list of your favorite activities. Then list new activities that you'd like to try. Think of ways to combine them. For instance, if you like to travel and to cook, take a cooking class somewhere you've always wanted to visit. Add more favorite activities to your weekly calendar. They'll boost your endorphins!

Identify Your Worthy Causes

When my friend, Sheva, needed funds to start an orphanage for street kids in Nicaragua, Brooke and I gladly wrote a check. We knew about her special connection with the children there, about her long-term sponsorship of a boy she'd met in front of the Managua Cathedral, who had overcome great obstacles and become a psychologist as an adult. They had already begun working together to help the children in his home country when she asked for our help. We know and love Sheva, and we were *elated to provide seed money for such a worthy cause.* (You can read more, and donate, at fyera.org.)

Of course, we aren't the only ones who experience joy through giving. Humans are hard-wired to help others. That's why toddlers, who are too young to speak, will instinctively comfort another crying baby. Kindness is humanity's most common character strength, one that needs nurturing and development, but the seed is there from the beginning.

Numerous studies have proven that the happiest, most satisfied and fulfilled people are those who devote their lives to caring for others. Arthur Brooks, a former professor, prolific researcher, and author, found that adults who donate to charity are forty percent more likely to say they are "very happy" than non-donors. And people who give money experience more positive emotions than the people who receive it.

When we help others, we help ourselves, while selfishness reduces our happiness. Nancy Etcoff, a Harvard psychologist, says, "The more selfish you are, the more unhappy you are. If you look at suicide notes they are filled with 'I,' 'me,' 'my.' "

Altruism improves your mental and physical health, and even helps you live longer. During a five-year study of 423 elderly couples, the people who helped others, even giving emotional support, were half as likely to die as those who didn't lift a finger for someone else.

We experience the most happiness and satisfaction when we support worthy causes that align with our values and purpose. Because helping and giving creates so much happiness, maybe the old plea to "give till it hurts" should be revised: "Give till you're ecstatic!"

Prioritize your top five worthy causes, the ones that make your heart sing and your spirit soar. Ask yourself,

> *What worthy causes or groups am I passionate about supporting with my time, money, and energy?*
> *Which ones are most closely aligned with my life's purpose?*
> *Which causes do I want to support more in the future?*

Share your time and money generously while you're alive so you can experience the joy of giving. Then leave money and resources to your favorite causes in your will or estate plan so your impact will last beyond your lifetime. It really does feel better to give than to receive!

Once you have identified your passions, look for ways to pursue them more often in your leisure time and your work. The more you integrate your passions and purpose with your personal powers, the more synergy, and positivity you'll experience.

But don't feel you have to integrate all your passions into your work. It's often better to pursue some passions for pure enjoyment. If you pursue your interests and favorite activities for extrinsic rewards, such as money, the pleasure and feeling of accomplishment can quickly fade. When I was a professional photographer, I often found myself thinking, *I didn't pursue this career to take these types of photos*. I experience much more pleasure and satisfaction now that I only take pictures that light me up.

Positive Places

When I accepted a new job, Brooke and I moved from a rural community on the outskirts of Sacramento to urban West L.A. We downsized from a spacious three-bedroom home on two acres to a cramped one-bedroom condo—with only one parking space for our two cars.

PURSUE YOUR PASSIONS IN POSITIVE PLACES

Even though the real estate agent assured us it was a "good area," Brooke and I felt like we were living in a tenement. The kitchen was so small that when we opened the dishwasher door, we couldn't stand at the sink, which made it extremely difficult to wash the dishes.

But the worst part was the units had only one window and one sliding door that both opened onto a central courtyard. The noise of the forty or fifty window air conditioners, kids playing, and people partying all hours of the night was distressing. On the street below, car alarms screeched and honked 24/7. We went from loving our home in Orangevale to hating our home in Brentwood. So we moved again, this time to a beautiful new condo in Marina del Rey.

Our unit was big, quiet, well designed, and attractive. But it soon became clear why there was an eight-foot block wall around it and two guards at the gate. It was in the middle of a blighted, gang-infested area, with massive traffic jams and rude people. I started calling it Marina del Rabies because of all the "mad dogs."

One day, Brooke came home crying after a short drive to our local shopping center turned into a two-hour ordeal. We agreed it was time to flee the big city. By then, we had learned that both the home itself and its neighborhood made a difference in our positivity.

We moved to a lovely, spacious home on one acre at the base of Camelback Mountain in Phoenix. The first night was blissfully quiet. The next morning, instead of car alarms or screaming kids, we awoke to the cheerful warbling of a Cactus Wren. We had a huge kitchen, a pool, and covered parking for both of our cars. Palo Verde trees, cactus, shrubs, and desert flowers surrounded us. Foxes, quails, and lizards roamed our property.

Our home overlooked the city of Phoenix and the Valley of the Sun. During the frequent summer monsoons, we'd sit on our porch at twilight with a cool drink. Heavy rain pelted the parched desert, instantly cooling the air. Periodically, lightning bolts flashed through the sky in a blinding light show. Thunderclaps rumbled towards us— *boom-Boom-Boom-BOOM!*—and exploded against our eardrums with a loud *Kaa'rrraAKK!* Remembering it still gives me goose bumps.

During most winter sunsets, purple, pink, and gold clouds spread out in cottony rows over the city below us, painting a mackerel sky. Golden halos framed each cloud's sunny side, and a charcoal border framed the shadowed side. As the sun went down, the clouds faded into darker shades of orange, pink, and grey. The buildings, mountains and cactus slowly vanished as red, blue, and yellow lights switched on and sparkled in the city below.

The community, neighborhood, house, and people in Phoenix were all wonderful. But from May to October, the heat was brutal. The temperature often soared to over 115. The burning sun cracked my lip and seared my skin like a blowtorch. When I got a heat stroke walking a few hundred yards outside in August, we realized that Phoenix was great for lizards but far too hot for these two humans.

So I accepted a new position, and we moved to Orange County in Southern California. We bought a perfect, compact home in a quiet neighborhood in an uncongested, friendly, and centrally located town. We have short commutes and rarely get stuck in traffic. We love our home, neighbors, neighborhood, and community. The weather is fantastic! But I do miss those glorious desert sunsets and awesome lightening storms.

Researchers aren't convinced that where we live affects our quality of life, because we quickly adapt to our circumstances. But Brooke and I know from personal experience that the region, community, neighborhood, and home *do* make a difference in our happiness and life satisfaction.

Positive places make you feel calm, secure, and inspired. They set the stage for creative and innovative behavior. That's why many companies that rely on new products and ideas are housed in buildings that resemble a bucolic campus instead of a downtown high rise.

The three subdomains of positive places are

1. region and community,
2. neighborhood and home, and
3. favorite places.

PURSUE YOUR PASSIONS IN POSITIVE PLACES

Just as each type of plant needs a unique combination of light, water, soil, and fertilizer, each of us needs a unique combination of aesthetics, amenities, income opportunities, culture, and weather. Some people thrive in the heat of Phoenix. Some wouldn't part with the seasonal display of the Shenandoah Valley, while others would much prefer the same, sunny view of the ocean all year in San Diego. Some people enjoy a quiet, rural life, and others crave the revved up pace and sounds of the city.

Think of positive places as perfect greenhouses that have all the ingredients *you* need to flourish.

Your Ideal Region and Community

Many people already live in their ideal home and community. But if you're considering a move, this section will help you make sure you're selecting the optimum place, for you.

When considering a new region, research the weather, traffic, and income opportunities. The relative importance of these three elements will depend on your current stage of life. When I was in my twenties, I lived in Aspen, Colorado. It was a beautiful and exciting place to be, since I loved to ski in the winter and hike in the summer.

But career opportunities for me were almost nonexistent, the traffic was miserable, the homes were unaffordable, and the men outnumbered the women by four to one, a real bummer for a single guy. It got so expensive to live there that the locals started lamenting, "The billionaires are driving out the millionaires." Aspen was a great place to live when I was young, but it wasn't the right place to find my soul mate, build my career, or retire.

To evolve to the next step towards the Endorphin Zone, sometimes you have to move to a more positive place.

Here are a few other things to think about as you define the ideal region and community for you. First, people who live in regions that are overcast a lot tend to suffer from seasonal affect disorder (SAD).

Sunny skies evoke sunny moods. That's one reason residents of the Sunbelt are happier than residents of any other area of the country. Warm climes also eliminate the hassles and dangers of snow and ice, while minimizing the effects of arthritis that often accompany aging.

Suburbanites are significantly more satisfied with their communities than urbanites, who suffer from higher rates of schizophrenia, depression, and other mental health problems than people who live in less stressful communities. Suburbanites also report higher life satisfaction than people living in small towns or rural areas.

Make sure your new community is a good cultural fit.

Each community has a dominant world-view, political orientation, and value system. People are most satisfied with their lives when the majority of the people in their community share their values and beliefs. If you love laid-back, intrinsically oriented Boulder, you'll probably be stressed-out in hard-charging, extrinsically oriented Manhattan.

Politics matter, too. Orange County, where I live, is generally more conservative than either Los Angeles or San Diego counties. But each city in the OC also has its own dominant values and culture. For instance, Laguna Beach is full of artists, liberals, people of diverse sexual orientations, and free thinkers. The locals affectionately refer to themselves as "Lagunatics." If you fit any of these descriptions, you'll be happier in this funky beach community than the master-planned and corporate suburbs of Irvine.

Keep your commute short.

The closer your home is to your work, the lower your stress and the happier you'll be. But many people don't understand how hard a long commute is on their mental and physical health.

In a study of commuters at the Stuttgart and Ulm railroad stations, about ninety percent of the travelers had daily slogs of more than forty-five minutes each way. Some of them traveled more than three hours daily. A control group of non-commuters reported half as many symptoms, such as pain, dizziness, exhaustion, and severe sleep deprivation as the long-distance travelers. Alarmingly, about one third of the extreme commuters needed immediate medical treatment. Ouch!

People who commute long distances don't have time for their families and friends, much less their passions. Often, their life partners feel more burdened than the commuters themselves do, since they are forced to take care of nearly all of the housework, childcare, and other family duties.

Many people move far from their work so they can afford a bigger home and yard. Sometimes they commute long distances for a higher paying job or better schools. They should consider this:

When Daniel Kahneman and his colleagues tracked the emotions evoked by daily activities of employed women, commuting proved to be the pits. It ranked dead last in positivity. The extra cost of commuting, running bigger homes, and being separated from loved ones for long hours is likely to reduce, not enhance, your quality of life.

If you can, make sure your home isn't more than twenty minutes from your work. If you do have a long commute, carpool or take public transportation so you can relax, read, or listen to music and personal development programs. That will reduce your stress and transform your commute time into key-interest or favorite-activities time.

Consider an intentional community.

Although she was rapidly losing weight and had fallen a few times, Marion didn't want to leave her family home. But, after she started her second cooking fire, her daughter Jennifer knew it was time to make a change. She found a suitable eldercare facility for her mom and sold the house, although Marion whined and resisted every step of the way.

Then an amazing thing happened. Within a few months, Marion got her sparkle back. Because the new home provided her with three nutritious meals a day, she gained weight and critical neuro-chemicals. Daily exercise sharpened her mind and toned her muscles. Marion quickly became the most popular "girl" in the home. She told Jennifer, "I love it here!"

One of the worst aspects of getting old is losing your spouse and being alone. Group living solves the three plagues of aging: isolation, boredom, and helplessness. Older people living with others live longer, healthier, happier lives and cost less to care for. But you don't have to wait until you are losing your marbles to live with others.

Our ancient ancestors evolved into modern humans over the past 200,000 years in close-knit clans of roughly fifty people. Until recently in our history, most humans lived in these small groups with relatives and friends of all ages. Because of this, living in a community of like-minded people, of all ages, naturally enhances our happiness and life satisfaction. That's why, today, many people seeking more fulfilling and sustainable ways of living are experimenting with intentional communities

The goal of these lifestyle pioneers is to forge meaningful relationships with others who share a common purpose. Residents often share religious, political, or other value systems, such as ecological sustainability. People living in rural intentional communities often farm the land and live simply. The Amish, who live without public power, automobiles, or TV, are some of the world's happiest and most satisfied people.

Unlike communes of the 1960s, intentional communities generally involve equity ownership, cooperative decision-making, and a well-defined business and political structure. Each family buys separate living quarters, shares common areas, and splits the common expenses. There's usually a community area where everyone can cook and eat together, host events, watch movies, and socialize. Residents celebrate milestones and share hardships together.

Living with people who share a higher purpose is a proven way to increase your well-being. It can also enhance your financial sustainability and reduce your impact on our small planet.

The number of intentional communities is growing rapidly around the world. They aren't for everyone, but consider this option if you're seeking a new, ideal community for you.

Moving to a new region and community is a common occurrence for happy, flourishing people. That's because we usually make major moves to advance our education, take a new job, enhance our quality of life, or retire. In the process, we experience new things, make new friends, and develop new routines. This breaks old habits, allowing us to reinvent ourselves and to evolve towards our best possible selves. So, if you seek more endorphins in your life, move to a more positive community—for you.

Take your new community for a test drive.

If you're planning a big move, or thinking about buying a vacation home, rent in your dream community first. Try it out and see how long your initial glow takes to fade to the new normal. Are the tradeoffs worth it?

Josie and Max saved up for a happy and secure retirement and then moved from a high-density Southern California community to a serene, resort-like, golf community near Spokane. It took them only about a year to become miserable in their beautiful new custom home. Why? Their children, grandchildren, and best friends—the most important people in their lives—lived a thousand miles away.

So, after a year in purgatory, they sold their retirement "dream home" for a loss and moved back to their old community. Their move cost them a bundle and reduced their financial security in retirement.

Moving far from family and friends is a common mistake made by well-off retirees. Similarly, people often buy vacations homes on a whim because they associate the good feelings of novelty, relaxation, and fun with the vacation location. Time-share resorts depend on this. But vacation homes can turn into money pits that you never have time to enjoy. They also reduce your financial sustainability, especially if you have to fly your entire family somewhere to enjoy them.

Make sure miswanting doesn't seduce you into buying a home in a community that will reduce your positivity and financial sustainability.

Your Ideal Neighborhood and Living Space

Community, region, and neighbors impact happiness. But, once you find your ideal community, what physical amenities in your home and its surroundings contribute most to your positivity and well-being?

An article in *Scientific American Mind* magazine, "No Place Like Home," explains what psychologists discovered makes a happy living space. One of the most important things to consider in a new dwelling is its neighborhood. Make sure the schools, parks, services, traffic; shopping, and cultural resources meet your needs and wants. Also, landscaped common areas and underground utilities dramatically improve the aesthetics. Neighborhoods built on cul-de-sacs are the quietest because there's no through traffic.

A critical ingredient that's high on everyone's list is personal safety and security. So, be sure to move to a low-crime area. Strong locks, alarm systems, fences, and outdoor lighting enhance feelings of personal security.

Good neighbors make a home even more enjoyable, while loud or troublesome neighbors are a good reason to move. When people are crowded, as Brooke and I were in our Brentwood condo, there are more problems with neighbors. Effective soundproofing minimizes noisy neighbor irritations, as well as traffic and other environmental noises. More perceived space around a home, with trees, shrubs, and fences, increases the feeling of privacy.

The happiest living spaces have courtyards, communal gardens, and places to sit and chat with neighbors. They have some high ceilings and open floor plans with large rooms that are customizable for different lifestyles. Skylights brighten otherwise dark rooms and halls. Plenty of private space allows family members to get away from others when they want to chill out. Small balconies, gardens, and courtyards also increase desirability. Functional kitchens, with plenty of workspace, are a must.

Living on a hill with a view of nature, mountains, and trees can boost endorphins. Looking out windows onto a garden or landscaping, and bringing nature inside with plants, flowers, and photos elevates our mood. Streams, lakes, fountains, and other water features also evoke positive emotions. In fact, just looking at a fish tank, even if it's only a projection on a big screen, lowers stress and blood pressure. *Ahhhh*.

Energy efficiency is becoming more and more important. Extra insulation, variable-speed pool pumps, solar panels, whole-house fans, shade trees, double pane windows, weather sealing, and water-wise landscaping all enhance positivity, lower the cost of running a home, and improve sustainability. Speaking of sustainability, instead of asking, "How much home can I afford?" Ask, "How much space do I need?" Big homes and yards sap wealth and deplete natural resources.

If you're considering a move, use the information in this section to prioritize the criteria for your ideal community and region. Then *prioritize the amenities you need and want in your dream neighborhood and home*. Consider your season of life, passions, values, and personal style. If you're happy with your current home, use this information to transform it into your personal Endorphin Zone.

Your Favorite Places

A few times a year Brooke and I suffer from "nature deficit disorder." Our work causes brain fatigue, which makes us a little cranky and unable to focus. Instead of turning on the boob tube, we engage in some Attention Restoration Therapy (ART). After work, we drive to one of our favorite places, a restaurant in Laguna Beach that overlooks the Pacific Ocean.

While savoring a glass of wine, and enjoying its mild euphoric buzz, we watch with "soft fascination" as the waves gently wash ashore, kids play in the surf and lovers stroll on the beach below us. Occasionally we see dolphins frolicking in the ocean. As the afternoon sun warms our skin and paints the shore with a golden hue, Mother Nature recharges our mental batteries.

All natural environments restore your ability to focus your attention and enhance your working memory. A one-hour stroll in nature increases cognitive abilities by about twenty percent.

Interacting with nature also increases creativity and intelligence. In one study, participants who immersed themselves in nature for four days increased their problem solving abilities by fifty percent!

Nature has such a positive effect that the mere presence of plants in your office boosts your ability to focus on "brain straining" tasks—even if the plants aren't real.

Nature also promotes healing, something shamans have known for thousands of years. Being in forests, parks and other natural places, especially green ones, reduces blood pressure, heart rate, muscle tension, and stress hormones. Nature also elevates our mood, which strengthens the immune system.

Patients recovering from surgery, who have views of trees and lawn instead of a brick wall, require less pain medication, and go home sooner. In another study, prisoners in cells facing farmland instead of a prison yard got sick less often.

My personal experience confirms what some scientists believe: spending time with Mother Nature connects us with our own nature, shifting our values away from extrinsic rewards and toward more satisfying intrinsic ones. Because of this, nature nudges us along the path toward the Endorphin Zone.

Do you have favorite places in nature that recharge your heart, mind, and spirit? Make a list of them. Then, *spend more time in natural environments, when you are home and when you go on vacations.*

The Value of Vacations

Vacations aren't optional; they're mandatory health and longevity therapy. For most people in modern society, work is stressful. All of us need periodic downtime to rest, renew, and recharge. But the average American spends far too much time working, taking only nine days off

PURSUE YOUR PASSIONS IN POSITIVE PLACES

a year. Many don't take any vacations at all.

Vacations interrupt your routine and open your mind. They allow you to step back and look at your life with a new perspective. But you don't have to fly seven thousand miles and spend a month in a tropical paradise to benefit. Long weekends to favorite spots, or to new places close to home, can be just as memorable as international vacations. In fact, there's no relationship between the length of a vacation, or how far you travel, and the positivity it evokes.

Even a "staycation," where you do all of the cool things you've always wanted to do in your own community, can put you in the Endorphin Zone.

Three types of vacations are especially engaging, memorable, and transformational.

Ecotourism takes intimate groups to visit magnificent, pristine environments that are off the beaten trail. They're often co-led by indigenous guides. *Spiritual vacations* take you to the holy land, India, Bali, South America, or other sacred places. They typically involve discussions with indigenous people, meetings with wise elders, healing sessions with shamans or rituals with holy leaders. *Service vacations* combine travel with volunteer work, usually with charities or religious organizations.

To maximize your endorphins, spend your money on novel experiences and activities instead of expensive lodging, international flights, or upgraded seats. Intersperse leisurely, unstructured days with more active, passion-pursuing days.

Read guidebooks and, if you can afford it, hire a local guide. Connecting with the local people is often the best part of a vacation. Travel with friends, and combine your vacations with your passions. Go on an archeological dig. Help save the rainforest or the whales. Visit fascinating historic sites. The possibilities for endorphin adventuress are endless.

Make a prioritized "bucket list" of all of the places you want to visit in the years ahead. Then schedule six to eight trips a year for the next three years. Mix it up with some weekend getaways and some longer vacations. *Take all the time off that you can.* Savor your adventures, and as soon as you return, start planning your next trip.

Your physical environments do make a difference in your emotional state. So pick them with care. Spending time in positive places soothes your stress, recharges your brain, and heals your soul. It expands your thinking and often evokes peak experiences that last a lifetime.

Savor Your Positive Experiences

Savoring is the art of prolonging and enhancing pleasurable and rewarding experiences. The more you prolong your positive feelings, the higher your positivity ratio. Savoring is also a great way to enhance sustainability. That's because it increases the positivity you experience for the money and resources you invest (more bang for your buck). Savoring enables you to boost your mood while spending and consuming less.

Here are four ways to maximize your endorphins while pursuing your passions or enjoying positive places.

1. *Anticipate the endorphins:* Plan, research, discuss, and prepare for your activities and experiences far in advance. For six months before my first adventure to Ecuador, I joyfully prepared for and anticipated the trip.
2. *Immerse yourself in each experience:* Block out distractions. Slow down and indulge each of your five senses. Consciously focus on and make mental notes of the details. Author and neuroscientist Rick Hanson says, "The more fully you feel something, the deeper the neural traces that are left behind in the brain. That solidifies your memory of the moment."

    So, savor the moment with all of your senses: inhale the smells, feel the sun on your skin, the wind on your face. Soak in the wonder, thrills, and sensory delights. Luxuriate in the pleasure, marvel at the beauty, and bask in the pride of accomplishment. Taking photographs or videos is a great way to savor the scene

and look at it from many different perspectives. But be sure to put down your devices, too, so you can fully experience what's happening in the moment without any physical filters.
3. *Reminisce and relive each experience afterward:* When I returned from Ecuador, I spent many hours selecting and editing my best photos. I smile every time they appear on my screen saver. Locally made souvenirs and diaries, or journals, also evoke positive memories.
4. *Share your experiences with others:* Talk about your hopes, dreams, thoughts, and feelings before, during, and after your experiences. On my third trip to Ecuador, my friends Eddie and Humberto joined me. Throughout the vacation, we constantly discussed and laughed about how much fun we were having. We remember and re-experience the highlights every time we get together. And I relive my adventures by sharing my photos with friends. (Slideshow anyone?)

By employing these savoring techniques, you can prolong the positive emotions generated by a short adventure or experience into a lifetime of happy memories.

* * *

Pursuing your passions will boost your mood and recharge your mental batteries. Pursuing your passions in positive places can help clarify your purpose and may even transform your life—for the better.

When I finished writing my first book, I was eager to start the next chapter of my life, but wasn't clear what it was. For the previous sixteen years, I'd been intensely focused on my business. Even though I was making more money than ever, it was becoming less and less satisfying. I knew what my purpose was, but I didn't know how to implement it. However, I did have an intuition about my path forward.

For thirty years, I'd been keenly interested in the Amazon rainforest, the animals, people, trees, plants, and shamans, the legendary visionaries and healers in indigenous communities. But I'd always assumed that traveling to the Amazon and meeting real shamans was a fantasy.

Then, as my book went to press, I learned of a former Peace Corps volunteer who took small groups on spiritual eco-tours to meet with Quechua shamans called *Yachaks* in the High Andes and Shuar shamans called *Uwishin* in the Upper Amazon. As I read the trip description, my interest turned into a burning passion. After consulting with Brooke, I reserved my spot.

An out-of-country experience takes you out of your comfort zone and often triggers positive change, especially if that's your intention. The more exotic the culture and environment, the greater the potential for meaningful insights and personal growth. Ecuador fits the bill. It boasts the highest concentration of indigenous people in the Western Hemisphere. Their values, beliefs, languages, and culture are mysterious and alien to North Americans.

For ten high-intensity days, I immersed myself in the strange and unusual culture of the Quechua families in the Andes and the Shuar communities in the Upper Amazon. In the High Andes, we hiked to sacred springs, lakes, waterfalls, and the summit of an inactive volcano. We shared meals, stories and our cultures with the local families.

To the Quechua, all of nature is sacred, especially the three mountains, Imbabura, Wymirasu, and Mohanda that surround the Valley of the Dawn, where we visited. The long hikes at high altitudes and climbing a fourteen-thousand-foot mountain completely exhausted me, wringing every drop of stress out of me. When, after leaving the Andes, we landed on the small grassy airstrip deep in the Amazon jungle, I was more relaxed than I'd been for sixteen years.

My hikes in the foothills of Upper Amazon immersed me in the rainforest, the most diverse and concentrated celebration of life on Earth. The alien culture and lush jungle opened me up to change. But the sessions with the shamans transformed me. These *curanderos* are the doctors, psychologists, and priests in their communities. For thousands of years, they've used medicinal plants and the healing power of nature to restore their patients' psychological, spiritual, and physical well-being.

During the healing sessions, they used the four elements of earth, air, water, and fire to "retune" and rebalance our psycho/spiritual energies. Their rituals, chants and *icaros,* or healing songs, induced non-ordinary states of consciousness—ecstatic states I'd never experienced before.

It seemed like the intensely strange and dramatic healing sessions overloaded my nervous system and forced a "reboot." Afterward, I felt more integrated, grounded, and peaceful. My center of gravity had shifted from my head to my heart. By the last day, I could see a practical way to fulfill my life's purpose. I would help heal the rift in the modern world between our logical "heads" and our emotional "hearts." I didn't use the words then, but I realize now that my purpose is to help people use science (head) to optimize their positivity (heart).

I returned home feeling more loving, focused, passionate, and purposeful. Most important, my values had shifted in a powerful way. Before my adventure, the most important thing in my life was my business. When I returned the most important thing in my life was my relationship with Brooke.

Pursuing my passions in positive places helped me find my purpose and transformed my relationship with Brooke in a profoundly positive way.

That's the subject of the next chapter: positive relationships with positive people.

ENDORPHIN EVENT #7
Connect with Your Passions in Positive Places

Summarize this chapter for your guests by going through the pages and using the subheads and graphics to share the key points. Then brainstorm on the following topics.

1. Prioritize a list of passions that light you up and trigger endorphins. Include your favorite activities, your key interests, and your worthy causes. Discuss how you could engage more often in the things that intrinsically motivate you.
2. Prioritize a list of new and interesting activities that you want to try.
3. Prioritize a list of all the places you want to visit in the next ten years. Brainstorm ways you can travel to as many of these places as possible.
4. Create a wish list of features of your ideal region, community, neighborhood, and home.
5. Discuss, plan, and enjoy a getaway or vacation that includes your key interests, favorite activities, worthy causes, and favorite places. Plan lots of time in natural environments. If appropriate, invite some of your favorite people to join you.
6. Consciously savor your peak experiences and endorphin moments. Share them and practice recalling them in your memory. Consider keeping a journal and taking photographs.
7. What will you do differently in the future, based on your insights from this chapter?

8

Identify Positive People

Life's greatest happiness is to be convinced we are loved.
—Victor Hugo

Aspen has some of the best spring skiing in the world, especially when the sun comes out after a big snow storm. One afternoon, after skiing fresh powder on a blue-sky March day, I was feeling unstoppable. So, I decided to visit a beautiful girl I had a crush on. When I knocked on her door, to my dismay, a bushy-haired young man answered.

Sheepishly, I asked if Barbara was home. "No," he said, "Barbara and John went into town to see a movie." Then he stuck out his hand and introduced himself: "My name's Bruce. I'm John's friend."

I shook his hand half-heartedly, as I realized my dream girl had a boyfriend. But my mood perked up when Bruce offered food, "I'm cooking sweet and sour pork. Do you want to join me for dinner?"

That's how I met my best friend for life, Bruce Weinstock. We connected instantly and remained close for more than thirty years.

Although he died when he was only fifty-two, my memories of his positive spirit and our shared Endorphin moments will stay with me forever.

Positive people, like Bruce, can have a profound impact on our success and happiness.

The Power of Positive People

It's probably impossible to truly flourish without a least a few positive people in your life. Positive people care about you and you care about them. They empower you to satisfy your needs, wants, and aspirations. They also encourage you to grow and evolve in a direction that you intrinsically want to explore. So, one key to flourishing is to surround yourself with positive people.

This important Endorphin Domain includes three groups:

1) family and friends,
2) soul mates, and
3) mentors.

When you work, play, or socialize with positive people you experience many satisfying positive emotions, including connection and empowerment. But the benefits of win-win relationships go far beyond feeling good.

George Vaillant, one of the giants of positive psychology, has followed the lives of more than eight hundred men and women for more than sixty years. The Study of Adult Development, at Harvard University began in 1938 and is still following participants today. The goal of this seven-decade project is to identify which key character traits form the foundation for a "good life."

As Vaillant examined the study's data, he discovered something profound: *the capacity for warm, empathetic relationships is the strongest predictor of health, wealth, happiness, and satisfaction.* Vaillant summarized his findings by saying, "The only thing that really matters in life are your relationships to other people."

Daniel Gilbert, the Harvard psychologist who studies "miswanting," came to the same conclusion: "We know that the best predictor of human happiness is human relationships and the amount of time that people spend with family and friends. We know it's significantly more important than money and somewhat more important than health."

We've Got to Have Family and Friends

The desire to bond with other people is hardwired into our DNA. When we interact positively, oxytocin, a chemical messenger, is released into our brains, triggering warm, gentle feelings of connectedness. It's this contact high that bonds us to individuals and groups. Paul Zak, a world renowned expert on oxytocin, calls it "the glue of society."

Positive people aren't only about connecting and bonding. They're also extremely important resources. As Mae West said, "It's the friends you can call up at four in the morning that matter." Family members, soul mates, and close friends provide emotional support in troubled times and encourage you to persevere. They calm you when you're stressed, elevate you when you're down, and share your joy when you succeed.

They also provide physical resources. They lend you tools, let your kids play in their pool, and help you when you need a hand. In tough times, they let you crash on their couch.

When separated from other people, most of us feel a painful longing for companionship and someone to talk to. Loneliness is usually highly distressing. That's why solitary confinement is such a dreaded punishment. Social isolation not only makes us feel bad, it creates health risks that are just as dangerous as smoking, high blood pressure, and obesity. But positive relationships dramatically enhance our health and longevity.

In a decade-long Australian study, scientists surveyed the social environment, health, and lifestyle of almost 1,500 people who were over seventy years old.

They were surprised to discover that *friendships increased life expectancy by a greater extent than any other variable.* In fact, people with the most friends outlived people with the fewest friends by twenty-two percent! A network of good friends is even more beneficial than close relationships with family members.

How Many Positive People Do We Need?

According to evolutionary psychologist Robin Dunbar, social networks are like three concentric circles. The innermost circle typically consists of a soul mate (life partner) and a few best friends. We have the deepest emotional bond with these people, typically because we share common experiences, values, beliefs, interests, and opinions with them. We usually minimize the small talk with these special people. Instead, we enjoy meaningful conversations about our feelings, relationships, frustrations, joys, experiences, and other people.

Because they support us during personal crisis, our inner circle contains the most important people in our lives. Dunbar discovered that the average American has only two people they can "discuss important matters with."

Our middle circle usually includes between 12 and 20 people. These are often work colleagues, neighbors, family, or members of churches, clubs, and other communities that we're actively involved with. We care about each other and share many mutual values, beliefs, and interests. This group is our main social network, representing people we like and enjoy being with. But we don't talk with them as intimately or frequently as we do with our inner circle.

The outer circle normally includes thirty to fifty distant family members and friends. You don't know them intimately or see them very often. But you enjoy socializing with them when the occasion arises.

IDENTIFY POSITIVE PEOPLE

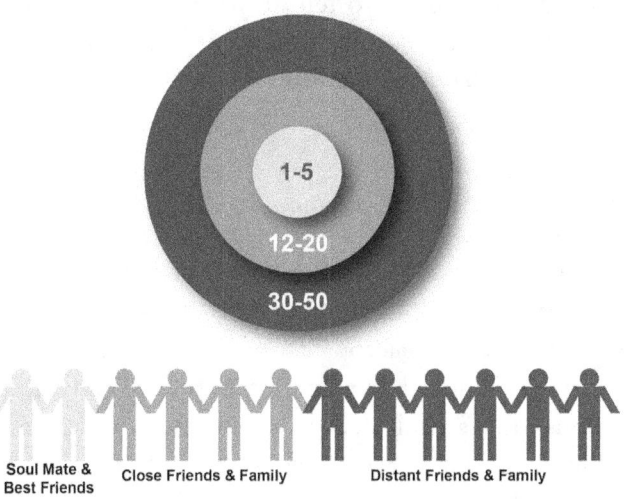

Figure 8.1. Three Circles of Positive People—Your "Personal Tribe"

The average person has a total of about fifty to sixty people in their three circles. In addition to our "personal tribe," of around sixty people, most of us can name about 150 other people that we know but seldom interact with.

However, not everyone is so lucky. Each year more and more people report they don't have anyone that they can "discuss important matters with." That's a sad statistic. So, count yourself lucky if you have one to three people in your inner circle. If you have another fifteen to fifty people in your middle and outer circles, you have all the positive relationships you need. If your tribe is smaller than average, don't worry. When it comes to relationships, it's wise to focus on quality instead of quantity.

The more you associate with people who help you satisfy your needs and wants, and encourage you to pursue your aspirations, the more you'll flourish. So, consciously associate only with positive people. The most positive people value relationships and positive experiences more than power, money, and possessions. They're conscientious and take their responsibilities seriously but have a sense of humor about life and themselves. They're open to change, agreeable, optimistic, and enjoy helping others.

Now, make a list of three to ten of your favorite positive people. What are their common denominators? *Make a commitment to build deeper, more profound, and empowering connections with your "Endorfriends."*

Avoid Toxic People

Have you heard the sick joke about why divorce is so expensive? "Because it's worth it!" Nothing relieves stress faster and more effectively than ending a toxic relationship. It could save your life.

In mice, stressful social interactions trigger a dangerous inflammatory response that's equivalent to septic shock in humans. In one study, socially stressed mice were twice as likely to die as those suffering physical hardships.

Because they cause stress, toxic relationships also damage human health. Toxic people are emotional vampires who make you feel disconnected, disempowered, used, and drained of emotional and physical energy.

Dr. Marco Iacoboni, the author of *Mirroring People: The Science of Empathy and How We Connect with Others*, says, "You can catch a mood, just like a cold." So avoid people who cause you stress and unhappiness, even if they're co-workers or family members.

In the Harvard Study of Adult Development, George Vaillant discovered a common happiness tactic used by successful people who grew up in dysfunctional families. As adults, they had totally severed relationships with their toxic family members.

Work on enhancing your key relationships. Get counseling if an important relationship is "suboptimal." But, if you decide the relationship isn't fixable, get out and don't look back. Life is too short to hang out with toxic people.

The Mother of All Positive Emotions

The most intense, meaningful, and fulfilling relationships are based on the deepest connection, love. According to "the genius of positive psychology," Barbara Fredrickson, love is the most common positive emotion because it encompasses most, if not all, of the others.

Love isn't just an awesome positive emotion. It's also a motivational state. And the ability to love and be loved is one of the most important character strengths. Many scientists are concluding that love is the most important positive emotion, the mother of them all!

The scientific concept of love is multifaceted, including companionship, affection, attachment, friendship, trust, commitment, romance, passion, intimacy, lust, contentment, and connection. There are many types of love including romantic, familial, friendly, patriotic, and team- or group-based. It varies in intensity, openness, and intimacy but always involves a strong commitment and the melding of many other positive emotions into a powerful win-win relationship.

One type of love stands out from all the rest.

The Bliss of Romantic Love

Romantic love is the wild side of this powerful emotion. It creates a potent bond between two people that makes them feel profoundly safe, affirmed, and empowered. Romantic love typically evolves through four stages:

1. the initial *attraction* and that magical spark of connection,
2. *infatuation* or passionate love,
3. *struggle* to overcome selfish instincts and build a solid "partnership" and (if compatibility and commitment remain high),
4. profound connection and contentedness, known as *companionate love*, the stage where you're convinced you've found your soul mate and commit to a long-term relationship.

Romantic attraction puts us in a deranged state of "psychological arousal," especially in the early stages when we're head-over-heels in love. Martie Haselton, a UCLA psychologist, believes we swoon into these altered states because romantic love is a "commitment device."

In the throes of infatuation, the neurochemicals that flood your limbic brain hijack your rational thought processes and you become temporarily unhinged. Your pulse races, your tongue gets tied, you take insane risks, and you even write corny love letters. Oxytocin, nature's love glue, creates intense feelings of connection and euphoria. It also makes you want to cuddle, hug, and touch your lover.

In addition to oxytocin, infatuation triggers the release of dopamine.

Biological anthropologist Helen Fisher says, "It (dopamine) is what triggers very goal-oriented behavior, where no one else matters but your new partner." You can't eat, you feel elated, euphoric, and manic all at the same time, swinging wildly from ecstasy to despair as you seek proof that your beloved loves you, too.

This powerful neurotransmitter overwhelms your logical brain with the same chemical cocktail that causes addiction and cravings for heroin. Dopamine makes you yearn for your beloved and focuses your attention and energy in a hyperactive attempt to win their affection.

Infatuation also releases the sex hormone testosterone, which triggers a fierce urge to make love with the person that's causing you so much "agony." When besotted with this powerful combination of oxytocin, dopamine, and testosterone, making love with your beloved seems like the only way to quench your burning desire.

If you pick your lover carefully, and are committed to the relationship, wild, passionate limbic-love tends to eventually evolve into a deeper and more spiritual hominoid-brain connection called companionate love. In this more mature love stage, you meld into your soul mate, finishing each other's sentences, laughing at the same things, and touching each other often. Companionate love usually lasts "until death do you part."

Many deeply loving relationships start as a platonic friendship based on shared interests and values. The romantic spark ignites after they get to know and appreciate each other.

Falling in love is one of the most exciting, intoxicating, and energizing experiences in life, the ultimate endorphin rush. I call this intensely euphoric state "love happy." It makes people crazy in an insanely wonderful way.

The Transformational Power of Love

Family bonds, deep friendships, and especially romantic love, can transform us for the better. For instance, parents often adapt and change for their children. And love makes you dream about spending the rest of your life with your loved ones.

Focusing on the future induces "global processing," which promotes out-of-the box thoughts and ideas. When you are in love, you envision and are willing to act on a much broader range of possibilities. You hatch all kinds of crazy scenarios for your future life together. These cognitive changes can permanently rewire some of your neuro circuits, which leads to changes in your behavior.

All of us learn and adapt through a process called neural plasticity. This refers to the brain's ability to grow new neurons, connections, and neurological networks. Oxytocin somehow "thaws" existing neural networks and prepares them to add, remove, and change long-established connections.

In *The Brain that Changes Itself*, Norman Doidge, M.D. explains, "What nature provides in a neuromodulator like oxytocin is the ability for two brains to go through a period of heightened plasticity, allowing them to mold to each other and shape each other's intentions and perceptions."

This is how love, especially romantic love, can permanently transform your life for the better. And when you're deeply in love, you naturally want to hold onto that wonderful feeling forever—which leads many of us to want to . . .

Live Happily Ever After

My father wasn't much of a philosopher, but he once told me something profound: "You can make all the money in the world, but it won't do you a darn bit of good unless you have someone you love to share it with."

He was right. Scientists have amassed overwhelming evidence that a successful marriage is the highest indicator of overall happiness and life satisfaction. In one representative poll by Pew Research Center, forty-three percent of married people rated themselves "very happy," compared to only twenty-four percent of single people.

Obviously, not all married people are happy and not all single people are unhappy. But, on average, happy people tend to get married and marriage itself seems to boost their happiness and life satisfaction even more. However, you don't have to be married to experience most of benefits associated with marriage.

So, if you're in a committed relationship, most of the following research on happy marriages will apply to you. And, of course, you can flourish without a life partner. My mom is one of the happiest, most satisfied people I know. And she's been a single widow for over 30 years.

However, numerous studies over the last 140 years have proven that, on average, married people are happier, enjoy better health, and live longer than single people. Statistically, marriage adds about two years to women's lives and about seven years to men's lives. Men become more responsible and abandon "stupid bachelor tricks" after they marry. They also start eating regular meals, party and drink less, and generally clean up their acts.

Being happily married can also increase your wealth and financial stability. Research shows that the average married person works harder, advances further in their careers, and saves more money than their unmarried peers. One study, by research scientist, Jay Zagorsky, discovered that, *on average, people in long-term marriages accumulate nearly twice as much wealth as people their same age who are single or divorced.*

One more small thing: children. Research shows that children improve married peoples' life satisfaction and sense of meaning. The more children married couples have, the higher their positivity ratio. Married fathers, especially, report much greater satisfaction and meaning than their childless peers.

Overall, children tend to increase life satisfaction for married parents who are ready for the responsibility and time commitment. But children also increase stress, generating both more positive and more negative emotions. That's probably why children don't increase the average single parents' happiness or satisfaction. Raising kids as a single parent, or as an unprepared young couple, can be extremely challenging and stressful.

Fortunately, when the kids move out and become financially independent, their parents' sense of satisfaction, meaning, and accomplishment rise dramatically and remain higher, compared to people who never had children.

A strong, loving, and deeply committed romantic relationship is a sure way to enhance your health, wealth, and happiness. And, you can apply many of the success tactics of happy couples to enhance any relationship. So, let's look at what it researchers have learned about building and maintaining long-term positive relationships.

The Keys to a Long and Happy Marriage

Selecting a lifelong partner is one of the most important decisions you ever make. Your decision can make you euphoric or miserable. Even though love can transform people, it's not a good idea to go into a relationship expecting your lover to change. It's much wiser to commit to the right person than to try to "fix" the wrong one.

That's why I believe in the carpenter's maxim: "Measure twice; Cut once." Here's what to look for in your ideal mate.

People usually like people who are like themselves. So the happiest couples tend to pair up with partners who complement them in all facets of their lives: biologically, financially, intellectually, psychologically, sexually, and socially.

The more naturally compatible two people are, the less they have to change to meld into a loving partnership. Long-term partners usually share the same values and beliefs, political and religious orientations, sense of humor, and cultural tastes. They often have the same interests, energy levels, and sleeping patterns. They typically have similar socio-economic backgrounds and are fairly equal in looks and intelligence.

All of these compatibility issues help reduce negative emotions, friction, and conflicts. Compatibility with spark is the key. With the right partner, you can be yourself while sharing adventures, activities, ideas, dreams, goals, and friends. When you share similar positive values and worldviews, you naturally encourage your lover to grow and evolve into their best possible self.

Communicate Authentic Love

Drs. John and Julie Gottman are international leaders in the field of couple's relationships. Their research has convinced them that the best way to stay in love is to give lots of love. In fact, they have concluded that romantic relationships have a positivity tipping point.

The Gottmans discovered that for a relationship to thrive, the partners must communicate at least five times as many positive "signs" to each other as negative ones. A sign is any communication that signals thoughts and feelings.

Signs include what you say, how you say it, your vocal tone, attitude, gestures, body language, eye movements, and facial expressions. They are the outward expression of your inner emotions. A romantic relationship with a five-to-one or greater positivity ratio is almost sure to last.

But when the positivity ratio falls below this tipping point, the relationships starts to languish and eventually falls apart. The more negative interactions, the faster the relationship crashes and burns.

Here are five positive signs that the Gottmans discovered are essential for lasting romantic relationships.

1. Show sincere *interest* in each other. ("Tell me more.")

2. Express *affection* such as hugging, touching, kissing, and eye contact (handholding and goo-goo eyes count, too).

3. *Validate* each other's ideas, beliefs, points of view, and concerns. ("I understand and agree with you.")

4. Express *empathy* for each other's feelings. ("I feel your pain. I share your joy.")

5. Make each other smile and *laugh*. ("You are so funny!")

Most people thrive on authentic appreciation from their lovers. I often tell people that I married Brooke because she laughs at all of my jokes. The truth is I laugh at her humor, too. We're constantly striving to trigger each other's endorphins. That will enhance any relationship.

Obviously, all of these loving signs must authentically emanate from deep within your soul. To have a flourishing relationship, you must appreciate your partner and make sure they know it.

Celebrate Good News

Shelley Gable has discovered that the way you respond to your lover's good fortune is a strong predictor of the strength of the relationship. Her research complements the Gottman's insights on flourishing couples.

In one study, she analyzed how men and women responded to a positive event in their partners' lives, such as earning a raise. She discovered that the best way to respond is *constructively* and *enthusiastically*, such as, "That's fantastic honey. I know it's because you always have good suggestions on how your whole team can be more productive."

A less enthusiastic response is, "Oh, that's nice." Moving into negative territory, you could respond with an uninterested, "The commute traffic was horrible today." The worst possible response, one that's guaranteed to shorten your marriage, is to focus on the negative, "It wasn't much of a raise, was it?" Why share any good news when your partner always sees the glass as half empty?

Savoring good news and being enthusiastic about happy events puts both partners in the Endorphin Zone. It focuses your attention on the positive and creates a shared endorphin moment.

A final tip is to focus on the good things that are working in your relationship and your life. Even your soul mate and closest friends can say or do things that bother you. So, don't sweat the small stuff; let it go. Practice the key character strengths of forgiveness and kindness. Consciously focus on what you love and appreciate about your soul mate and friends. Let them know what makes you feel loved and appreciated. Then teach them how to evoke those positive emotions.

Keep in mind that we need five times as many positive interactions as negative ones, for any relationship to flourish. So, think about the impact of what you are about to communicate, before you express it. If you can't think of anything good to say, say something constructive, enthusiastic, and loving anyway. Because, in any relationship, the more positivity you give, the more you get.

Make Your Partner Ecstatic

One of my goals is to make Brooke ecstatic that she married me. My strategy is to make sure she experiences a flood of endorphins a few times each day. So, every day I tell her how much I love her (11 on a scale of 10) and point out at least one specific thing that I admire, appreciate or love about her; "I appreciate how you always take such good care of our garden and how hard you work to keep it looking nice."

What could you say to light up the person you love?

Focusing on and expressing the things you admire, appreciate, and find attractive about your lover increases their endorphins and your own.

Be sure to show your love with your actions as well as your words. For example, you can ask your sweetheart, "On a scale of one to ten, how happy are you today?" Listen to the answer and if it's less than a 10 (ecstatic), you can ask, "What would make you even happier?" Then enthusiastically do what it takes to boost their positivity.

Once you learn what makes them happy, do what they want without being asked. Encourage and empower them to pursue their passions, spend time with their friends, and listen to them when they need to share or vent. Don't hover, cling, or "glom onto" them. Give them freedom to be themselves and they'll love you even more.

If you want to optimize your relationship with your soul mate (or anyone else) focus on their good points and forgive their shortcomings. Consciously communicate more positive signs and celebrate good news. These simple recommendations will help boost the positivity ratio over the tipping point so your love lasts forever.

Do You Need Somebody to Love?

I hope you have all the positive relationships you want. But, if you're looking for your soul mate, it's helpful to make a list of all the positive things you need and want from them.

Use the information in this book to define the positive character strengths, personality traits, values, beliefs, interests, and other factors that are important in your ideal life partner. Identify what you want, not what you don't want. And don't go into to much detail about their looks. Just list the key physical features that turn you on and those that turn you off. Focus more on how they make you feel then how they look.

Separate your list into two categories: 1) need to have and 2) nice to have.

Once you have a written description of your ideal mate, review it every morning and evening. Visualize being with your soul mate in your ideal future. Pre-experience what you will be doing and saying and how connected, empowered, and loved you will feel.

This process may seem simplistic, but it works. Two months after I wrote a description of my ideal soul mate, I met Brooke. As I got to know her better, I realized she had every one of my "need to haves." The only "nice to have" she didn't do was downhill skiing. That was no biggie. You'll learn more about visualizations in the chapters ahead, but for now, just realize that you can't get what you want until you know what you want.

Writing things down on paper is the first step to turning your dreams into reality.

When you do find someone to love, you'll naturally want to enjoy the ultimate romantic experience with them: hot, loving sex.

The Amazing Benefits of Loving Sex

As Mae West once observed, "Too much of a good thing . . . can be wonderful."

Nobel prize–winning psychologist Daniel Kahneman and his colleagues at Princeton asked 909 employed women volunteers to keep a diary of their daily activities. The next day the participants ranked the intensity of various emotions they experienced during each activity. After crunching the numbers, the researchers discovered the activity the women enjoyed the most was intimate relations, including *sex*.

They aren't unique. In a study of middle-aged professional women, sexual satisfaction was the second strongest predictor of life satisfaction. We don't need a scientific survey to know that sex is at the top of most men's list. Loving sex is the pinnacle of hedonic pleasure. So, let's talk about sex! (Don't get too excited. This section isn't about technique. Get a video for that.)

My goal is to share some of the little-known benefits of loving sex, and give you permission and encouragement to make love more often.

Sex gets you "high."

It's no surprise that we enjoy sex so much. After all, it's critically important for the survival of our species. We're hardwired to want lots of it. Unlike other hedonic pleasures, no matter how many times we do it, sex never loses its appeal. All we need is a little time to recharge between our romantic encounters.

The brain chemicals oxytocin and vasopressin are released in both men and women when we are sexually aroused during foreplay. Even more are released during intercourse. In women, oxytocin levels rise to up to five times their normal levels just before orgasm. After sex, our brains continue to release oxytocin and endorphins in waves.

This powerful chemical cocktail creates a calm, euphoric afterglow that alleviates pains, including headaches, arthritis, and even migraines. Oxytocin is the safest tranquilizer in the world and is about ten times more effective than Valium. This is why *sex is a powerful stress reliever and instant cure for mild depression.*

Together, oxytocin and endorphins reduce our fear of intimacy and create a warm, trusting connection. That makes us more empathetic, supportive, and open to sharing our feelings, which strengthens our bond with our lover. Sexual activity also increases the dopamine level in our brain, which enhances our problem-solving abilities.

Finally, the increased levels of testosterone released before, during, and after sex improves our self-confidence. These synergistic emotional, psychological, and physiological effects can come to a climax in a profoundly pleasurable and satisfying "Endorphigasm."

Not having sexual intercourse makes some women (and, I'm guessing, most men) depressed. And the longer they go without sex, the more depressed they can become. Why is this?

One factor is the "injection" a woman receives during intercourse. A survey of almost three hundred adult female students found that women whose male partners made love without a condom were far happier than women were whose partners always used condoms. The explanation for this is that mood-enhancing hormones in the men's semen reduced their lover's stress and lifted their mood. (Don't use this as an excuse to skip protection unless you're in an exclusive relationship and use another form of family planning.)

Because it has so many positive effects on our bodies and our brains, sex can create a "drug like dependency." This may cause us to become "addicted" to someone who's totally incompatible and sometimes downright bad for us. So, to avoid stress and drama, choose your sex partner carefully for personal compatibility, not just physical attraction.

And, for maximum positivity, stick with the optimum number of lovers at a time—one.

Monogamous sex makes you look younger.

Want to look ten years younger? You'll love the treatment.

Dr. David Weeks, a neuropsychologist and the author of *Secrets of the Super Young*, led a ten-year study involving 3,500 people. Amazingly, he found that people who have sex four or more times a week with a committed partner look at least ten years younger than other people their age who have sex only two times a week. Regular, loving sex is one of the most effective ways to look younger than you are.

Some people might say that the youthful looking people have more sex. But, Weeks theorizes that endorphins and oxytocin help preserve youth. Other researchers have noted that when women make love, and especially when they achieve orgasm, they produce large amounts of estrogen. This hormone makes their hair shine and their skin smooth.

Week's study showed that *the full benefits of frequent sex were enjoyed only by couples involved in long-term, monogamous relationships*. Playboys take note: sex with lots of partners was more likely to make you look older than younger.

Although you obviously don't have to be in love, or even have a partner, to have an orgasm. But, women who are in love with their partners report more satisfying and easily achieved orgasms. It's clear that the best sex is with a loving, committed partner with whom you're totally smitten. That's why making love is much more rewarding than just having sex.

Frequent, enthusiastic sex increases health and longevity.

Today, many doctors encourage their patients to have lots of sex. This is based on numerous research studies of both mental and physical health benefits of frequent sex. One study reported that men in their twenties who ejaculated more than five times a week were one-third less likely to get aggressive prostate cancer than men who ejaculated less than twice a week.

When researchers at the Queens University in Belfast tracked the death rate of one thousand middle-aged men for ten years, they discovered a direct correlation between not enough sex and early death. The men who reported the highest frequency of orgasms had a death rate that was half that of the men who had the lowest number of sexual encounters. In a follow up study, men who had sex three or more times a week cut their risk of heart attack or stroke in half.

And regular, enthusiastic sex stretches or tones just about every muscle in your body. It improves your posture while firming up your stomach and butt. It's also one of the safest and most enjoyable ways to raise your heart rate. Maybe that's why *Men's Health* magazine called the bed the "single greatest piece of exercise equipment ever invented."

Sex, Money, and Happiness

More good news! Making love more often will make you happier than earning more money. So, if you're not achieving your income goals, you can make up any endorphin deficits in the bedroom.

Economists David G. Blanchflower and Andrew J. Oswald are leaders in a new field called happiness economics. Their research team analyzed the sexual activity and happiness levels of more than sixteen thousand adults who had participated in various American social surveys since the early 1990s. After crunching the numbers, Blanchflower and Oswald came to some interesting conclusions.

The happiest people had the most sex with a committed partner and never had sex with anyone else. Significantly, unlike more income, which has diminishing impact on happiness, sex increases happiness in direct proportion to the amount you have.

The team also compared sex's positive lift with the good feelings we experience from earning more money. Their conclusion was that an average, monogamous American couple that revved up their love making from once a month to once a week would increase their happiness and life satisfaction as much as earning an extra $50,000 a year! So, supercharging your intimacy, connection, and sex life will boost your endorphins much, much more than a big increase in your income.

After reading dozens of scientific studies on the benefits of loving sex, I've come to this conclusion: as long as you practice it in moderation, occasional abstinence probably won't hurt you . . . much. When it comes to making love with a committed, adult partner, as long as you avoid unwanted pregnancies, more is better.

Loving sex is an important aspect of human flourishing. So don't let anything stop you from fully experiencing its many benefits. If you aren't able to fully express and satisfy your sexuality, seek counseling or therapy from a qualified professional. Don't miss out on one of life's greatest joys.

If you are in a loving relationship, commit to making love more often and to savoring your intimacy more deeply and passionately. Simply say this to you lover, "Honey, do you know what would be good for our health—and would make us both really happy?"

Now that we've explored the benefits of positive relationships with soul mates, family and friends, let's look at the transformative power of mentors.

Mentors Can Change Your Life

Humans learn best by modeling the behavior of others. Interacting with, watching, listening to, and reading about people you want to emulate can make a huge positive difference in your life.

When I was younger, Alan Watts, the author, speaker and radio personality who popularized Zen Buddhism in the West, made a big impact on my thinking. When I was an investment wholesaler, my boss, Frank Terzolo, told me, "I'm going to change your life." His mentoring and tough love sent me on the trajectory that I've been on for the last three decades.

In addition to personal relationships, biographies and historical novels are engaging ways to learn and grow from virtual mentors. Workshops, conferences, and classes are great ways to meet real mentors. When I read a book or article that resonates with me, I often attend workshops and conferences to meet the authors. That's how I met Martin Seligman and found out about his six-month teleclass on positive psychology, *Coaching Towards Happiness*. I also met Ed Diener and many other leading positive psychologists at conferences.

Engaging a mentor isn't usually an imposition: happy people enjoy helping others. So, most successful people will be happy to share their wisdom and insights once they realize you're passionate about learning what they know.

If you want to accelerate your learning and growth, mentor and teach others. Teaching forces you to think clearly and articulate your knowledge and insights. It's an important strategy for personal development and a positive win-win experience.

Make a list of people who have made the biggest positive contribution to your life. Identify what they did to help you learn, evolve, and prosper. If possible, tell them how grateful you are and how the contributed to your success and happiness.

Then list five to ten possible living mentors that you want to meet, learn from, or build relationships with in the future. Make a similar list of historical figures you want to learn more about. Then build relationships with mentors. Don't be shy to ask for help and advice. They'll probably benefit more from the relationship than you will.

* * *

Surrounding yourself with positive people is a proven path to health, wealth, and happiness.. So, consciously identify and spend more time with people that put you in the Endorphin Zone. They will light up your life, increase your positivity ratio, and put you on the upward spiral of flourishing.

Building positive relationships takes commitment, time, and effort. However, nothing is likely to have a greater impact on your quality of life.

ENDORPHIN EVENT #8
Plan and Go On an Endorphin Date

Summarize this chapter for your guests by going through the pages and using the subheads and graphics to share the key points. Then brainstorm on the following topics.

If You're in a Relationship with a Soul Mate (Or want to have a great time with someone you are attracted to.)
1. Discuss, plan, and enjoy a romantic all-day date with your lover. Exchange flowers or small gifts. Do new things together that allow you to both express your powers and passions. Spice up your day with a little danger, novelty, and physical activity. That will arouse your libido.
2. Then, enjoy a romantic dinner at one of your favorite places. Take turns sharing what you love, appreciate, and find sexy about each other. Savor your meal and conversation. Look deeply into each other's eyes. Practice active and constructive responses. Show positive signs. Tell your lover what you want to do together later. Build positive anticipation. Then go home, or someplace special, and enjoy a wild, romantic time making hot, loving sex.
3. Repeat often.

If You're Happily Single
1. Determine who you want to invite a platonic or romantic friend to join you on this Endorphin Quest.
2. Plan and carry out a series of "random acts of kindness" with perfect strangers to brighten both their day and yours.
3. Pay the toll for the car behind you, let someone cut in line, buy someone a cup of coffee, give a gift or compliment, etc. Or volunteer to help others in need or for a worthy cause.

4. Savor and then discuss the experiences, and the responses of the people you meet. Tell your friends what you like, admire, and appreciate about them. Focus on active and constructive responses to their good news and ideas.
5. End the day with a fun dinner. Go somewhere new that's relaxing and comfortable. Discuss the joy of giving, helping, and contributing to the happiness of others. Be open to romantic possibilities, if that's an option.

If You're Looking for Your Soul Mate
1. Invite a friend who will support you in this adventure. Plan and go somewhere you can new meet people who are likely to be in your age group and share your interests, beliefs, and values. The more opportunity you have to interact with others, the better.
2. Practice engaging people in conversations about their favorite subjects—their passions and themselves. When you meet someone you're interested in, ask them, "What lights you up and generates energy in your life?"
3. Listen deeply and respond with active and constructive comments. Listen to your inner guides; they will guide you to your soul mate. When you connect with someone you're attracted to, communicate positive signs to express your feelings for them.
4. Continue this activity until you find your soul mate. Then do Endorphin Event 1 with them.

SUMMARY:
Maximize Your Endorphins in All Your Life Domains

It's time to give yourself a pat on the back. You now know more about the keys to human flourishing than ninety-nine percent of the people on the planet. You've learned about the four inner Endorphin Domains: your personal operating system, your powers, your passions, and your purpose. And you've learned about two of the three outer Endorphin Domains, positive places and positive people. Here's a quick review of this section.

Chapter 4. Upgrading your "personal operating system" will increase your positivity more easily and quickly than changing your life circumstances. The ideal operating system will empower you to satisfy your biological needs and key emotional desires, and encourage you to follow your higher aspirations.

The happiest people are optimists who take full responsibility for their lives and focus on what they want, not what they don't want. Their positivity enables them to constantly grow and adapt to the changes around them. They're grateful for what they have and are satisfied with who they are, but they aspire to be, do, and accomplish even more.

Chapter 5. Identifying what generates success and happiness in each of your Endorphin Domains will empower you to do it more often—and spend less time doing things that stress you out. Endorphin Data from your past and Endorphin Dreams for your future will lead you to the Endorphin Zone.

By recalling your past work successes, you can identify the natural talents and learned character strengths that are responsible for your greatest successes and happiness. Pursue work that allows you to express your powers and that doesn't require you to use your weaknesses (if you have any).

Chapter 6. Discovering your life's purpose unlocks your highest potential. Your purpose is to contribute to the well-being of other people, other living things, and our planet. When you're expressing your personal powers in the service of your life's purpose, your work becomes your calling. You'll find clues to your purpose in meaningful life experiences, by clarifying your values and through the inspiration of role models. To clarify your purpose, imagine what you would like people to say about you at your eulogy.

Chapter 7. Your passions add spice, spark, and adventure to your life. We invest energy and resources in our passions solely because of the intrinsic rewards we enjoy from them. Identify your top passions so you can take steps to enjoy more of them in your life.

Your physical environments make a difference in your emotional state. Spending time in positive places soothes your stress, recharges your brain, and heals your soul. So pick your region, community, neighborhood, and home thoughtfully. Spend time in natural places and bring nature into your home. Travel breaks your routine, opens your mind, and gives you time and "space" to become who you are.

Chapter 8. You need people to love, and they need you. Humans are social animals and need the companionship, care, cooperation, and love of others. You feel connected to positive people, and they empower you to be more successful and happier, or both. Avoid toxic people you don't feel connected to, and/or who sap your personal power.

By connecting with a soul mate, a best friend or two, and a "tribe" of about fifty other people, you build a network of family, friends, mentors, and advisors who support you in your quest for a flourishing life.

After completing the exercises in this section, you'll have a list of your Endorphin Data and the Endorphin Dreams that you want to test drive in the future. Now, it's time to use this information to envision yourself living your best possible life—when you're doing all of the things that make you successful and happy, and are test-driving new things that may make you ecstatic!

STEP THREE

Envision a Flourishing Future

9

Visualize Your Ideal Work and Play

Behold this day, for it is yours to make.
—**Black Elk**

The Great Pyramid of Khufu was Earth's tallest structure for more than four thousand years and was known as one of the Seven Wonders of the World. Have you ever thought about the person who first envisioned such an iconic structure?

In my mind's eye, I see an Egyptian priestess waking abruptly in the middle of the night. She jumps out of bed and shouts, "I just had this insanely great dream! Let's enslave tens of thousands of workers for decades. We'll make them quarry gargantuan stone blocks and drag them to the middle of nowhere. Then we'll force them to build a colossal monument to Khufu.

"I know the Pharaoh's gonna LOVE THIS!"

We'll never know exactly what happened. But, it's certain that before the pyramids were designed and built, they started as someone's impossible dream. In fact, everything that humans have ever invented or created started as a dream, or vision, in someone's imagination. Our ability to create internal representatives of things that don't exist and events that haven't happened, and then turn those visions into reality, sets us apart from every other species.

Why You Need a Positive Vision

For thousands of years, wise people have understood the importance of vision. Modern scientists are confirming the Old Testament's wisdom that, "Where there is no vision the people perish."

Andrew MacLeod's research team analyzed interviews with para-suicides, people who survived a suicide attempt, to try to understand their motivations. They reported a surprising conclusion: it's the lack of a positive vision, not the presence of a negative vision, that drives many people to attempt suicide. Substantial other research supports MacLeod's findings.

Why does the absence of a positive vision make people take their own lives?

The average person spends about seven minutes out of every waking hour thinking about their future. Without a positive vision, the future is unknown, which creates uncertainty. Because of our negativity bias, uncertainty evokes fear, causing withdrawal from life and a focus on avoiding pain instead of pursing pleasure. That's why people without a positive vision often move from a bad situation to one that's worse. They flee from the frying pan into the fire.

Constantly anticipating the pain they seek to avoid barrages them with negative thoughts and emotions that lead to rigidity and paralysis—languishing. They become Old Fogies, habitually repeating unsatisfying behaviors with no motivation to change, since they can't envision anything better. Their options narrow, depression closes in, and taking their life can seem like the only way out.

Management guru Peter Drucker, says, "The best way to predict the future is to create it." A positive vision helps you do just that by projecting an upbeat mental image of the future, replacing fears and uncertainty with optimism and confidence. Vision provides direction and focus for your life. It becomes the basis for your plans, goals, and actions. It empowers you to ask the right questions, solve the right problems, and take appropriate actions to consciously create a life you love.

One of the most powerful benefits of a positive vision is that you don't have to wait until some vague future date to experience its benefits. Lee Berk, a world-renowned expert on positive emotions and health, discovered why positive visions are so powerful; anticipating positive future experiences evokes positive emotions in the present.

Since positive emotions are attractive, a positive vision lights you up and pulls you toward your ideal future every time you think about it. In fact, anticipating a positive experience often generates more endorphins than the experience itself.

Try it!

Think about a positive event you're looking forward to in the future. Close your eyes and imagine yourself enjoying the experience. Savor it with all your senses: visualize it, hear it, feel it, taste it, and smell it. Did you notice your muscles relaxing? Are you smiling? Just *thinking* about the future experience enhanced your positive emotions, instantly.

When you envision positive future events and experiences, positive emotions cause you to think and act in novel and innovative ways, enhancing your intuition, creativity, and problem-solving skills. They inspire you to try new ideas and approaches. Most important, positive visions focus your resources on the strategies and behaviors that will lead you towards your ideal future.

What is a positive vision?

While your *purpose* inspires you as your *raison d'être*, your reason for being, your vision gives you a sense of destination. A positive vision is a mental representation, or image in your mind's eye, of your ideal future. Although the most powerful visions are based on a meaningful purpose (you can see your purpose being fulfilled), any positive vision will help you flourish.

To better understand what a positive vision is, it's helpful to distinguish it from fantasies and dreams.

1. A *fantasy* is something you daydream about that isn't likely to happen. Some fantasies are fun to think about, but you'd get in a lot of trouble if you acted on them. It's best to keep your fantasies where they are, in your imagination.
2. A *dream* is something that you think about, a lot, and you want it to happen. But you haven't made any plans or taken any action to make it happen.
3. A *vision* is a compelling dream that you are committed to making happen. You're emotionally attracted to your vision and think about it all the time. It calls you on an exciting and challenging adventure that will bring out the best in you. You've probably already taken some steps to turn it into reality.

Walt Disney said all of your dreams can come true if you have the courage to pursue them. "If you can dream it, you can do it," he encouraged. But how? To the right, you can see my process for transforming intangible dreams and visions into reality.

This process starts with vague thoughts and feelings, evolves into specific mental images, which you can turn into measurable goals, plans, actions and, finally, results. After evaluating the results, you can adjust your behavior until you're satisfied. Psychologist, Ray Baumeister says, "The function of consciousness is to simulate the future, and then choose among the simulations."

12 Steps to Turn Dreams into Reality
1. Dreams
2. Vision
3. Aspirations
4. Goals
5. Plans
6. Schedules
7. Actions
8. Results
9. Evaluation
10. Insights
11. Adaptation
12. Flourishing

Think of a positive vision as an emotional lighthouse. It inspires and guides your every thought and action. It becomes an important and powerful mental resource.

The Building Blocks for Your Positive Vision

My mom has traveled to more than a hundred countries. She once told me proudly, "Whenever I want, I can close my eyes and go back to anywhere I've ever been." We all have this uniquely human capacity to vividly remember past experiences. We can also envision future experiences that haven't happened yet.

Unlike lower mammals, humans can create mental representations of highly detailed alternative scenarios for our future. You can mentally step into the future without risk, test various actions, and envision probable outcomes. The more accurate your mental models are, the more accurately you can predict the results of your actions.

This ability to "see" the future helped our ancient ancestors avoid threats and envision the best way to pursue opportunities. Using MRI images, neuroscientists are shedding light on the biological foundations for this incredible human ability.

When you remember the past, or envision the future, the same network of neurons and neuro clusters lights up in our brains, and in similar patterns. This shows that these circuits are used for both memory and for imagining the future. When people lose their memories, they can't form clear mental images of the future, or even imagine what they want to do next week. These facts indicate that your memories of past experiences are the raw material for your visions of the future.

Since your memories are the building blocks for your vision, your past defines and often limits your thinking about the future. Fortunately, your personal experiences aren't the only source of your memories. You can consciously fill your memory banks with positive thoughts, information, and images by reading, watching movies, and exchanging information with others. So make a conscious effort to fill your memory banks with success stories, positive role models, ideas, and information that will help you think outside the box of your past experiences.

Our Visions Evolve as We Evolve

Visions take a while to form in your mind, becoming clearer as you invest time and thought in them. Like an object in the distance, you can see more details as you move closer to them.

The process of defining your vision is similar to designing and building a custom home. There are thousands of decisions when you build a new home. But you don't have to make them all at once. The process usually unfolds over several years. You start with a general desire, eventually deciding on the big issues, such as the architectural style and location.

Then you hire an architect who draws a beautiful rendering of your dream home, turning your intangible vision into a tangible image: out of your mind and into the real world. Once you have it on paper, you decide on the myriad details, typically over one to two years. You answer all the questions the same way you'd run a marathon, one step at a time.

That's the process you'll use here, too. Start with a vague vision and fill in the details over time. The Endorphin Data and Endorphin Dreams that you worked hard to define in the previous section are the raw material for your positive vision.

Since you've read this far, and done the exercises that called to you, you already have most of the important elements of your ideal future in your mind. You just haven't put all the pieces together yet. But you're getting clearer on what makes you happy, successful, and fulfilled in each of the seven Endorphin Domains. The knowledge you've gained reading this far will help you separate your dreams from your fantasies and your visions from your dreams. It will also minimize miswanting.

Your goal is to synthesize your self-knowledge into a positive vision. Picture yourself at your best, expressing your personal powers, pursuing your passions, and fulfilling your life's purpose. Imagine working with positive people in positive places, making an enormous contribution to the world, and growing and evolving in meaningful ways. Once you have a vision, your inner circle of positive people can help you to turn it into reality.

The most important elements in your ideal future are your ideal work and positive people. Since identifying positive people is usually easy and discovering your ideal work is usually hard, let's start by defining a vision of your ideal work. Then you'll define a positive vision that includes all of your domains.

In the process, you'll answer the three big question of life:

What do I want to be when I "grow up"?
Who do I want to "play" with?
What types of conversations and interactions do I want to have with them?

Satisfying Work:
The Foundation for a Flourishing Life

When you meet a new person in a social setting, what's one of the first things you typically ask them? Isn't it, "What do you do?" The answer tells you a great deal about them. In fact, what people do, or did, for a living, before they retired, usually defines them more accurately than any other single characteristic. Current or past work indicates social status, income level, education, personality, and even values.

For most people, work also dictates how they spend over half of their waking hours, defines most of their social interactions, and is a primary determinant of their life satisfaction. If you're retired, you still need to identify how you can express yourself in the most fulfilling ways. If you're a student, this section will help you identify your ideal future work.

Your ideal work is a vehicle for expressing your powers, purpose, and passions. It makes you feel secure, competent, autonomous, connected, and proud of your accomplishments and contributions.

But, for many people, the only thing positive about work is their compensation.

In a Spherion Emerging Workforce Study, over half of the American workers surveyed were unsatisfied and wanted a different job. Seventy-five percent of these unhappy employees wanted to change jobs as soon as possible. This leads me to a distressing conclusion: for many people, work is a major source of stress in their lives instead of a source of joy and fulfillment. Apparently, they don't know it can be enjoyable and meaningful.

Endorphins at Work

The summer I graduated from high school, I took a road trip from my home, just north of San Francisco, to Seattle. Along the way, I stopped to visit my father's sister in Corvallis, Oregon. Aunt Mackie was a professor of plant genetics at Oregon State University. She was working on a project to improve Bing cherries, an important crop in her state.

I can still see Mackie's ear-to-ear smile and floppy straw hat when I met her in the middle of a cherry orchard. I looked at all the trees, heavy with ruby-red fruit, and asked her incredulously, "Aunt Mackie, is this where you work?" She smiled even bigger, held her palms up, and spun around in a circle. With a childlike laugh she answered, "Yes, this is my lab. Isn't it fabulous?"

Then she said something I'll never forget: "I love my work. I can't believe they pay me to do this."

I was stunned by the contrast between my father, who hated his work, and his sister, who loved hers. It was a revelation that work could be fun and rewarding. My father's stressful work led to disabling arthritis and an early death. But his sister, who enjoys her work, is still alive, healthy, and passionate about her projects, forty years later. After she retired, Mackie traveled the world for more than a decade, collecting cuttings for a genetic plant bank in St. Louis. She once gleefully told me, "I get all turned on by plant variability."

Now in her late eighties, Aunt Mackie is working on a project to transform a wild Japanese blueberry, the Haskap, into a commercially viable crop. Although she never earned a high income, she's lived a wonderful life, full of purpose, passion, and flow, in a place she loves. Mackie found rewarding work that gave her life a sense of meaning and joy. And you can, too.

Determine Your Current Work Orientation

Abraham Maslow wrote, "Self-actualizing people are, without a single exception, involved in a cause outside of themselves. They are devoted, working at something precious to them—a calling, a vocation." Psychologists tell us that people think about their work as either a job, a career, or a calling.

Which of these three definitions describes how you feel about your current work?

1. A *job*. Jobs are stressful and energy draining. You feel bored and disengaged at work. You watch the clock, looking forward to "quittin' time" and the weekend. Your motivation is strictly to earn money. The song, *Take this Job and Shove It*, describes how you feel about your work.
2. A *career*. You try to achieve success and happiness by "climbing the career ladder." You accept long hours and major stress as part of your work. You're willing to "temporarily" sacrifice your quality of life and time with your loved ones for increased status and pay. You like some, or even many, aspects of your work but are mainly in it for money and status. You fantasize about early retirement.

3. A *calling*. Like my Aunt Mackie, you "get all turned on" by your work. It's a key part of your identity, an integral part of your life, your vehicle for personal growth and self-expression. A calling has something that jobs and careers lack: a transcendent, spiritual dimension, a higher purpose than just making money. You know it's your destiny to do this work because it makes you feel fully alive. Your work is meaningful and it's making a positive contribution to the world. You often work long hours and weekends. You never want to retire.

Interestingly, it isn't the work itself that determines if it's a job, a career, or a calling; it's your personal fit. The young orthodontist who bought my father's practice was passionate about his work. He flew a private plane to small villages in the rugged mountains of Northern Mexico, where he straightened people's teeth for free. For my dad, orthodontia was a stressful job. For Tom, it's a fulfilling calling.

Aristotle said, "Where your talents and the needs of the world cross, there lies your calling." To flourish, we must discover our calling, work that supports us and contributes to the greater good.

Start by matching your powers, passions, purpose, and values with a specific work personality.

Identify Your Work Personality

Discovering your calling requires introspection, research, and the belief that your life actually has a higher purpose. You can get the ball rolling by identifying your "work personality." John Holland developed this widely used career counseling technique based on his observation that "the choice of a vocation is an expression of personality."

In Western societies, most people fit one of Holland's six work personalities. These work orientations are a synthesis of your unique talents, interests, character strengths, and values—your personality.

Groups of people with the same work personality create a work environment. For instance, imaginative and innovative people working together on a film create an artistic work environment.

Each of us typically has varying levels of interests and skills in all six of these work personalities. If you took an online interest inventory, such as the Campbell Interest and Skills Inventory (CISS®, http://psychcorp.pearsonassessments.com), it would rank each of the six (other career counseling profiles may use different names and definitions). If you haven't taken a profile, you can rate each of these descriptions based on how well you believe they define you. Use a scale of one to five, with five meaning "very much" like you, and one meaning "not at all" like you.

The Six Work Personalities and Environments

1. *Enterprising*: influencing others through leadership, politics, public speaking, sales, and marketing.
2. *Conventional*: organizing the work of others, managing, and monitoring financial performance.
3. *Social*: helping others through teaching, healing, coaching and counseling.
4. *Artistic*: creating artistic, literary, or musical productions, and designing products, services or environments.
5. *Investigative*: analyzing data, using mathematics, and carrying out scientific experiments.
6. *Realistic*: producing products, using hands-on skills in farming, construction, and mechanical crafts; includes physical risk taking through athletic, police, and military activities.

Each of these six work environments has dozens or even hundreds of specific job classifications. But you need to start in the right environment, where you can express and develop your natural talents and pursue your passions. Your specific activities and responsibilities will evolve as you develop your unique abilities.

To help pin down your ideal work environment, review your Endorphin Data from chapter 5. In which work environment did most of your peak successes occur? Which environment is most supportive of your values, beliefs, and purpose? *Which one are you intuitively drawn to?*

For another perspective on your ideal work environment, imagine you're at a party where people from the six work personalities are socializing in six different rooms. Which group is most like you and your closest friends? Which personalities would you feel most connected with? Which groups would you probably not connect with?

Martin Seligman says when you're deciding which type of work to pursue, you must answer the following questions:

How much *positive emotion* will it provide?
How *engaging* will it be?
How *meaningful* is the work for you?

At a Stanford commencement address, Apple founder Steve Jobs said, "The only way to do great work is to love what you do." Imagine you have a magic wand and can do anything you want. What would you love to do? What would make you feel proud of yourself? *What type of work calls to your heart?* What do you want to be known for?

Use the answers to the questions above, your insights about your personal powers from chapter 5, and any career profiles you've completed, to identify and prioritize your top two work environments—where you know you will do great work that you love. Also, identify work environments that you want to avoid. The wrong work environment will be a dungeon where you languish instead of a greenhouse where you can flourish.

Don't focus on job titles, status, or income. Instead, focus on what you'll be doing and who you'll be doing it with. Write a detailed description of your ideal work, including responsibilities, daily activities, travel, etc. Describe a work environment and position that enables you to express your powers, while pursuing your passions, for a higher purpose, with positive people, in positive places.

If, after doing all these exercises, you still don't know what you want to be when you "grow up," ask yourself this question:

If I did know what my calling was, what would it probably be?

Trust your gut for the answer. Deep down you already know what you're destined to be. It's in your DNA. So listen to your inner guides to discover your calling.

Transform Your Current Work into Your Calling

Before you decide to take your current job and shove it, consider a few things. Hardly anyone starts out with their calling. Normally we evolve from a job to a career and then, if we identify our natural talents, purpose, and passions, we can evolve into our calling.

If you currently have a good job or career, but it's not ideal, here are a few things that will make you happier and more satisfied, right now. First, focus on the things that you're grateful for, including your teammates and how your work contributes to a better world.

The second strategy is to change your work responsibilities and tasks. If you can demonstrate strengths and interests that match the type of work you really want to do, your current employer may have an opportunity for you. To convince them you can do the work, tell them about your past successes, and explain how they qualify you for your desired position.

Consider Self-Employment

When I met Melinda, she was an art director for a magazine publishing company. But she was frustrated. She eventually started a thriving advertising and marketing agency. A while ago, she wrote me an email with a story about how she started her business.

"Once upon a time I was looking for a company where I would be challenged, and only be limited by my own ambitions, where I would be able to give back to others without having to ask someone for permission. Steve, you were the one that asked me, 'Why don't you start your own business?' I replied, 'What, I never thought about owning my own company.' The rest is history." Melinda is now the master of her own destiny, free to express her creativity and use her time according to her priorities.

As you define your ideal work, don't limit yourself to working for someone else. About one in ten people in America are self-employed, but that percentage is much higher for mature workers. In fact, almost one in five workers over sixty-five is self-employed. Andrew Oswald, a researcher who studies money and happiness, says, "Everything associated with self-employment—independence, autonomy—is associated with being happy."

In a recent Gallup-Healthways Well-Being Index report, business owners had the highest overall well-being and work satisfaction of any occupational group. Successful business owners also earn the highest incomes and have the highest net worth of any occupation in America.

The second most satisfied group, professionals, also has a large percentage of self-employed people who earn above average incomes. Self-employed workers can organize their work to maximize the use of their strengths and minimize the use of their weaknesses. They are masters of their destiny.

The income and quality of life associated with self-employment explains why the Department of Labor predicts the number one employer in the future will be "self." That prediction is supported by a recent Internet poll in which ninety percent of twenty-five to forty-four year olds wanted to own their own businesses. Because of these factors and corporate downsizing, the twenty-first century is likely to see a major boom in self-employment. However, self-employment isn't for everyone.

Running a business can be demanding and exhausting. On average, self-employed people work much longer hours than employees. One of my clients joked that his business entailed "long hours, low pay, and high risk to capital. Other than that, it's not a bad job."

How do you know if you could be successful as a self-employed business owner? The clues are in your peak successes, especially from your earliest years. Everyone I know who is successfully self-employed demonstrated their entrepreneurial drive at an early age. So the question you need to answer is, *What have I done in my past that indicates I'll be successful running my own business in the future?*

If the answer is *nothing*, but you're determined to work for yourself, don't quit your day job. Instead, work in the field of your calling. Develop your contacts and skills. Then start a business while you're still employed. Work on it nights and weekends. That will give you a taste of the long hours all new businesses require. And you can maintain positive cash flow until your new business is able to support you.

Experts say we're likely to have seven to ten completely different occupations in our lifetimes. Defining your ideal work, or your calling, will empower you to turn each new situation into a *BCR*, a beneficial career readjustment that takes you closer to your ideal.

Envision a Positive Future

What if you were the writer, director, and star in a movie of your life? Would it be a drama? A tragedy? A comedy? A farce? Or would you write an inspiring story about a healthy, happy, and successful person who is making a positive difference in the world?

Well, you *are* the writer, director, and star of your own life. You have the ability to make your life a fascinating work of art or a boring waste. Just as a movie needs a script, you need a vision. Your positive vision is a story about your future: the better your story, the better your future. As Albert Einstein said, "Your imagination is your preview of life's coming attractions."

An easy and fun way to start defining your vision is to imagine an ideal day when you're living in the Endorphin Zone. Review your Endorphin Data and Dreams. Then I'll guide you through an exercise to transform them into a positive vision of your future.

Relax, smile, and suspend disbelief. Think about the possibilities, not the obstacles. I'll explain how to refine your vision to make sure it's realistic, achievable, and sustainable, in the pages ahead.

Envision an Endorphin Day

Imagine it's five to seven years in the future. Your life has turned out exactly the way you envisioned it. You've worked diligently and achieved most of your key goals and many of your aspirations. Read and envision the section below and answer the questions with as many sensory details as you can. Remember, you have to envision your ideal future before you can create it.

Your Ideal Home and Community

It's morning and you just woke up. Look around your room. It's your ideal bedroom. What does it look like? How is it furnished? Look over to see your soul mate lying next to you. You feel the warmth of their skin. They gaze into your eyes and you both smile, knowing you are the perfect match for each other. You cuddle for a few minutes before you get up, savoring the love you feel. *Describe your soul mate and the things you love most about them.*

Now, get up, and look at yourself in the mirror. You look marvelous, just as you have always wanted. What do you look like? Describe your health, fitness, and vitality.

Put something on and walk into the kitchen. Pour a cup of you favorite morning beverage. Look around your ideal kitchen. What do you like about your kitchen and your mornings at home?

Is anyone else living with you? Who are they? What makes them ideal housemates for you?

Now, look around and appreciate what a wonderful home you have. What is the architectural style of home is it? How big is it? How is it furnished? When you look out the windows, what do you see? Trees, houses, buildings, mountains, the ocean, your landscaped yard? *What do you like and appreciate about your home?*

When you finish savoring your home, eat a healthy breakfast. What type of diet are you maintaining to optimize your health and vitality? After breakfast, take a shower and get dressed. What is your ideal bathroom like?

Now, go outside. When you step out your front door, what do you see? Is your home in an urban, suburban, or rural community? *Describe the key features of your neighborhood, yard, and lot.* What makes them ideal for you?

Who are your neighbors? What do you like about them? Smile to yourself knowing you live in such a wonderful place.

Your Ideal Work Environment

Now, it's time to start the productive part of your day, where you contribute to the well being of others, and the planet. If you're retired or financially independent, replace the words "work" and "office" with whatever is appropriate.

If you work at home, simply walk to your work area. If you work farther away, what type of transportation do you take? Do you ride your bike, take the bus, captain a boat, canter a horse? If you drive, what type of vehicle is it and what do you like about it?

On your way to work, notice how beautiful and inspiring your surroundings are. You feel safe and secure in your community. *What do you appreciate about your region and community?*

You arrive at your work place in less than fifteen minutes, inspired, invigorated, and eager to get started on your day. As you enter, pause to admire how perfect it is. Describe your work place. Is it an office building, a remodeled home, a warehouse, a lab, a recording studio, an orchard? *What do you like about your work place?*

As you enter, one of your coworkers greets with you a cheerful smile. "Good morning. It's a great day!" Seeing and hearing them lights you up, and you smile back.

You're working on projects that you're passionately interested in. You're challenged to use your unique abilities at your highest level. You are all turned on by your work, experiencing large doses of eustress and flow, with very little frustration or stress. You're learning and growing in exciting and meaningful ways.

You feel that it's your destiny to do this work. You know you're contributing to a better world. You're delighted that you're being paid so well to do work that you love. What types of work are you doing, and what types of projects are you working on? How are you expressing your powers and contributing to a bigger purpose? *What makes your work so rewarding for you?*

Your co-workers are competent and fun. They also enjoy their work. You work harmoniously together as you strive to achieve shared goals toward an important purpose. Their skills compliment yours, and they enjoy doing things that you'd rather not do. You feel connected to them and empowered by them. They share many of your values and beliefs.

If you have supervisors, they empower you to grow and evolve in directions that are engaging and interesting to you. All of your co-workers appreciate you and are grateful for your contribution. *What do you like about your teammates?* What makes them a good fit for you?

If you interact with clients or vendors, almost all your conversations are positive. They value your expertise and enjoy working with you. *What do you like about your clients and vendors?*

You laugh and smile a lot at work. It brings you great joy.

Family, Friends, and Fun

You love your work, but you have balance in your life. So you leave after working less than nine hours. You exercise in an inspiring location. After about ten minutes, you start to feel the endorphins flowing. Where and how do you exercise? *What do you like about exercising?*

After working out, you spend about an hour on your favorite activities, interacting with your family members, playing with your dog, reading or enjoying a hobby. *What are your favorite activities after work and before dinner?* What do you like about them?

Since today is an ideal day, you're getting together with your soul mate and some of your closest friends for dinner. You're anticipating a wonderful evening with them. You're going to one of your favorite places to eat. What do you like about it? What makes it ideal for you?

As you connect with your friends over dinner, you realize the food, friendship, and great conversation are putting you in the Endorphin Zone. You feel fortunate to have such great friends. *What do you like and appreciate about them?* How are your friends empowering you? How do you connect with them?

After a fantastic evening, you and your lover return home. You discuss your plans for tomorrow and the week ahead. You're deeply in love and happy to be spending your life with your soul mate. *What do you love and appreciate about them?*

Before going to sleep, you take a few moments to review the day's Endorphin Moments and to count your blessings. Just before turning out the light, you kiss your soul mate and whisper, "Honey, do you know what would be good for our health—and would make us both really happy?" Then visualize a happy ending to your day.

Envision Positive Achievements and Experiences

Variety is the spice of life. Even when you're engaged with meaningful work, you soon adapt to your predictable routine and get a bit bored. So mix up your daily and weekly activities and schedules, add some novelty to your life. Pursue your passions in positive places with positive people. Always have positive events and activities to look forward to in the future.

In addition to envisioning your ideal day, envision positive achievements and experiences in your ideal future. These activities involve your powers, passions, and purpose. For instance, running a marathon, participating in cooking class, or taking a photography workshop. They also include graduations, retirement, marriages, new babies, get-aways, vacations, parties, holidays, workshops, adventures, family gatherings, etc. Think of a metaphorical year that's comprised of four seasons. Then envision endorphin moments and peak experiences in each season. Here are a few questions to help you with this exercise.

What dreams and aspirations did you have when you were younger that you'd like to accomplish or experience in the future? What people do you want to meet and get to know? What aspirations and goals do you have? What passions do you want to pursue? What causes do you want to support?

Make a list of all the places you want to visit and all the things you want to accomplish and experience before you die. Collect images, make a scrapbook or a collage, or post images on your social media site or personal website to help you visualize your ideal future. To make it more concrete, *write a 250- to 750-word story that describes the key elements of your vision in a way that lights you up when you read it.*

Share your vision with you inner circle. Simply tell them a story of where you "see yourself" in your ideal future. The more you think about it, visualize it, and share it with positive people, the clearer your vision will become, and the more likely it is to actually happen.

Famous psychoanalyst Carl Jung advised listening to your inner guides: "Your vision will become clear only when you look into your heart. Who looks outside, dreams. Who looks inside, awakens."

Over time, additional thoughts and insights will come to you when you least expect it, bubbling up from your subconscious mind. It could happen when you're driving, walking your dog, exercising, daydreaming, or just relaxing. Be ready to write your insights down when they hit you.

* * *

I know the value of this exercise not only because I've done it for myself, but also because I've helped hundreds of people imagine and create the life and business of their dreams. I recently spoke with John, a client who participated in one of my workshops about a decade ago. This is what he told me about turning his dream into a vision and his vision into reality.

"Remember when we did that exercise to envision our ideal future? At the time, I thought it was a bit hokey. Since numbers drive most of my decisions, it seemed too touchy-feely for me. But now, I'm sitting in the office that I visualized during your workshop. The furniture, décor, staff, and layout are exactly what I imagined. It's very comfortable and calming and feels like a home instead of an office. I'm even generating the gross revenue and net income that I envisioned and wrote down over ten years ago."

What we think about comes about. Your vision is a seed that will grow into reality if you invest time, energy, and resources into it. Once John had a clear vision, he didn't just dream about it; he took action, using his problem-solving skills, resources, and personal powers to turn it into reality. But it all started with a clear mental picture of what he wanted—that he wrote down on paper, thus making the intangible tangible.

Our visions are powerful catalysts for positive change in our lives, because they become self-fulfilling prophesies.

John said, "The visioning exercise really helped me define and connect with the business and quality of life that I wanted in the future. Now I'm living it."

ENDORPHIN EVENT #9
Share Your Positive Vision

Summarize this chapter for your guests by going through the pages and using the subheads and graphics to share the key points. Then brainstorm on the following topics.

1. What is your work personality and what is the ideal work environment and job description for you? Describe your ideal co-workers.
2. How can you enjoy more engagement and fulfillment in your current job?
3. Verbally guide your family and friends through a visualization of their ideal day and a few future positive experiences. Use the text in the Envision Your Endorphin Day and Envision Positive Events and Experiences sections of this chapter as a script or starting point.
4. Then write down any additional insights and details from this exercise, and share your visions with each other. Help each other "flesh out" your ideal futures. Make them as specific, emotional, and concrete as possible.
5. Collect images, words, and concepts that evoke your positive vision. Use them to create a "vision binder" of photos and pictures representing your ideal future from magazines and the Internet. Build a Facebook or website montage, or other visual representation of your ideal future. Share your vision with your inner circle.
6. Commit to supporting each other's vision. Share ideas and resources for bringing them closer to reality. Encourage and empower each other.
7. Review your vision binder and story of your ideal future often. Use it to connect with your ideal future, boost your positivity, and pre-experience the Endorphin Zone.
8. What will you do differently in the future, based on your insights from this chapter?

10

Optimize Your Personal Finances

My problem lies in reconciling my gross habits with my net income.
—**Errol Flynn**

On a hot summer day, a not-so-young plastic surgeon fell in love with a beautiful young blond. Laurel had been a part-time model and full-time receptionist. Men were mesmerized by her soft feminine curves, sparkling blue eyes, and full, pouty lips.

The doc and Laura met at a charity polo event. She was wearing a big ol' cowboy hat, a fire engine red mini dress—and not much else. The balding surgeon couldn't resist Laurel's youthful charms. Soon the happy chemical messengers dopamine, oxytocin, and endorphins were flooding through their minds and bodies.

The blissful lovers were lost in an orgy of hedonism and consumption. He bought her a new wardrobe and a red Jaguar to complement his blue one. Within months, they were living together, taking ridiculously expensive vacations, and planning an extravagant wedding.

There was only one problem: they were spending money faster than he was earning it.

"They both loved to shop. It was like an addiction." My informant was the former bookkeeper for the love-struck surgeon.

She looked over her glasses at me as she dished out the details. "He was earning almost $1 million dollars a year, but they were spending even more. They bounced checks, or maxed out their credit cards, a coupla times a week. I was supposed to fix everything—because I was his bookkeeper."

She shook her head. "I felt more like his mother."

Since the doc didn't have enough cash to pay for their lavish wedding, his bookkeeper arranged for a $75,000 bank loan. "But on their wedding day, neither the wedding planner nor the banquet manager asked for the checks I'd prepared."

She lowered her voice and confided, "Since they had money in their bank account, they spent it. They blew the entire seventy-five grand on new clothes, furniture, and decorating, in just two weeks."

After that, the loony lovebirds lurched from one financial crisis to another. The bank cut off their credit line; their bills kept piling up. "I had to fend off the resort, the banker, the IRS, and a bunch of collection agencies," the bookkeeper told me. "One day, we couldn't meet payroll. I walked out and never looked back."

Unfortunately, Laurel and the doc had a common problem: their net income didn't support their gross habits. Their lifestyle wasn't sustainable; they were heading for financial disaster.

Up to this point, you've learned about many of the subjective measurements of well-being. Now let's turn our attention to a key objective measurement of your well-being, positive personal finances.

Financial sustainability is the last of the Endorphin Domains. This is an important one because it supplies the cash flow you need to satisfy your needs and wants, and to pursue your aspirations.

To flourish financially, you must do three things competently:

1. achieve and maintain positive cash flow in the present,
2. build resources for a better future, and
3. plan and achieve lifelong financial independence.

When you're successful and happy, and know it's financially sustainable, you experience key positive emotions, including autonomy (financial independence) and optimism. But flourishing financially doesn't happen naturally in our complex modern society; you have to make it happen.

Probably the biggest obstacle to flourishing financially is most of us never had any personal financial management training. But competent management of personal finances is a required skill if you want to flourish. So this chapter is an introduction to personal financial management skills. The next chapter presents proven strategies for achieving lifelong financial independence.

Incidentally, the information in these two chapters doesn't come from positive psychology or related fields, it comes from my twenty-five years of running a successful business and my experience training thousands of entrepreneurs to build and successfully run their own firms. You can apply many of my business efficiency strategies to simplify and get control over your personal finances.

I'll make the process as engaging, fun, and easy as possible. If some of the information is too basic for you, consider sharing it with someone you care about who needs it.

I recommend you tackle the exercises in this chapter with your soul mate, if you have one. The process will be a lot more fun, and you'll be more likely to implement it, if you do it with the person you're sharing your life with.

Let's start by looking at the most important character strengths for financial success.

The Keys to Wealth and Sustainability

In the late 1960s, Stanford psychologist Walter Michel conducted a famous experiment that involved more than six hundred hungry four-year olds—and almost a thousand marshmallows.

He seated each subject at a desk in a small room. Then he placed a single marshmallow on a plate in front of them and said, "You can eat this marshmallow right now, if you want. But, I have to run an errand. If you can wait until I get back to eat this marshmallow, I'll give you a second marshmallow as a reward for your patience." Then he left. Colleagues in an adjacent room videotaped the kids through a one-way mirror.

The average kid held out for only about three minutes. A few gobbled down their marshmallows immediately. Others distracted themselves by singing, covering their eyes, smelling, or even petting the marshmallow. In one hilarious scene, a little boy licks the table around the plate, humming happily to himself. Almost one third of the kids exhibited high self-control by waiting the entire, agonizing fifteen minutes. When he returned, Michel rewarded these kids with a second marshmallow.

Think about the significance of this experiment. The kids with good self-control doubled their marshmallow resources. That's a valuable and profitable character strength. But the benefits of self-control go way beyond marshmallows.

The Surprising Benefits of Self Control

Michel continued to track his subjects through time. In adulthood, many of the quick marshmallow gobblers were on a downward spiral toward career failure and financial ruin. They earned below-average incomes, were unsatisfied with their jobs, suffered from more physical health problems, and generally weren't going anywhere in life. They were classic examples of underachievers.

As adults, the self-controlled group earned higher incomes, enjoyed greater work satisfaction, and more fulfilling lives. They also maintained better health and were more energetic. In short, they were flourishing.

Michel's research challenged the existing personality theory. It convinced skeptics that when it comes to flourishing," self-control is more important than raw intelligence. It also validated Aesop's classic ant and grasshopper fable about the benefits of deferring gratification.

Self-control is one of the essential character strengths for financial prosperity. The other two are prudence, wisely and cautiously planning for the future, and persistence, industriousness and perseverance, aka the "work ethic."

Achieve and Maintain Positive Cash Flow

The first rule of financial management is to never, ever run out of money—always have plenty of cash available to pay for your living expenses and emergencies. Achieving that goal requires you to balance your spending with your income, and to maintain a cash reserve.

The first step to flourishing financially is to spend less then you take home.

If you're already managing your cash flow effectively, have cash reserves, and are saving at least ten percent of your income, you may want to skip to the following section: Build Your Resources. If your current cash flow management systems are suboptimal or non-existent, this section will help you get control over your money.

The money you have left, after paying your taxes and salary deductions, is your "take home income." That's the amount of money you have available to pay your living expenses. Any money left, after paying all your living expenses, is your net cash flow or personal profit. The higher your net cash flow, the more money you'll have for fun, emergencies, opportunities, personal development, saving, and investing for your future.

Write your total monthly take home income in the space below.

My current take home income is $_____ each month.

Spending less than you earn seems like simple advice, but it doesn't happen automatically; you have to make it happen. You can balance your budget one of two ways, by increasing your income, or by reducing your expenses. The optimum strategy is to do both. We'll start with the fastest and easiest way, reducing your expenses.

You can manage your spending only if you have timely information on where your money is going. But the concentration required for bookkeeping puts most people in a negative emotional state. We naturally go into a slightly dour mood when we're intensely focused on details. It helps exclude distractions and focuses our mind on our task.

These common negative feelings cause many people to avoid personal financial management altogether, or to do it as little as possible. Believe me, I understand. Bookkeeping is one of my least favorite things to do, but I'm committed to competent financial management. So, I've made it as fast and easy as possible. Now it takes less than one hour a month, each, for Brooke and me to pay our bills, review our spending, and reconcile our accounts.

To minimize the time and effort you spend managing your personal finances, and to do it effectively, I recommend using financial management software, such as Quicken. There are also on-line services that help you manage your money. This type of software links to your checking and savings accounts, credit cards, investment accounts, etc. Once you set it up, it dramatically simplifies and streamlines all of your personal bill paying and expense tracking. Here's how to use it to manage your cash flow.

After installing the software, or setting up an online account, enter the websites and passwords for your bank and credit card accounts. Start with the ones you use all the time and add more as needed. Customize the expense categories in your software to match the categories in the worksheet. Add sub categories if you want more detailed information.

At least once a month, sync the information in your software with your bank and other spending accounts. You can do this with the click of a button in Quicken. Many on-line services update constantly. When this information downloads into your software, it's collected into a folder, waiting for you to assign it to a specific Cash Flow category.

Initially, you'll have to allocate each deposit to an income category and each expenditure to an expense category. But, you only have to do this once for each vendor and payer. Then the software automatically allocates future transactions with them to the same category.

To further reduce the time and effort you spend doing personal bookkeeping, automate all of your recurring bill payments, like your mortgage and utilities. You can do this through your bank website, vendor, or personal finance software. The more you use and customize the software, the quicker and easier it gets. If you don't "automate" your personal finances, as you earn more, spend more and build wealth and resources, managing everything gets more complicated, time consuming, and unpleasant.

But with the right software, set up correctly, your financial management becomes faster, easier and "less unpleasant" each year. The easiest way to get up to speed with personal finance software is to hire an expert to set it up and train you to use it. Once you get your financial management software set up, you can start tracking and managing your expenses.

Determine Where Your Money Goes

Understanding where your money goes, each month, will help you identify changes you want to make. So, at the beginning of each month, print a spending report from your software, for the previous month. Review all of your expenses category totals and the individual expenditures. Look at your net cash flow, the money left over after you've paid all your monthly expenses. Is it a positive or negative number?

Positive cash flow leads on an upward spiral of optimism, increasing opportunities, and financial prosperity. Negative cash flow leads us on a downward spiral of stress, anxiety, and scarcity.

Just one month of expenses won't tell you the whole story, because expenses vary from month to month. But it should flag some expenses that you want to cut right away. The longer you use your personal finance software, the more accurately you'll be able to project future expenses and net cash flow.

After a few months, you'll have enough information to start prioritizing, reducing, and eliminating unsatisfying expenses. After the first year, you'll be able to project your average monthly expenses with great accuracy. At the beginning of each year, I recommend reviewing all your expenses for the previous year. Then set target spending and income goals for the following year.

For now, print three copies of the Cash Flow Worksheet (Figure 10.1). You can download a printable PDF file from my website, EndorphinZone.com. Label the first one CURRENT EXPENSES. As soon as you have enough information, complete that work sheet for an average current month's cash flow. You can use this information about your current spending, to make some positive changes in your future spending.

OPTIMIZE YOUR PERSONAL FINANCES

Cash Flow Work Sheet ☐ Current ☐ Ideal Current ☐ Ideal Future 20___		
Gross Income for _____	**Monthly**	**Yearly**
W-2 earnings from employment		
Business income, profits and dividends		
Other income, alimony, gifts, royalties, etc.		
Retirement income, Social Security, pension, etc.		
Investment income; stocks, bonds, annuities, etc.		
Total Gross Income (from all sources)		
Gross Income Deductions		
- Retirement plan contribution (10%+ of income)	-	
- Other payroll deductions, college funding	-	
- Federal income taxes, Social Security, etc.	-	
- State and local income taxes	-	
Net, Take Home Income (available to spend or invest)		
Living Expenses		
Fixed, non-discretionary expenses		
Rent or mortgage		
Property taxes, home insurance, etc.		
Household repairs, maintenance and services		
Food and household supplies		
Clothing		
Life, health and disability insurance and expenses		
Medical, dental, eye care, prescriptions, etc.		
Transportation, auto payments and upkeep, etc.		
Utilities, phone, on-line services, electricity, etc.		
Other fixed expenses		
Total Fixed Living Expenses	-	
Variable and discretionary expenses		
Education, classes, workshops, etc.		
Electronics, TVs, stereos, computers, phones, etc.		
Entertainment, hobbies, passions and fun		
Household appliances, furnishings, etc.		
Maintenance and repairs		
Misc. expenses, lunch, pets, parking, etc.		
Personal services, misc. cash expenses, etc.		
Vacations and adventures		
Other discretionary expenses		
Total Variable and Discretionary Expenses	-	
Net Cash Flow (+ or -)		

Figure 10.1. Cash Flow Worksheet

Optimize Your Expenses

Knowing what generates endorphins in your current life and what you'd like to change, in your future will enable you to thoughtfully allocate the money you have available to spend each month.

Evaluate each expenditure and category total to answer these questions:

1. What are you spending money on that isn't generating endorphins now or contributing to a better future?
2. What categories and specific expenses can you cut back on, without reducing your overall happiness and satisfaction?
3. How can you shift some of your current spending to more rewarding categories?
4. How can you experience more endorphins while spending less money?

By simply identifying where their money is going, most people can cut ten to twenty-five percent out of their monthly expenses without reducing their quality of life at all.

So now, label a second Cash Flow Worksheet IDEAL CURRENT EXPENSES. Considering the questions above, *write down monthly spending goals for each category. Evaluate every expense from a cost/benefit perspective: what is the cost and how much does it add to your positivity?* Write your total monthly expense goal in the space below.

My ideal current spending goal is $_____ each month.

Next, determine your projected net cash flow for the next twelve months. Aim for a positive cash flow, or personal profit, of at least ten percent of your net, after-tax income.

My projected "personal profit" for the next 12 months is $_____.

Once you've established your monthly cash flow goals, start implementing the changes needed to achieve them. Cut your unsatisfying expenses to the bone. Stop all impulse buys. Only use credit cards for emergencies and frequent flyer miles. *Make it a fun game to see how little you can spend and how much happiness, meaning, and engagement you can experience.*

Do whatever it takes, including downsizing your home, to ensure you're spending less than you're earning each month. Savor the things that you decide to spend money on. The less you spend today, the sooner you'll be financially independent and living in the Endorphin Zone.

Fewer expenses translate to less stress and greater freedom, financial security, optimism, and sustainability. If you do it thoughtfully, cutting your expenses will enhance your quality of life.

Remember, the Maasai are about as happy as America's wealthiest billionaires. In America, the Amish, who live simple, frugal lives, are one of the happiest groups of people. You, too, can be happy *and* frugal.

Build Liquidity and Banish Debt

As soon as you achieve positive cash flow, you'll have money left over each month that will enable you to accumulate cash reserves. Start by building working capital. Allow your extra monthly cash flow to accumulate until you've saved three months of living expenses in your checking account.

Then, at the end of each month, have your excess cash flow automatically transferred from your checking account to a savings account. Keep these transfers flowing until you've accumulated six months of living expenses in your savings account. Now, you will have nine months of living expenses in liquid cash. That will enhance your feelings of security, autonomy, and optimism. It will also dramatically lower your stress.

As soon as you have three months of cash reserves, direct a portion of your excess cash flow to pay off any credit cards and consumer debt, starting with your highest interest accounts. Once, you have six months of cash reserve, stop saving and direct all of your excess personal profit to banish any remaining consumer debt. At this point, you are on your way to financial security and will soon be building substantial resources for a better future.

Review your cash flow together with your soul mate, monthly. Discuss your progress and make adjustments to achieve your financial goals.

Cash flow management is a learned skill. It requires commitment, prudence, and self-control. It takes time to determine where you are now, set goals, and change your habits and expectations. But you must be able to put money away, if you want to build wealth and achieve financial independence in the future.

Reducing your expenses is a great place to start, but it addresses only one side of the cash-flow equation. So let's look at the happier side of cash flow, increasing your income.

Optimize Your Income

The more resources you have throughout your life, the more opportunities you'll have to pursue your visions, aspirations, and goals and to make a positive contribution to the planet. Financial prosperity empowers you achieve your full potential to experience, express, explore, evolve, and enjoy life. Increasing your income will boost your self-esteem, and feelings of competency, autonomy, and satisfaction.

But, to flourish in all your Endorphin Domains, optimize your income; don't maximize it. Your optimum income will provide plenty of money to fund a happy, meaningful, and fulfilling lifestyle today and enable you to save enough to fund your ideal future.

Start by estimating the gross income that you need to sustain a high quality of life in the present and save at least ten percent of your income for a better future. Use your current income as a benchmark.

My optimum current income is $_____ a year.

For most people, their optimum will be higher than their current income. If you already earn enough money, focus on enhancing your quality of life by applying your insights from this book. But if you need more income, here are some proven ways to earn more money, happily.

The optimal way to increase your income isn't to work more hours; it's to increase your income per hour. To earn more per hour, you must increase the market value of your knowledge and skills. Your value depends on how effectively and efficiently you solve problems and produce results—and how difficult it is to replace you. In our information-based economy, knowledge is power, and one sure path to a higher income is higher education.

On average, higher education leads to more income, greater social status, better health, and longer life expectancy. And college graduates have much higher rates of employment than people without degrees.

One of the biggest benefits of pursuing a calling instead of a career is you enjoy getting better and better at your job. That's because your work is intrinsically rewarding. Once you have a solid basic education, continue learning. Remember that it take about ten years to truly master any field. Be smart; more education and skills will increase your value only if they're in demand. And only learn things that you want to use. Getting paid more and more to do something you don't like doing isn't flourishing.

As you increase your expertise, share your knowledge, wisdom, and skills with others. Write, speak, and contribute to your industry events and publications. If you really want to increase your value and your income, write a good book. You'll become a bona fide expert in your field.

Finally, consider work that pays for your results, not your time. Sales, management positions with bonuses, and contract work offer opportunities to achieve your full income potential and often to have more control over your schedule. Just be sure the work is a good fit for your work personality and skills.

There's plenty of room at the top in every field, so do what you love, become a world-class expert on the practical application of your knowledge, communicate your benefits effectively, and watch your income and quality of life skyrocket!

Build Resources for a Flourishing Future

There are two ways to accumulate capital that will support you at some point in the future: by saving aggressively in a retirement plan or by building a valuable business. You can also do both.

As your knowledge and skills grow, your income will naturally grow, too. So keep your expenses low and max out your retirement plan contribution. Every dollar you invest today will compound and grow, so you'll have even more investment income in the future. This is how most people eventually accumulate enough wealth to make full-time work optional.

The other way to build wealth is through equity ownership in a thriving business. You can earn equity for your contribution through stock options or similar strategies. Combining aggressive retirement plan funding with equity in a profitable business is a sure way to achieve financially independence.

However, if you have a big vision, a compelling purpose, or an exciting idea, or all of these, you'll probably have aspirations to build a business of your own. Few things are more satisfying than doing what you love, working on important projects, with people who empower you, in a thriving business, with a higher purpose.

You can support a flourishing lifestyle as a small business owner, with few or no employees. But if you want to build serious wealth, you'll have to build a highly valuable business. Successful business builders earn the highest incomes and accumulate more wealth than any other occupation. They're the backbone of all prosperous societies.

But not all businesses are successful. Here are some strategies for building a thriving one.

In free-market, capitalistic societies, people become wealthy through innovation—combining existing ideas and technologies in new ways to achieve better results. I pointed out in chapter 2 that innovation is behind all new technology, business growth, and wealth creation. In fact, the American Academy of Sciences estimates that new ideas generate eighty-five percent of all economic growth. Businesses that don't innovate, adapt, and evolve, languish and eventually die.

Since innovative ideas and technologies are so important for business success and national prosperity, an obvious question is, "What fosters innovation?" You already know the answer: it's the Endorphin Effect. Curiosity, optimism, learning, research, imagination, problem solving, resilience, perseverance, risk-taking, and action are the "secret sauce."

Positive emotions are the psychological foundation for innovation, entrepreneurial risk-taking, team building, and ultimately, wealth creation. Without optimism, innovation, and perseverance, we'd be stuck in the Stone Age.

If you have a burning desire to build a business, or if you already own one, use the science of human flourishing to foster a positive, innovative, and creative culture, a culture that encourages new ideas and technologies, optimism, action, resourcefulness, and perseverance. These emotional states and associated ways of thinking and behaving only happen when team positivity ratios are greater than five to one. Using the science of human flourishing to make sure your team stays above this tipping point will almost guarantee your business will flourish.

As an innovative entrepreneur, you'll have to work hard, overcome many obstacles, and defer gratification. But in the long run, you'll feel the exhilaration of accomplishing something important, and you'll probably end up with a lot more "marshmallows."

No matter how much you earn or how valuable your business is, you'll always have to balance your finances with your happiness.

* * *

Considering the optimal balance between money and quality of life isn't just my idea. It's a planet-wide idea whose time has come.

In 2004, Martin Seligman and Ed Diener wrote a landmark paper entitled "Beyond Wealth: Towards an Economy of Well-Being." In it, they recommend creating a system for tracking our national well-being to complement existing economic indicators. Seligman and Diener wrote, "Economic indicators omit, and even mislead about, much of what society values." To remedy these shortcomings, they envision one or more sets of "optimum well-being indicators" for nations and communities.

Seligman and Diener make a critical point: "If economic and other policies are important because they will, in the end, increase well-being, then why not assess well-being more directly?" Seligman and Diener argue that well-being measurements should be the primary indicators of a society's "success" and that economic indexes, such as the Gross Domestic Product (GDP) and the Standard and Poor's 500 stock market index, should be secondary.

This concept of measuring national subjective well-being isn't a distant fantasy; it's already happening. In 1972, the King of Bhutan, a small Buddhist country high in the Himalayas, made a startling announcement: henceforth, the happiness of Bhutan's citizens would be the primary focus of all economic development, and the policy of enhancing Gross National Happiness (GNH) would guide all government policies and decisions.

Today, Bhutan is sharing its experiences and processes for "Operationalizing Gross National Happiness" with delegations from all over the world. National Well-being Accounts are now being used in twenty-two European countries. Other measuring tools are being developed and introduced in the United States, Canada, and other countries. More are on their way.

All over the world, policy makers, social scientists, and pollsters are identifying new and better ways to track individual and communal progress toward the good life. As we learn more about human flourishing, new measurement techniques will supplant traditional economic indicators.

You can see signs that this tectonic paradigm shift is already happening in some of our leading institutions.

Harvard University is one of the world's top leadership training institutions. Graduates go on to run many of the biggest organizations on the planet. Because of their skills and intelligence, many of them become leaders in their industries and governments. Their values will help shape the future.

In the spring of 2006, something amazing happened at Harvard that should make us all optimistic. For decades, the most popular class at Harvard was Economics 101, an introduction to the dismal science. The students referred to this popular class as "how to get rich." But in February of that year, Psychology 1504, "Positive Psychology," the study of the science of happiness, officially became Harvard's most popular class.

Each week, 855 eager students packed Harvard's largest lecture hall, to hear charismatic professor Tal Ben-Sharar explain the scientific basis for a "fulfilling and flourishing life."

Almost one out of four students who took the class said it "changed their lives." Ninety-nine percent said they'd recommend the course to fellow students. The young leaders were captivated by the class, even though the instructor's key message is that the ultimate currency isn't money; it's happiness.

This huge interest in positive psychology in so many of our future leaders is an encouraging sign. There are now more than two hundred colleges and universities around the world that offer positive psychology classes.

Each year, thousands of well-educated and motivated young people are learning about and applying the science of human flourishing. The seeds for "an economy of well being" have been planted and are ready to sprout.

ENDORPHIN EVENT #10
Optimize Your Personal Finances

Summarize this chapter for your guests by going through the pages and using the subheads and graphics to share the key points. Then brainstorm on the following topics.

1. What areas of personal finance would you like to change, get under control, or improve? How can you make it happen?
2. What expenses can you eliminate that aren't adding much to your quality of life?
3. Make a list of ideas for earning more income by better utilizing the knowledge and skills you already have.
4. What new knowledge and skills do you want to develop so you can express more of your natural talents and interests—and make more money?
5. How could you earn extra income by pursuing a passion, or interest, of yours?
6. How can you maintain balance between your need for income and your desired quality of life?
7. What subjective quality of life indicators, such as vacation days, should you track in addition to your objective income and wealth?
8. What will you do differently in the future, based on your insights from this chapter?

11

Build Wealth for Financial Freedom

....

> *Wealth is the ability to fully experience life.*
> —**Henry David Thoreau**

Greg had owned a successful asbestos removal business for over twenty years, but his passions were custom cars and art. He was an avid and accomplished painter who had always wanted to be a commercial artist, but assumed it was just a fantasy. Then he met Tom, a financial advisor who helps his clients clarify their ideal future and then creates plans to support it financially.

Over the next few years, Greg worked with Tom to optimize his business and personal cash flow. As the business profits increased, it became more valuable. He invested most of his profit in a tax-advantaged retirement plan. When he had enough value in his business and retirement account to ensure life-long financial freedom, he sold the business and cleared several million dollars. Then he went back to college, got a degree in art, and set up a gallery in Maine.

Tom says he provided Greg "reassurance that he could follow his passions." Tom also created a financial plan and helped Greg implement it. Together they optimized and then repositioned Greg's wealth so he could pursue his creative passions: a lifelong dream fulfilled.

Carol, an investment advisor, built a thriving practice and a healthy retirement account balance. She continues to work in her sixties, organizing her life to take several months off each year. She uses that time to pursue her higher purpose: as a volunteer with World Vision International, she helps vulnerable women and children in Africa.

In this chapter, I'll explain a process to plan and achieve financial freedom when full time work is optional and you have enough time and money to pursue your passions and purpose.

Build Wealth for Future Income

Achieving lifelong financial independence means being able to generate income for your entire life. Typically, most people work for their money (earned income) from the ages of about twenty-five to sixty-five. If they invest prudently, their money works for them (investment income) when they retire. If you follow the suggestions in the last chapter, you'll be investing to build wealth for a better future.

The table below shows an ideal wealth-building scenario. Your wealth, or net-worth, grows while you are working through contributions to your retirement account or the increased value of investments or equity in a business. When you stop earning income from work, your investments generate more than enough income to pay all your expenses, and then some.

Your wealth continues to grow, as in the dotted line A. At the very least, your income from your accumulated capital will last much longer than you're expected to, as in the solid line B. The earlier you start building wealth, the more resources you'll have later in life.

BUILD WEALTH FOR FINANCIAL FREEDOM

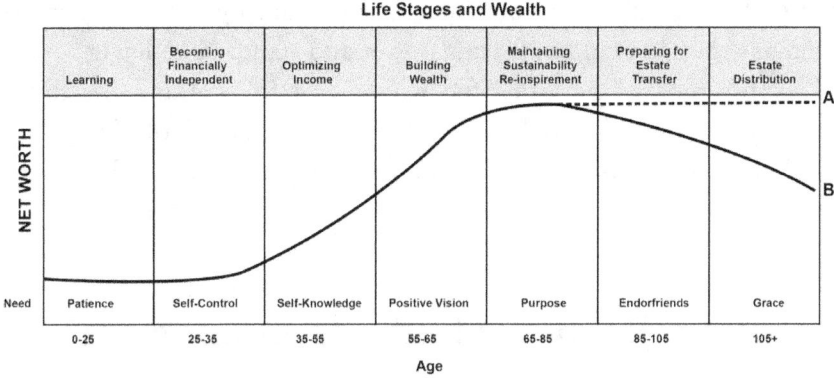

Figure 11.1. Life Stages and Wealth

Having enough resources to pursue your purpose and passions and never run out of money is the goal of building wealth, not just having enough to retire. The very term *retire* means to "withdraw," an unpleasant prospect for healthy, happy, and financially independent people. That's why, for many people, the traditional notion of stopping work completely after the age sixty-five is obsolete.

The average person lives approximately twenty years after they leave full-time work. But happy, healthy, and wealthy people, who have a compelling vision and purpose, can expect to live for thirty or forty years after formal retirement. And, as science finds new ways to extend the length and quality of our lives, life expectancy is rising fast. In the future, living past one hundred will be commonplace.

If you're a "Wise Happy" who'll retire in your mid sixties, plan on having enough money to support yourself for another forty years—or more.

Funding that many years of living expenses, rising healthcare costs, taxes, and inflation will require more money than most people can accumulate during a normal working life. With three to four decades to fund, one of the biggest challenges is inflation, which quickly erodes buying power and raises living expenses. Historically, inflation has shaved about three percent every year off the purchasing power of your dollars. That means your future income must grow that much to maintain your current purchasing power and standard of living.

So, for most Americans, the whole idea of working for thirty or forty years and then living at the same standard of living, for another thirty or forty years, without working is a fantasy. But that's not a problem, if you change your beliefs about retirement.

Transform Retirement into Re-Inspirement

Instead of planning for a traditional retirement, think about planning for "re-inspirement," when you're living and working (contributing) in the Endorphin Zone. Re-inspirement is that magical time after leaving your "primary career" or selling your business when you shift into more engaging and meaningful work. If you plan it out, life after your first "retirement" will be the happiest, most fulfilling years of your life.

Once you've accumulated a comfortable level of wealth, you will have a lot of options. You can start a new business or take a part-time job. Another possibility is to cycle back and forth between work and leisure, or take a phased retirement, working fewer hours each year until you finally stop working. Or you could "downshift" to more rewarding and less stressful work.

You may even want to completely reinvent yourself to align your outer life with your inner values and aspirations. Hopefully, you'll pursue a calling that you want to do forever. This brings me to a key point about retirement: people who love what they do will never want to fully "retire," no matter how much money they have.

All this means Wise Happies will probably want to continue working long beyond the traditional retirement age. Earning income for as long as you can will make a huge positive impact on your financial sustainability. It will give you more time to accumulate savings and reduce the time that you'll need to rely on your savings for income.

But, even if you want to work longer, you aren't going to want to work as hard and, eventually, you won't want to or be able to work at all. Aristotle said, "Happiness belongs to the self-sufficient." Being dependent on charity and the government to take care of you when you're old won't make you happy. So each of us must plan and build wealth to sustain our own financial independence—for as long as we live.

Use Software to Plan for Life-Long Financial Independence

In hunter/gatherer societies, people have no need for numbers, investing, or personal financial management. Most indigenous tribes in the Amazon share a simple economic concept: there is either enough or not enough. So, deep in the rainforest, many people can't count much beyond three. I once watched a Shuar *Uwishin,* or wise elder, use all his fingers and toes to count out twenty leaves for a medicinal tea. Counting using fingers and toes may work for hunter/gatherers, but we live in a vastly more complex world.

Most of us can handle basic math. But, no matter how smart we are, we can't make complex cash-flow projections, in our minds, for up to forty years into the future. To plan for and achieve financial freedom in the concrete jungle, we need more sophisticated "tools" than our fingers and toes.

Making financial decisions today that will ensure you never run out of money in the distant future requires retirement planning software or online retirement calculators. This software projects cash flows over many decades and displays them on color charts and graphs. It shows you how much you must save while you're working, and how long your money will last when you slow down or completely stop working.

A positive vision, combined with a realistic plan, will dramatically increase your chances of achieving financial independence. But most people never do this on their own. So, I'll explain how to create a life-long Financial Sustainability Plan, with the guidance of a competent and trustworthy investment advisor. If you're committed to developing your own plan, modify this process to fit your situation.

I call this my Life and Wealth Optimization Process. Over the last decade, I've trained hundreds of investment advisors to use it with their clients. (Bookmark or dog-ear this page, because you'll want to refer to it again later, especially if you seek the help of an investment advisor.)

Going through this process will turn your most cherished dreams into visions, your visions into goals, your goals into action plans, and your action plans into lifelong financial sustainability.

This type of process is often called "right" to "left" brained thinking. It starts as intangible thoughts in your brain and ends as tangible resources that will support you.

The Life and Wealth Optimization Process

1. Envision your ideal future.
2. Set preliminary spending goals for your ideal future.
3. Hire a competent, caring investment advisor.
4. Share your vision, aspirations, concerns, and goals.
5. Organize and assess your current resources.
6. Test various future financial scenarios, select the best one, and set realistic goals.
7. Prepare an action plan and implementation schedule.
8. Implement your action plan.
9. Monitor your results and
10. Make adjustments as necessary to achieve your goals.

This process will help you determine where you are now, financially, and where you want to go. It enhances the traditional financial/retirement planning process, primarily by starting with your vision instead of your goals. Since only a small fraction of financial advisors use my process, I suggest you find one who does something similar. Then ask them to collaborate with you on this quality-of-life based process.

1. Envision your ideal future.

This step is one of the main reasons I wrote this book: to help people clarify their ideal future *before* they create a retirement plan. Most planning-oriented investment advisors start by asking about your goals. Their "big question" is typically, "When do you want to retire?"

The most common answer: "As soon as possible. It's stressful working here."

But setting goals to move away from something negative is much different from setting goals to move towards something positive. The moving-away approach leads to strategies for surviving in the future. A more empowering question is this: "What do you want to do, be and experience in your ideal future and roughly how much will it cost?" This approach leads to strategies for flourishing in the future.

Maybe this is why, in a survey by Harris Interactive, pre-retirees rated "helps me visualize my future," as the most desirable characteristic in an investment advisor. But few investment advisors have processes, or meaningful questions, to help their clients envision their ideal future. Most advisors haven't studied coaching, positive psychology, or human flourishing. They focus on the numbers and don't understand the importance of a positive vision. This is a huge "missing link" in the industry. But you don't need their assistance. You've already created your positive vision of the future.

Your vision is the basis for your preliminary goals. With these as a starting point, a competent investment advisor can run various scenarios, discuss them with you, and together, you can establish realistic and achievable goals.

2. Set preliminary spending goals for your ideal future.

To set preliminary financial goals for your future, identify and prioritize the most important differences between your current life and your future life. For instance, after you put your kids through school and pay off your mortgage, your expenses will go down dramatically. When you stop working, you'll stop investing thousands of dollars a year into your retirement plan, but you'll probably spend more on travel and entertainment, and you may have higher medical bills. Your earned income will stop, but your Social Security, pension, and retirement plan income will start.

Identify and describe the key changes in your future financial situation. For example, "Trade down to a smaller home that costs $100,000 less than our current home. Pay off the mortgage and stop funding our retirement accounts to reduce our current outgo by $25,000 a year." Set preliminary targets for each income and expense category by adjusting them up or down from your current situation, based on your expected changes.

Complete a cash flow projection for your ideal retired future, when you aren't earning any income from work. If you're planning big changes in your financial situation before you retire, complete a worksheet for your ideal working future. (See the simple worksheet below or use the detailed worksheet from the last chapter.) Put a date on each worksheet to indicate the year you expect that phase to start.

Your Ideal Working Future Cash Flow
    $ _____ Ideal Working Future Income
− $ _____ Ideal Working Future Living Expenses
= $ _____ **Ideal Working Future Net Cash Flow**

Your Ideal Retired Future Cash Flow
    $ _____ Ideal Retired Future Income, when full time work is optional
− $ _____ Ideal Retired Future Living Expenses
= $ _____ **Ideal Retired Future Net Cash Flow**

Once you've identified your future cash flow, prepare a schedule of anticipated major capital outlays, such as a new home or car, and the date you plan to purchase them. Use the Internet to establish price ranges for all major purchases required for your ideal future. Estimate everything in today's dollars.

When you've completed this exercise, you'll have achieved an important milestone: you'll have transformed your intangible vision of your ideal future into tangible income and spending goals.

3. Hire a competent, caring investment advisor.

Now you need to determine the sources of your future income. Determining your future capital needs and income sources, after inflation and taxes, and where it will come from, gets complicated. But it's easy with the right help. So finding the right investment advisor is one of the most important things you'll ever do.

Let's segment investment "professionals" into two different groups: product-centered salespeople, or *sharks*, and client-centered advisors, or *dolphins*. Shark advisors are cold-blooded and transaction-oriented. They focus on maximizing their YTB—yield to broker.

Dolphin advisors are warm-blooded and love people.

They are
- knowledgeable, trustworthy, client-centered experts who use a holistic approach in their work; and
- good coaches who use meaningful questions and empathetic listening to understand your dreams, vision, goals and concerns.

They will
- always put your interests before their interests;
- empower you to clarify and successfully achieve your financial and life goals;
- develop written financial, retirement, scenario, or sustainability plans;
- offer comprehensive advice, strategies and services;

- help you simplify, monitor, and control all of your resources to reduce stress; and
- meet with you periodically to help you avoid costly mistakes, and keep you on track.

They provide
- specialized knowledge and services to help you achieve lifelong financial sustainability;
- access to professional investment management and insurance solutions; and
- comprehensive services and follow through.

They are motivated by
- the joy they experience helping people maximize their financial independence and quality of life;
- a win-win, lifelong relationships with their clients (not their clients' money);
- sincere caring for every client; and
- a sense of their work as their calling.

Dolphin advisors are life coaches who specialize in money. They are ideal for Wise Happies, because they reduce negative emotions and increase positive ones. Since their recommendations are based on your wants and needs rather than their compensation, you're more likely to achieve your financial goals.

However, according to research by CEG Worldwide, a firm that focuses on investment advisors, only about one out of seven financial advisors are client-centered; the other six are product-centered. Additionally, it's important to realize that though they may be well intended, not all client-centered advisors are competent dolphins. So, take the time to find a top-tier advisor who is both client-centered and competent.

The best way to find a dolphin advisor is through a referral. Ask your friends and professional advisors for recommendations. A second option is to search the Internet for investment advisors, financial planners, retirement strategists, and wealth managers. Look for the terms such as *life coaching, life planning, financial life planning,* and *vision coaching.* They indicate a holistic and client-centered approach to financial and investment advice.

Favor advisors who have strong credentials and have been in the industry for ten years or more. Only work with a newer advisor if they collaborate with a seasoned advisor on the plan and recommendations. Avoid pure investment brokers and insurance agents. You want a trustworthy, planning-oriented advisor, that offers both investments and insurance, not a product-centered salesperson.

If you like what you discover, contact the advisor and share your situation. Make sure they work with clients like you and develop written retirement plans. Interview at least three financial advisors who fit the criteria above. I recommend interviewing at least one woman, because women are often more relationship oriented than male advisors. (Sorry for the generalization, but that's my experience.)

When you meet, check out the office, staff, and location. Does it make you feel good? Does everyone you interact with ask good questions and listen thoughtfully to your answers? Are they focused on understanding the payoffs you want and the things you want to avoid, or on selling you something? Dolphin advisors will encourage you to do most of the talking during the first few meetings.

Do they prepare a single written plan or run various "what if" scenarios for your review and discussion? Review a sample plan. Is it concise, simple, and clear? Is it easy to understand? Does it document vision, values, goals, and concerns? Is it clear how the advisor's recommendations will accomplish the stated goals? Does the plan include a written implementation schedule? Determine exactly what deliverables you'll receive, how long it will take and how much it will cost.

Ask about the advisors' professional experience and credentials. How do their specialized skills and knowledge match your needs and goals? Show them the 10-step Life and Wealth Optimization process in this chapter, and make sure they're excited about implementing it with you.

After you've met with the three advisors, consider how you felt with each one. Dolphin advisors will make you feel understood, competent, empowered, optimistic, and eager to meet again. Sharks will make you feel uncertain, confused, incompetent, worried, and pressured. If you don't feel good, cross that advisor off your list.

Don't stop interviewing until you feel a strong sense of connection and empowerment with one or more dolphin advisors. Decide who you feel the most connected with and empowered by, and whose expertise and processes will add the most value for you. Then check out their references, licenses, and credentials carefully. Remember, the person you hire will be a key resource for you and your family, hopefully for the rest of your life.

(Additional resources to help you find a dolphin investment advisor are available at EndorphinZone.com.)

4. Share your vision, aspirations, concerns, and goals.

Once you hire a dolphin advisor, set up a meeting to share your vision of your ideal future. Schedule ninety minutes to two hours to discuss your vision, what's important about it, your preliminary cash flow and retirement goals, and any challenges and concerns that you have.

Clarifying this "soft data" is the most important step in the entire planning process. How can anyone help you get what you want if they don't know what it is?

Brooke and I recently went through my Life and Wealth Optimization process with my friend, Eddie, who is a dolphin advisor. He used many of the questions that you've read in this book to *fully* understand our vision and dreams for our ideal future. Just talking with him about our future transported Brooke and me to the Endorphin Zone. Discussing the places we want to go, things we want to do and people we want to spend time with connected us with the positive possibilities our future holds.

When Eddie finished asking us about our vision, he clarified and documented our personal success criteria, meaning what would have to happen for Brooke and me to be happy and satisfied in the future. Then we celebrated with a bottle of champagne. When he left, Brooke said, "That was fun!" We talked about how good it felt to be truly heard and understood. We both eagerly anticipated our next meeting when we'd learn what we needed to do to turn our vision into reality.

After you discuss your vision, values, goals and concerns with your advisor, the critical soft data, your advisor's next task is to gather, organize, and assess all of your hard data.

5. Organize and assess your current resources.

Your advisor will give you a list of all the documents and information they'll need from you, including your current income and expenses, last year's tax returns, employee benefit plans, retirement assets, bank and brokerage statements, insurance policies, wills, trusts and other important papers. This information will provide a starting point for decades of secure, comfortable, and happy living—in the Endorphin Zone.

Once they receive the information, your advisor will enter the important numbers and details into their software program. Then they'll prepare and print several reports, typically your net worth (wealth), which includes your current investments and other assets, and your liabilities, or debt. Finally, they'll review your personal success criteria and then create several different future financial scenarios to discuss at your next meeting.

6. Test various future financial scenarios, select the best fit, and set realistic goals.

Most financial advisors will conduct this meeting in their office and show you various scenarios on a large monitor. But, since

Eddie's a friend of ours, we held this meeting in the comfort of our family room, and reviewed our future financial projections on our flat screen TV.

No one can actually predict the future, but an experienced professional can make reasonable projections based on historical facts and realistic assumptions. By looking at several scenarios, instead of just one, you get a better understanding of how your current decisions and actions, and economic conditions, could impact your future finances and, by extension, your quality of life. With multiple options, you can choose the scenario that is the best fit for your resources, vision, and aspirations.

Plus, you'll be mentally prepared for a wide range of future outcomes and will be working to stay on course toward your ideal.

Before he turned on his laptop, Eddie asked us to review a Personal Success Criteria report that he prepared specifically for us. It was a wish list that documented our vision, values, goals (preliminary), and concerns that he discovered in our previous meeting. After we'd reviewed it and confirmed he'd gotten it right, Eddie told us the purpose of the meeting was to discover the best-fit scenario. This would be the one that checked off the most important boxes for us.

Turning on his laptop, Eddie said, "Scenario planning is a lot like Visine, because in both cases our goal is to get the red out." We all laughed and then Eddie got started. As Brooke and I held hands, relaxing on our favorite couch, Eddie operated the software. He displayed our base line scenario showing our annual projected income until I was one hundred years old.

At first, our income comes entirely from our earnings, and then it shifts over time toward unearned income. Eventually, we stop working and all of our income comes from our retirement investments and social security. The software converted the numbers into color graphs. The baseline only had a little red in it, indicating years, we'd have to take income from principal.

Then we started the "what if" part of the session. We'd ask a question, and Eddie would adjust the numbers, instantly displaying the new scenario. He also asked us questions and made suggestions as all three of us worked together to "get the red out." We could easily see the consequences of different personal and financial decisions, such as how much we contributed to our retirement plans each year, when we stopped earning income, and how much we'd be able to spend in the future.

To stress test the scenarios, Eddie had prepared several that included unexpected expenses or reductions in our income. We reviewed what might happen if one or both of us became disabled, died prematurely, or needed long-term care. The whole process was engaging, fun, and enlightening.

After looking at about a dozen alternatives, Brooke, Eddie, and I agreed on the best fit scenario. It included realistic and achievable savings and return targets and would generate enough income when we retired, even if we both live beyond one hundred. It checked off all the boxes on our Personal Success Criteria report, and more. Eddie, who has been an investment advisor for more than thirty years, made sure our assumptions were realistic and achievable.

Scenario planning empowered us to turn our preliminary hopes and dreams into a realistic vision and, then, achievable goals. It gave us confidence that our most cherished hopes for the future will become reality, if we follow the plan. This process is much more engaging and enlightening than traditional one-scenario financial plans.

People like Brooke, who had dreaded the planning process because of all the "numb-ers," actually enjoy discussing the future and seeing the projections in color graphs. Scenario planning is like a fun game; all you have to do is try various scenarios until you "get the red out."

Once you agree on a specific scenario, you'll need a blueprint to follow.

7. Prepare an action plan and implementation schedule.

After our meeting, Eddie printed the key goals and numbers. Then he used that information and our Personal Success Criteria to draft a step-by-step financial sustainability plan, which included specific personal, financial, and investment recommendations, and an implementation schedule.

Once you have a written plan, and realistic and achievable goals, you have a blueprint to transform your positive vision into reality.

8. Implement your action plan.

A financial sustainability plan (aka retirement plan) will tell you how much you need to save each year to achieve financial independence. This information will help you refine your current expenses and savings targets. If you're retiring, your plan will tell you how much you can spend and never run out of money.

At this stage, you'll probably have to set up some new accounts and reposition some of your assets to increase your probability of achieving your goals. Today, a broadly diversified portfolio may have as many as fifteen thousand different securities in thirty-five different countries! Many highly sophisticated portfolios are assembled with up to a dozen different types of investments, or "asset classes." Broad diversification, strategically planned, is a hallmark of high-quality investment management.

After you get everything set up, stay on plan, save monthly, invest with professional management, and watch your money grow.

9. Monitor your progress.

Managing cash flow and investments isn't an event or a transaction; it's a lifelong process. To make sure you achieve your goals, you need to monitor your spending, savings, and investment results. Meet with your financial advisor at least once a year to review your progress. They will provide structure, discipline, accountability, resources, and encouragement to keep you moving confidently toward your goals.

As you review your progress, keep in mind that professional money managers manage your money, but they can't manage the markets and can't predict the future. So don't expect any investment advisor to consistently beat the market—*and don't hire anyone who claims they can.* In the investment world, anything that sounds too good to be true is almost always a scam. Ask Bernie Madoff.

Professional investment advisors aren't in the business of making people rich; they're in the business of helping people manage their money so they don't become poor. They have the knowledge, skills, and resources to manage your investments prudently, which means "wisely cautious in planning for the future."

Aim for slow, steady progress. Don't watch the market too closely; it will raise your blood pressure. Expect wild swings up and down in your stock portfolio. The only real benchmarks that make any sense to track are the ones you establish with your advisor.

10. Make adjustments as necessary to achieve your goals.

Like any journey, you're likely to drift off course over time and your situation or goals may change. That's when your investment advisor will recommend appropriate adjustments to your spending, saving, or investment portfolio. They'll help you avoid costly mistakes during volatile economic times, when greed and fear urge you to take insane risks or to sell out at the worst possible moment.

If you work with a dolphin advisor and follow the recommendations in this chapter, you'll have the best chance of building the wealth you need to turn your retirement into re-inspirement—the happiest and most fulfilling years of your life.

Hire Professional Investment Managers

In the six other Endorphin Domains, your emotions are reliable guides to success and happiness. But, when it comes to investing, your emotions and intuitions are usually wrong. As Benjamin Graham wrote in

The Intelligent Investor, "The investor's chief problem—and even his worst enemy—is likely to be himself." In fact, scientists in the emerging field of behavioral finance have learned that even brilliant people do really dumb things when it comes to money, investing, and financial decisions.

How can that be? Remember that humans evolved in the savanna of eastern Africa, not the canyons of Wall Street. Over millions of years of natural selection, the human brain has become perfectly adapted for surviving and thriving in natural environments, not for making successful investment decisions.

DALBAR, a research and consulting company, has quantified how our emotions sabotage investment success. By analyzing flows into and out of equity (stock) mutual funds, they can calculate the investment performance of individual investors. Their analysis has proven that unsophisticated investors (again, not stupid investors, but those unsophisticated in the ways of Wall Street) are their own worst enemies.

For instance, during the twenty-year period ending on December 31, 2012, the Standard and Poor 500 Index (S&P 500), an indicator of the overall stock market, returned 8.2 percent a year. During this same period, the average equity fund (stock) investor earned only 4.25 percent a year. This was just enough to keep up with inflation, which was 2.4 percent a year and increasing taxes.

The average fixed income (bond) investor earned only .98 percent a year, which means they lost substantial buying power after taxes and inflation. The reason for this dismal performance is that the emotions of fear and greed consistently prompt us to buy high and sell low, a prescription for disaster.

If the individual investors simply bought and held the S&P 500 stock index over the twenty years measured, $100,000 would have grown to almost $484,560. But, on average, $100,000 invested by individuals grew to about $229,891. That means it cost the average investor, with $100,000, over $250,000 to manage their investments themselves! No matter what time periods you look at, amateur investors always underperform the market averages.

BUILD WEALTH FOR FINANCIAL FREEDOM

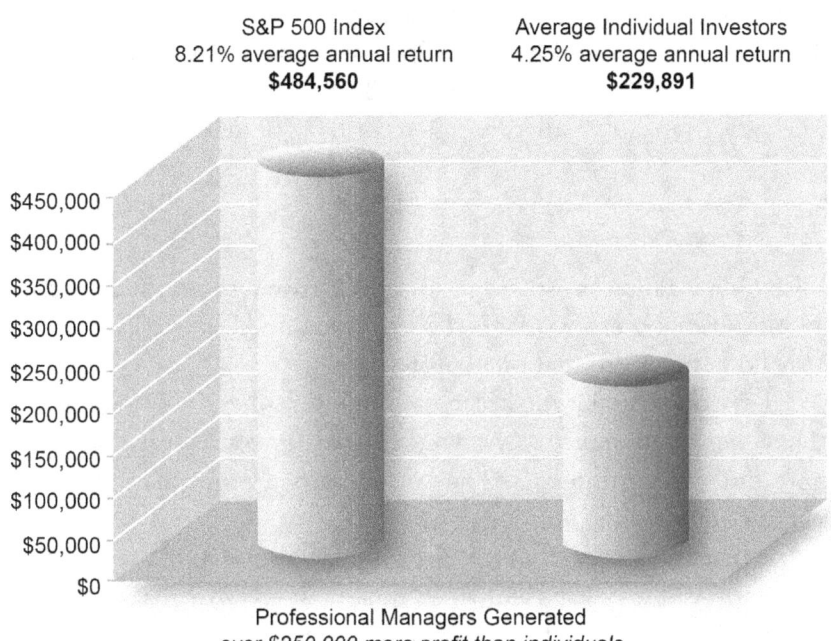

Figure 11.2. Individual Investors Versus the S&P Stock Index

If you aren't a highly sophisticated investor, making your own investment decisions is more likely to diminish your financial independence than to enhance it.

The more you know about humans' cognitive shortcomings, the more you'll appreciate professional investment management. That's why I'm not going to try to turn you into an investment professional. For most people, there's a much better solution: hire expert investment managers with the guidance of a dolphin investment advisor.

So, make sure your advisor recommends a diversified group of world-class investment managers for your retirement portfolio. Outsourcing to professional managers is the competent and prudent thing to do. It will give you peace of mind and will, in all likelihood, make a huge positive impact on your financial future.

Now you have a positive vision of your future that's grounded in realistic and achievable financial goals and strategies. And you have a competent, client-centered investment advisor, written goals, and plans to make your vision financially sustainable. Now, all you have to do is to continue to invest systematically and make adjustments, when necessary, to make steady progress towards your ideal future.

* * *

One day, Linda, a financial advisor I know, mentioned that her favorite clients were working-class millionaires. *Working class millionaires?* I'd never heard that one before.

"I have one couple who are in their mid seventies," she volunteered. "They were both nurses. She worked part-time so she could spend more time raising the kids. They never earned more than $90,000 a year in combined income.

"But they always lived in a well-maintained house that they paid off years ago. And they have almost $2 million in investments."

"Did they inherit that money?" I asked incredulously.

"No," she said. "They worked with a competent investment advisor for years. They lived below their means and invested for retirement every month. When they got raises, instead of spending more, or buying a bigger house, they increased their monthly investments. Their advisor invested their money with professional managers, and over time, it grew to over two million dollars."

Linda's clients are what I call *prudent delegators,* because they were wisely cautious in planning for their future. Their keys to financial independence were getting a practical education, taking responsibility for their personal finances, working with a competent investment advisor to develop and implement a retirement plan, deferring gratification, contributing monthly to their retirement account, and investing with professional management for decades.

You can use the same strategies to achieve financial freedom so you can turn your retirement into re-inspirement.

To learn how to flourish in retirement, visit endorphinzone.com.

ENDORPHIN EVENT #11
Build Wealth for Financial Freedom

Summarize this chapter for your guests by going through the pages and using the subheads and graphics to share the key points. Then brainstorm on the following topics *with your inner circle*.

1. What areas of your personal finances, retirement planning, and investments would you most like to change, get under control, or improve? How can you make it happen?
2. What type of help, advice, or services would contribute the most to your feelings of financial security and your success at achieving financial independence?
3. Share your desire to find a dolphin advisor, or create a financial plan to turn your positive vision into reality. Determine the best way to get a written plan with financial goals, savings goals, transition dates, etc. Who do you know who may be able to introduce you to a dolphin investment advisor?
4. Discuss what you want in your ideal investment advisor and get feedback and opinions. Ask them what they would look for and how they would find an exceptional advisor who fits your description.
5. Discuss the differences in your future expenses, compared to your current expenses. Ask for other opinions, viewpoints, and ways to achieve your goals. Do the same for your income.
6. What passions do you want to "monetize" by turning them into a business or source of additional income, at some point in the future?
7. What will you do differently in the future, based on your insights from this chapter?

SUMMARY
Envision and Plan a Happy, Fulfilling, and Sustainable Future

Good work! You now have something very few people ever have: a clear and compelling vision of yourself flourishing. And it's based on scientific research of what actually works in the real world—and your self-knowledge and insights. You also know how to create a solid financial foundation to support your vision throughout your entire life. Let's review this section.

Chapter 9. Your vision is the preview of your future. Your Endorphin Data and Dreams are the raw material for your vision of a flourishing future. One of the most important determinants of your future success and happiness is your work.

The more closely your work environment and job requirements match your talents, interests, skills, and values, the more joy, success, and fulfillment you'll experience at work and in life.

Knowing what you want is the first step to getting it. So envision yourself living, working, and playing in the Endorphin Zone.

Chapter 10. Achieving positive cash flow is the first step to building wealth. Spending less than you take home will reduce your stress, build your resources, and enable you to seize opportunities. It will also make you feel more autonomous and optimistic. Optimize your income and cut your expenses. Build up your liquidity and pay off your consumer debt, then start investing for your future.

Chapter 11. To accumulate enough wealth to achieve lifelong financial independence, you will need a plan. Scenario planning software enables you to project your income and expenses for your entire lifetime.

Consider hiring an expert, dolphin investment advisor to help you. The right person will help you create a realistic and achievable plan to turn your future vision into reality and your retirement into re-inspirement.

All right, breathe easy! The hard part is over. All of this thinking, introspecting, decision-making, and insights could overwhelm anyone. But you're not anyone, you're unique because you're committed to flourishing—and now you know how.

But there's a giant chasm between knowing and doing. So the final chapter will show you how to apply your new knowledge and insights to evolve and flourish—as you've defined it.

STEP FOUR

Align Your Life with Your Vision

12

Go Confidently in the Direction of Your Dreams

> *"Vision without action is merely a dream: vision with action can change the world."*
> —Joel Barker

Downhill ski racing is the original extreme winter sport. The no-holds-barred event tests the limits of human courage, strength, and skill. Imagine throwing yourself into a barely controlled fall down the face of a snow- and ice-covered mountain, doing everything possible to maximize your speed. Feel the exhilaration of blasting from zero to seventy-five miles per hour within ten seconds of leaving the starting gate!

Your skis hiss and chatter on the snow while you press forward on the balls of your feet, driving your edges aggressively into each turn. The bamboo gates slap your legs and shoulders with a rhythmic *whap, whap, whap.* You're in the flow. The forest and crowds disappear as you focus all your attention on the course ahead. While carving through wicked turns, G-forces crush you to the snow with three times the force of gravity.

One cloudless spring day, I skied Whistler Mountain, in British Columbia, with some friends. One of them, Jeff, was a former world-class downhiller. He showed us the course he raced with the Crazy Canucks, Canada's famous and reckless ski team. It was so steep that many of us pointed our skis sideways across the fall line and side-slipped down the hill. At the Fallaway pitch, which was basically a cliff, Jeff beamed, "I hit over seventy miles per hour on this section."

At these insane speeds, downhillers must negotiate deeply rutted and icy turns, abrupt dips, bone-jarring bumps, harrowing blind drops and eighty percent grades—all while maintaining the most aerodynamic position possible. The deadliest hazards are the blind jumps that launch them, helplessly, two to three hundred feet across the snow. Since mid-air corrections are impossible, they must line up each jump perfectly.

Small mistakes can lead to disaster. Hooking a gate, catching an edge, or blowing a jump can mangle knees, fracture bones, rupture spleens, crush vertebrae, compress disks, and rip groins. Ow! Some downhillers have suffered brain damage, and a few have died.

Looking at the body-breaking pine trees lining the narrow ski run, it was hard to image how Jeff, *or anyone,* could ski so fast and ever hope to survive.

Jeff explained their strategy, "We weren't allowed to ski the course before a race. So we side slipped along the edge, just like you guys are doing, and we memorized every gate, jump, and turn. Before a race, we'd close our eyes and visualize skiing the perfect line down the entire course."

We marveled at his ability to memorize a two-mile course and "see" it in his mind's eye. Jeff explained that visualizing wasn't optional. "When you're skiing seventy or eighty miles an hour, you need to know what's around the next bend and over the next jump. If you don't have a good mental map of the course, you could get badly hurt, or die."

Jeff told me that his whole team practiced memorizing important details and relationships for each gate, turn, jump, or transition. They visualized skiing the runs many times every day, and, of course, winning. Eventually, it became second nature to them.

He confided, "Before I retired from ski racing and started meeting people in the 'real world,' I thought everyone visualized." He was shocked to learn that most "normal" people don't intentionally use visualizations to achieve their goals.

What he didn't realize is that most "normal" people don't have meaningful goals to visualize. It's a good thing you're not normal.

The Power of Meaningful Goals

Establishing goals based on your positive vision unleashes powerful subconscious motivations and processes. Meaningful goals are congruent with your values and purpose, and synergistic with each other. They coordinate, support, and reinforce your powers, purpose, passions, positive people, positive places, and financial sustainability.

Meaningful goals transform intangible desires and aspirations into concrete words and measurable objectives. These goals are the foundations for your plans and the motivation for your future actions. Written goals enable you to develop step-by-step implementation schedules, monitor your progress, and adjust course when necessary.

When you're intrinsically motivated and working to fulfill your life's purpose, you don't quit. You persevere until you accomplish each goal, not because you're driven, but because you can't imagine doing anything else. You're being pulled from the future instead of being pushed from the past.

One of the most powerful things about meaningful goals is the person you become while you pursue them. They motivate you to learn new things, evolve your thinking, and change your behavior to achieve them.

Meaningful goals trigger your dopamine reward system. This powerful neuro transmitter is the biological driver behind all desire, motivation, and goal-oriented behavior. When triggered, dopamine focuses your attention and energy on pursuing and achieving desired rewards: in this case, your meaningful goals.

When you take action on meaningful goals, you feel a pleasurable sense of control, optimism, and accomplishment. The more you fire up your goal-driven reward circuits, the greater your sense of satisfaction, especially when you get positive feedback. When you're frustrated, your dopamine reward system reminds you of the pleasure you'll feel when you achieve your goal. That motivates you to overcome setbacks and to try different strategies until you achieve your "reward." When you see clear connections between your efforts and your progress, your endorphins and self-esteem both get a boost.

There's another reason meaningful goals are essential if you want to flourish. Most people are distracted by information overload. Without clear, specific, and meaningful goals, people wander though life, squandering their powers and potential. Goals help you screen out unimportant information and stay focused on the most important things in your life, the things that will enhance your health, wealth, and happiness.

Meaningful goals literally program you for success.

The Ruler of Our Consciousness

At the base of your skull, a small cluster of neurons, the reticular formation, sits on top of your spinal cord where it attaches to your brain. It's the central structure in an extensive neurological network called the reticular activating system (RAS). The RAS intercepts, evaluates, and prioritizes all of your thoughts and the data your five senses transmit up your spinal cord to your brain.

Your brain can consciously process only a tiny percentage of the millions of bits of data your nervous system generates each second. To prevent information overload, your RAS blocks non-essential information and only alerts your conscious mind to potential opportunities and threats. Like a well-trained executive assistant, it screens out information that doesn't help you survive or flourish.

When you set a meaningful goal, your RAS immediately starts to scan your thoughts and environment for information and resources that will help you achieve it. For example, if you decide you want to buy a specific model of car, you'll immediately start to see them everywhere. They were always there, but your RAS didn't let them into your conscious awareness until you "told" it what you wanted.

Another benefit of written goals is you can share them with other people. The positive people in your life can help you achieve your goals only if you tell them what they are. That "alerts" their RAS to be on the lookout for ways to help you achieve them.

When you take time to define meaningful goals, focus your attention on them, invest your emotions in them, express your powers to pursue them, and enlist others to help you achieve them, opportunities and resources will magically appear. Doors will open where you didn't know there were doors. The universe will conspire to help you!

Because of all the reasons mentioned above, meaningful goals are essential "tools" for flourishing. In fact, Ed Diener says that one of the best predictors of well-being is having "meaningful goals."

Identify Your Endorphin Gaps

It's normal for people to be happy and satisfied most of the time, in most domains of their life. But in some situations, improvements in one or two key domains can make a big positive impact on your overall quality of life.

So, let's start the Endorphin Effect, for you, by identifying the highest priority changes you want to make in your life. Identifying your important Endorphin Gaps (the difference between where you are now and your ideal) will enable you to focus your energies on closing them. Then you'll turn each important Endorphin Gap into achievable goals, action plans, questions, visualizations, and, soon, changes in your thinking, behavior and life.

To identify your highest pay-off Endorphin Gaps, complete the Current Life Satisfaction Survey below.

In column 1, rate the *importance* of each of the 21 subdomains on a scale of 1 to 3. Ask yourself, *How important is this subdomain to my health, wealth and happiness right now?*

Then, in column 2, rate your *current satisfaction* for each one on a scale of 1 to 10. Ask yourself this question: *All things considered, how satisfied am I in this subdomain right now?*

If you're not sure what each category includes, review the chapter or section on that subject. If a subdomain is not important to you, give it a 5, or neutral, in the satisfaction column.

Go with your gut instinct when answering these important questions. Don't think too much about your answers. Your first impulse is the right one.

For a PDF version of this survey, go to EndorphinZone.com.

Now, put an X in column 3 to indicate High Importance/Low Satisfaction Categories.

Add up the "How Satisfied" column (3) and divide the total by twenty-one. The result is your current average life satisfaction, with ten being extremely satisfied, five being neutral and one being extremely dissatisfied. Any score lower than a 10 means you have room for improvement. A score of 10 means you need to set higher goals and expectations—to grow and evolve.

Current Life-Satisfaction Survey

Domains and Sub Domains	Importance Step 1 **How important** is this element of my life, right now? Rate 1 to 3 1 = low or not at all 2 = moderately 3 = very important	Satisfaction Step 2 **How satisfied** am I with this element of my life, right now? Rate 1 to 10 1 = very dissatisfied 5 = neutral 10 = very satisfied	Focus Step 3 Put an X in the box below to mark your biggest Endorphin Gaps
Your Personal OS			
1) Your Aspirations			
2) Your Beliefs			
3) Your Habits			
Your Powers			
4) Your Unique Abilities			
5) Your Character Strengths			
6) Your Health & Vitality			
Your Passions			
7) Your Key Interests			
8) Your Favorite Activities			
9) Your Worthy Causes			
Your Purpose			
10) Transformative Events			
11) Your Values			
12) Role Models			
Positive People			
13) Soul Mates			
14) Family & Friends			
15) Mentors			
Positive Places			
16) Region & Community			
17) Neighborhood & Home			
18) Favorite Places			
Financial Sustainability			
19) Positive Cash Flow			
20) Build Resources			
21) Financial Independence			
Total of lines 1 - 21	(a)		
Divide (a) by 21 to calculate your **Life Satisfaction**		=	

Figure 12.1. Current Life Satisfaction Survey

After completing the survey, answer these questions for yourself:

Which Endorphin Domains and subdomains are the most important to me? Prioritize them by importance.

In which Endorphin Domains and subdomains am I currently the most satisfied? What am I most satisfied about?

In which Endorphin Domains and subdomains am I currently the least satisfied? What am I least satisfied about?

What are my most important Endorphin Gaps? Identify and prioritize them, focusing on your least satisfying subdomains.

Which Endorphin Gaps will generate the greatest, success, happiness, and satisfaction when I reduce, or eliminate, them?

In which Endorphin Gaps can I achieve the biggest and fastest results, with the smallest amount of cost, effort, and stress? Prioritize them.

Once you've answered these questions, you can use your insights to create and prioritize meaningful goals, goals to close your highest-priority Endorphin Gaps. To rapidly boost your endorphins, focus on the subdomains where you are the least satisfied where you can achieve the fastest and easiest results.

Create Meaningful Goals

Create a goal for your top ten to fifteen Endorphin Gaps. Start by answering three questions about each one.

What is the name and "problem that needs solving" in each gap?

What's important to me about closing each gap?

What has to happen for me to feel that I have successfully closed each Endorphin Gap?

These three questions will help you define the problem you need to solve, the value that's motivating you to solve it, and how you will keep score as you work to close it.

There are two types of meaningful goals, SMART and HEART goals. You'll use a balance of both. SMART goals are about doing or achieving things that increase your objective well-being. They're Specific, Measurable, Action-oriented, Realistic, and Time-bound. They are best for measurable results and activity levels.

Here's an example of a measurable SMART goal: "I weigh 180 pounds." This is an activity level SMART goal: "I exercise and stretch for at least forty-five minutes for five days every week."

SMART goals are usually about achieving extrinsic, or external, rewards: money, possessions, status, power, image, etc. But recall that your external life circumstances are only responsible for about twenty percent of the variations in your happiness that you can control. Your intangible attitudes, beliefs, mental models, expectations, and intentional thoughts and behaviors are responsible for the remaining eighty percent.

That means you need to balance extrinsic SMART goals with intrinsic HEART goals. HEART goals are Happiness-generating, Empowering, Aspirational, Reprogramming, and Timeless. They are best for improving our subjective well-being. Use them for intangible goals that are difficult or impossible to measure objectively.

These types of goals are about our positive intentions to think, act, feel, or be a certain way. An example of a "being" HEART goal: "I am a loving and considerate husband and father." An example of a "feeling" HEART goal: "I am in the Endorphin Zone at least ninety percent of the time." And a thinking HEART goal example: "I focus on what I want, not what I don't want."

As you work on writing and prioritizing, ten to fifteen meaningful goals, keep these things in mind.

Tips for Creating Goals

Set goals that you have direct control over, such as your thoughts, attitudes, intentions, actions, expectations, etc. Don't create goals based on what other people think or do. Set goals around what you intrinsically want to accomplish, experience, and be.

Not all goals are equal. Some goals are dependent on achieving other goals. For instance, if you want to move to a nicer home, you'll probably need to earn more money. To accomplish that, you'll have to enhance your knowledge and skills. So improving your knowledge and skills is an overarching goal that will empower you to accomplish other "smaller" goals. Focus mainly on overarching goals.

For best results, prioritize your goals in this order:

At the top are the ones that are the fastest and easiest to accomplish, so you experience some early wins,

Next are the overarching ones that will help you achieve many important sub goals,

Last are the ones that will take the longest, and the most effort, that will make the biggest positive impact on your happiness and life satisfaction. You can make progress on all three types at the same time.

Make sure each goal is congruent with your vision, powers, passions, and purpose, and synergistic with the others. When your goals are closely aligned with your flourishing self, you'll experience more joy and vitality pursuing them, achieve them more easily, and feel more satisfied throughout the process.

Set inspiring goals. Small goals don't have much emotional pull. So set some Big Hairy Audacious Goals (BHAGS) that are big enough to inspire you but realistic enough that you know you can achieve them.

The closer you come to achieving a goal, the more motivated you'll be. So break big goals into smaller milestones. The rewards of achieving them will keep you motivated to persevere.

Once you've written and prioritized your goals, create plans to achieve them. Researchers discovered that written plans, which detail when, where, and how you will take action on your goals, triple your chances of success. Don't just say, "Exercise for forty-five minutes, five days a week." Decide which days you will exercise and schedule it on your calendar.

Prepare for setbacks. If you anticipate and identify future potential obstacles, you can prepare to overcome them. So, be sure to have a plan

B and C if your first plan doesn't get the results you want. Nothing of value is easy, so expect challenges. They make you grow! So make written plans, and back-up plans, to achieve your important goals.

Your biggest challenge will probably be homeostasis, the tendency of all living things to maintain the status quo. Changing long-held mental models and habits, even if they're hurting your happiness, requires focus, commitment, and time. By recognizing that nothing of significant value is easy to accomplish, you'll be more resilient and persistent when you encounter the inevitable detours and setbacks.

Once you've written your goals and plans, you will feel a profound sense of accomplishment. Now, let's increase the potency of your goals by turning them into Empowering Questions.

Turn Your Goals into Empowering Questions

Many people use positive self-talk in the form of affirmations to stay focused on achieving important goals. However, recent research by Ibrahim Senay and his colleagues discovered a more effective way to direct our thoughts and actions: start with empowering questions, then answer them with positive affirmations and visualization. I'll explain this powerful technique in a moment.

Here are a dozen tips, based on the latest research, for turning the key goals you just defined into empowering questions.

How to Craft Empowering Questions

Use the first person singular tense: *I*, not *we*, or *they*.

Focus on what you do want, not what you don't want.

Include a balance of both SMART and HEART goals.

Make each one a positive and emotionally compelling question, not a statement. Start each one with "Will I . . .?" For example, "Will I stick to my budget every week?" not "I stick to my budget each week." You can also start with the interrogative phrase, "How can I . . . ?"

Include questions about both tangible results and intangible feelings, as well as the thoughts and behaviors that will create them.

Use positive verbs to denote action: *earn, accomplish, create, produce,* etc. Use positive emotions to denote feelings: *love, connection, self-esteem, fulfillment, flow,* etc.

Ask questions that empower you to see, feel, hear, taste, and smell the desired behavior, and to experience the emotional payoffs, when you achieve your goal.

Keep your questions short, simple, and concise—one sentence each.

Refine them until they resonate with your values, beliefs, purpose, and passions.

Make your questions big enough to inspire you, but small enough that you know you can answer them in the affirmative.

Transfer the questions to 3x5 index cards, about three or four to each side.

For samples of Empowering Questions and other resources to help you complete the steps in this chapter, go to EndorphinZone.com.

Now you can use your Empowering Questions to stimulate internal dialogues and images. These internal representations and discussions are powerful ways to "program" and motivate yourself to accomplish your goals.

Visualize Yourself Achieving Your Goals

Just as plants are heliotropic, growing in the direction of light, human beings are *visiotropic*; we grow in the direction of our visions. Think about what this means. The more you focus your attention, energy, and resources on your vision, the more you grow toward it. This is how daily visualizations can radically change your life.

Former California governor Arnold Schwarzenegger, the world famous action star who won five Mr. Universe and seven Mr. Olympia bodybuilding titles, is one of the world's most successful visualizers.

He once explained how he used them to shape his muscles into their winning form: "In my mind, I saw my biceps as mountains, enormously huge, and I pictured myself lifting tremendous amounts of weight with these superhuman masses of muscle."

Schwarzenegger continued to use visualizations as he pursued and achieved international superstardom and nearly a billion dollar net worth. Clearly, visualizations with action work spectacularly, if you do them. But it takes more than visualizations to turn your goals and visions into reality. It takes work.

Arnold didn't just visualize; he would hit the gym and "pump iron" for hours and hours. Visualizations alone won't accomplish anything in the material world. Freud called that type of belief "magical thinking."

To turn your goals and visualizations into reality, you, too, must "hit the gym" and do the work that will transform your vision into reality. Here's how to use your empowering questions, affirmations, and visualizations to turn your goals, and ultimately, positive vision, into reality.

Achieve Your Goals with Affirmations and Visualizations

If your kindergarten teacher ever read to you during naptime while you lay quietly on the floor, following the story in your mind, you're already an accomplished visualizer. In fact, everyone is. It's estimated the average person has about ten thousand mostly random thoughts or images every day that briefly flicker through their conscious awareness.

Today, doctors, actors, politicians, athletes, business people, entrepreneurs, writers, and soccer moms are using visualizations to achieve their goals. In a comment about today's elite athletes, Rebecca Smith, a sports psychologist at the U.S. Olympic Training Center in Colorado Springs, said, "There's no one who doesn't use imagery."

Here's how to use your imagination to purposely focus and harness your personal powers for positive change in your life. You'll use empowering questions to start an inner dialogue about your intentions for daily or weekly goals. Then you'll respond with a positive affirmation of your commitment to each goal, and visualize yourself doing the actions, expressing your personal powers, feeling positive emotions, thinking positive thoughts, overcoming obstacles, and achieving your goals.

You already envisioned many of your goals being achieved during the Endorphin Day and Future Positive Experiences exercises in the previous chapter.

Commit to reading your Empowering Questions and practicing your affirmations and visualizations for at least fifteen minutes, twice each day. Spend about two to three minutes on each question. After you wake up and before you go to sleep, are excellent times, when you are quiet and relaxed.

Turn on relaxing, instrumental music and sit or lay in a comfortable position in a safe, quiet place where you won't be disturbed. Shut the blinds and lower the lights. Close your eyes and relax your entire body by tensing and then releasing each muscle from your toes to your scalp. Breathe slowly while you count down from ten to one. Feel yourself sinking deeper and deeper into tranquility with each breath. Focus on the pleasant sensation of c-a-l-m-n-e-s-s.

When you feel deeply relaxed, open your eyes and read your empowering questions to yourself. Always start with something like, "Will I practice my affirmations and visualizations for fifteen minutes every day when I wake up and when I go to bed?"

Questions about your intentions motivate you more than traditional affirmations. They give you free choice and expand your mind to new possibilities, causing you to reaffirm your commitment to your goals. They inspire you to think, and allow you to choose to commit and act, instead of just commanding you to act. This self generated power and choice increases your intrinsic motivation to pursue and achieve your goals.

Read your Empowering Questions to yourself and then engage in some positive self-talk. Close your eyes after reading each one and answer the question by restating it as an affirmation, such as, "Yes! I will ____ (hit the gym)."

Then visualize yourself doing your desired behaviors and experiencing your desired material and emotional payoffs. Visualize the things you want to accomplish and experience exactly as you want them to be in the future. See yourself doing the work, overcoming obstacles, and adapting, evolving, and prospering.

You'll be in a lucid, waking dream state and can use your imagination to consciously control the plot, characters, details, and outcomes of your vision. See the scenes happening right in front of you, as if you're actually experiencing them, through your own eyes. Take the time to vividly visualize each scene for several minutes.

Don't just see it. Experience it with all your senses, adding sounds, smells, dialog, and tactile objects to your visual representation. Savor the positive emotions your inner representations evoke. See yourself succeeding, achieving, enjoying, laughing, smiling, and flourishing. Feel yourself being happy and successful.

When you hit obstacles, use this time to have an inner dialog with yourself about different ways you can overcome them. Let your conscious mind ask questions and present problems for your subconscious mind.

The more vivid your experience and the more intense your emotions, the more powerful your affirmation and visualization sessions will be. Suspend any doubts; you're consciously reprogramming your brain with positive intentions and expectations.

Don't be concerned if you can't visualize all the details, or if things fade in an out. Just create your best mental representations of positive thoughts and actions in your ideal future. You'll get better and better with practice, and sooner than you might imagine. Over time, you'll master this powerful skill.

When you complete a session, you'll feel the endorphins and dopamine surging through your brain and your body. That chemical cocktail will motivate you to take action to turn your goals into reality. To keep your most important priorities on the top of your mind, repeat your key affirmations to yourself throughout each day.

How Affirmations and Visualizations Work

The brain receives and stores information from all five senses. But it processes about ten times more visual information than all the rest of the senses combined. These mental images are the innate language of the subconscious mind.

This process of talking with yourself and visualizing future experiences integrates logic and emotions in a profoundly catalytic way that words alone don't. That's why visualizations and affirmations are far more powerful than affirmations alone.

Here are some of the underlying psychological processes that make this technique so effective.

Harness cognitive dissonance.

When you encounter information or situations that conflict with your inner representations of the external world, it evokes an unpleasant psychological condition called cognitive dissonance. This causes you to either ignore the new information or try to change it. But, humans vigorously resist changing mental models. Once you understand cognitive dissonance, you can harness it for positive change.

By consciously "programming" your mind with the reality you want instead of the reality you have, it changes its inner representations of the "real world." You physically grow new neurological connections, networks, and mental models in your brain. When this occurs, your subconscious mind automatically goes to work to bring your outer reality in alignment with your new inner representations.

So picture this. After doing his visualizations, Arnold looks in the mirror and sees that his biceps aren't as big as the mountains he expects to see, reminding him that he isn't Mr. Universe—yet. The more vivid and emotionally compelling his inner mental models, the greater his cognitive dissonance.

That inner tension motivates him to take action to close the gap. He hits the gym and pumps iron for years until his biceps really are as massive as "mountains." With focus, visualizations, cognitive dissonance and effort, he eventually becomes Mr. Universe, Mr. Olympia, an action star and the governor of California. Apparently, visualizations work for him. You probably know dozens of other examples from all fields of endeavor of people who "saw" their future before it came to life.

Engage your subconscious mind.

Another reason affirmations and visualizations are so effective is they harness our creative subconscious where ninety-five percent of our thinking processes occur. When you turn a meaningful goal into an empowering question, you give your subconscious mind a problem to solve. Your reticular activating system (RAS), described above, immediately starts scanning for knowledge, experiences, ideas and creative solutions.

Your subconscious mind works relentlessly, 24/7, as it synthesizes information, creates new neurological pathways and "test drives" possible solutions to obstacles. All this happens without any conscious thought or effort.

In fact, your brain does some of its best work while you sleep. Then one day, in the shower, walking the dog, or taking a nap, lightening strikes. You have an *aha!* moment, a profound insight, an out-of-the box solution to achieving a goal.

Rehearse success in your mind's eye.

When Jeff visualized skiing the perfect line, he was mentally rehearsing his future race. While he was blasting through gates and over the jumps, he could compare his actual course to his imagined, ideal course. Then he could, hopefully, stay on course and, sometimes, win. If he hadn't envisioned his ideal line down the hill, he wouldn't have known when he was off course, or how get to back on it.

Mental rehearsal is a great way to train your mind on your desired behavior and emotional state. Immersing yourself in your ideal future, your desired behaviors, ways of thinking, and ideal outcomes, reprogram your thinking patterns and reminds you of your highest priorities. It also triggers endorphins, which compound the positive effects.

Positive anticipation elevates your mood.

Thinking about your future, positive self-talk, visualizing, planning, and goal setting, all focus your attention on pleasurable rewards, experiences and feelings.

Anticipating a future reward activates the pleasure center of the brain, often creating more positive emotions than actually getting the reward!

That's another powerful Endorphin Effect; positive visualizations release endorphins, relax you, lower your blood pressure, enhance your immune system, and speed recovery from medical procedures. All by just anticipating your positive future.

As soon as you start visualizing, you'll be on an upward spiral of flourishing. There's absolutely no cost, risk, or downside, only positivity. This type of visual meditation can literally rewire your brain to enhance your quality of life.

Visualizations Can Rewire Your Brain for More Positivity

For more than 2,500 years, Tibetan Buddhist monks have practiced visualizing detailed "movies in their minds" to consciously cultivate positive emotions. For instance, to cultivate compassion, monks envision themselves in a stressful situation that makes them angry or irritable. Then they visualize and "experience" themselves relaxing and transforming their negative emotions into compassion. Practicing this type of visual meditation for decades creates profound changes in the emotional processing center of the monks' brains.

Neuroscientist Richard Davidson has studied Tibetan Buddhist monks' brains for more than seventeen years. He's an expert on brain plasticity, the ability of brains to grow new neural connections. The first time Davidson and his team hooked up experienced Tibetan meditators to brain scanners; he thought his machines were broken.

When the monks went into a deep visualization meditation, the recording needles went off the charts. Their consciousness, attention, learning, and memory brain waves all averaged about thirty times stronger than the non-meditating control group.

The scientists also found the happiness-processing neural circuits in the monks' left pre-frontal cortex, above and behind their left eyes, were much larger than normal. And the negative emotion processing centers, in the right pre-frontal cortex, above and behind their right eyes, had shriveled up like a prune. These changes in the emotional processing clusters in their brains' dramatically increased the monks' ability to experience positive emotions and dramatically reduced their ability to experience negative ones!

Davidson's research proved that we can consciously program, and physically change, our brains to enhance our positivity!

The monks Davidson studied had typically meditated for thousands of hours over many years. But even short-term visualizations have a profound impact on our positivity. In a European study of "mental time travel," participants practiced daily self-guided visualizations for two weeks. Not surprisingly, the visual meditators reported significantly more happiness than the control group.

In other studies, participants who envisioned their "best possible selves," anticipated a vacation, or looked forward to watching a humorous video all reported greater positive emotions than control groups. Keep in mind that the subjects in the above studies didn't take action to realize their goals. They simply imagined them.

Focused Action Will Transform Your Life

Visualizations alone, without action, may contribute to your moment-by-moment happiness. But visualizing *and* taking action is a proven way to adapt, evolve, and prosper.

When I became an investment wholesaler, I'd already gone through career counseling. I knew the job was a good fit for my talents and interests. I'd been successful in sales before. But my new job was way out of my league.

My boss had recruited a stellar team of overachievers. In my region, all my peers had attended Stanford on sports scholarships. They were savvy, competitive, and driven. I was a lot more laid back. As you might imagine, my peers kicked my butt. I wasn't cutting it. But failure wasn't an option. I needed to make a quantum leap in my productivity.

During a performance review, my boss let me know that I needed to either step up or step aside. He "recommended" I attend Lou Tice's Pacific Institute in Seattle. Tice had been a successful high school football coach. After becoming famous for transforming losing teams into winners, he started sharing his performance-enhancing techniques with business people.

Over a four-day weekend, I learned how to create and use affirmations and visualizations. When I returned, I used them to dramatically upgrade my personal powers and performance. Like a laser, I focused intensely on learning new skills and the most important thing—meeting with lots of qualified prospects. My daily visual meditations empowered me to break old habits, master new skills, adapt, and prosper.

I set BHAGs, big hairy audacious goals, became an effective public speaker, and managed my time for maximum productivity. I got into the flow and unleashed my natural talents. In a typical week, I shared my investment opportunities with more than two hundred people! My commitment, daily visualizations, and subsequent personal growth rocketed me to success!

GO CONFIDENTLY IN THE DIRECTION OF YOUR DREAMS

I grew my territory from last place (22nd) in sales to third place in just eighteen months. I won an award at our annual sales conference. I had met the challenge and triumphed. My peers were stunned; my boss was impressed. I felt a deep sense of satisfaction and accomplishment! Plus I tripled my income.

It was a wonderful period of growth, accomplishment, and prosperity in my life; I had met and conquered a serious challenge. I really liked the work, my teammates, and my income. But I still wasn't feeling fully satisfied.

I had to face my own Endorphin Gap. It wasn't a serious case of miswanting. But my inner guides told me a few areas of my life were suboptimal. Although I was expressing many of my personal powers, I wasn't expressing some of my most satisfying ones, or pursuing a higher purpose.

An aspiration slowly came into focus. I yearned for an integrated life that balanced my head and my heart, one that provided personal expression and financial independence. I didn't want some fantasy "have it all" life. I just wanted a comfortable blend of those things that feed my soul and make life engaging and fulfilling.

I'd learned a powerful technique for personal change and growth. Now, I made a commitment to discover which changes would lead to my best possible life, a healthy, wealthy, happy, *and* fulfilling one.

I quit a good job with great people to pursue what has been calling me for a lifetime, and set up my consulting and publishing business. I visualized my affirmations every day, slowly building my company and eventually tripling my income from my previous wholesaling job. But my real passion was human flourishing; helping my clients achieve success and fulfillment and helping their clients do the same.

I read everything I could find about positive emotions, positive character traits, and business and financial success. I attended workshops, and studied with shamans and scientists. The indigenous healers taught me to use my subconscious mind, imagination, and visualizations in new and powerful ways. As I learned about human flourishing, I implemented my new knowledge in my own life, and then started using it with my clients, and in my presentations and workshops. I soon realized that a wide variety of people would benefit from insights I'd learned on my quest.

Because you've now read the best of what I've learned, if you look in the mirror, you'll see a mini expert on the science of human flourishing. You know more than ninety-nine percent of the world's population knows about the good life and how to attain it.

You know about the Endorphin Effect, that you're designed to learn, adapt, evolve, and prosper. Your positive feelings automatically direct your attention and energies to areas that are ripe for personal growth and opportunities for acquiring resources. If you feel uplifted from just reading about flourishing, think how good you'll feel when you actually do the exercises, and start evolving and prospering.

If you have the courage to follow them, your "inner guides" will lead you on an upward spiral of flourishing—to the Endorphin Zone. So, if you feel positive about what you've read, do the most rewarding thing you can do from all the recommendations in this book. Then reread this book and follow the four-step process: commit to flourishing, discover your flourishing self and envision a flourishing future. Then align your life with your vision.

Transform Your Life and Our World

Human beings have transformed our culture and technology more during the last one hundred years than in their previous two hundred thousand years. And this transformation is accelerating. Scientists are cracking the Endorphin Code, discovering the biological, emotional, and spiritual foundations for living a good life. I believe research into human flourishing will foster a more positive transformation than the Enlightenment.

This book is a framework and catalyst for personal evolution and cultural transformation. Endorphinomics is a seed that will grow and evolve with the help of readers like you. I envision a global community of Wise Happies using the science of human flourishing to imagine and create a better life for themselves and a better world for all.

I invite you to join in at EndorphinZone.com.

* * *

It's time to celebrate! You now know how to adapt, evolve, and prosper—with the science of human flourishing. The next step is up to you. Only action will transform your knowledge and insights into reality.

So I hope you'll apply what you've learned and become a role model for others. Most of all, I hope you'll soon be living the life you've imagined . . . in the Endorphin Zone!

ENDORPHIN EVENT #12
Tell the Story of Your Journey to the Endorphin Zone

Summarize this chapter for your guests by going through the pages and using the subheads and graphics to share the key points. Then brainstorm on the following topics.

Imagine that this Endorphin Event is taking place five to ten years in the future. You have used the information in this book to start your journey to your ideal future and you have now arrived. Everything is as you imagined it in your positive vision.

1. Tell your friends exactly what you did to transform your old, suboptimal life into your new, flourishing life. Explain your key insights and actions in as much detail as possible.
2. Explain how you aligned your goals and behaviors with your values, purpose, passions, and powers in positive places, with positive people. How did you create synergy so that your goals and behaviors supported each other?
3. What beliefs and behaviors contributed most to your health, wealth, happiness, and fulfillment?
4. How did you achieve financial freedom?
5. What role did positive people play in your transformation? Who are they?
6. Take notes as you brainstorm with your loved ones. Then write a short story about your success called "My Journey to the Endorphin Zone." Refer to it often and upgrade it when appropriate. It's your personal road map to your ideal future. Follow it daily.

Acknowledgements

A book like this takes many hundreds of hours of researching, brainstorming, and thinking. This intense focus turned my wonderful wife, Brooke, into a "book widow" for many years. Through it all, she was one hundred percent supportive and encouraging, and she even came up with the brilliant concept for the cover. So thank you, Brooke, for all your empowering ideas and patience. You made this book possible. I love you with all my heart.

Every writer must have a "writer's buddy," to bounce ideas off of. Eddie Bryant is not only my writing buddy; he's my best friend and the creative consultant on this project. From the very beginning, Eddie has "beta tested" many of the processes in this book with his investment clients. He was also actively involved in every step of this project, especially the final look and feel of the book. Eddie will be the first investment advisor to use *Endorphinomics* with clients. Thanks, Eddie, for all the time and love you invested in this book.

A number of my friends and clients volunteered for the grueling task of reading and critiquing early versions of the manuscript. First and foremost is Barry Garapedian, who is using many of these concepts in his own life and coaching his clients to use them in theirs. Thanks for all the encouragement and coaching, Barry. You are a wonderful friend.

The following friends invested their time to read my manuscript and provided me with useful feedback: Bill Hortz, Lisa Wheeler, Mary Moore, Kathy Rowley, Humberto Medina and Steve Sanduski. Julie Stone made many helpful suggestions, especially on chapter 8. Sheva Carr provided some great insights on the three brains and how they work in synergy with our entire body when we experience positive emotions.

Thank you all for bringing out the best in me.

Larry Chambers, a friend and successful author, sent me a memorable email from a Hanoi hotel room after reading Chapter 8, telling me how much he enjoyed it. Thanks for the memory, Larry. I now envision people reading *Endorphinomics* all over the world.

A number of my clients tested many of the ideas in this book and gave me feedback. Lance Blount, Matt Louis, Scott Danner, Stephen Barrett, and Terry Hill all are "dolphin" advisors who helped shape the finished book. Over the years, many of my other clients tested my processes, challenged my ideas, and helped me refine my thinking. Thanks to everyone who has supported me on my journey to the Endorphin Zone.

My editor, Karen Risch, did a fantastic job of making my ideas shine and my voice sing. Thanks, Karen, for proving once again that, in writing, less is more.

When you look at a book, artists and graphic designers create what you see. Alex Vulchev did a fantastic job translating Brooke's concept into a powerful cover. Krista Donnelly created all of the technical illustrations, and Phil Boyd created the whimsical illustrations at the beginning of each section. GKS Creative designed and formatted the interior of the book, putting it all together with their layout skills. Thanks, team, you all did a fabulous job!

Finally, Amy Collins of New Shelves Book Distributors provided valuable guidance on the cover design and other important considerations. Thanks, Amy, you are a great book consultant!

Appendix

Flourishing vs. Languishing	
Optimism.	Pessimism.
Believe in your ability to make a positive difference in your life, the lives of others, and the world.	Believe your destiny is preordained and you are helpless to change the trajectory of your life, or make a difference in the world.
Strong religious, spiritual or faith-based beliefs and active participation in that community.	No right or wrong answers to the big questions of life. No connection with a spiritual community.
Virtuous values and character strengths.	If it feels good, do it, little thought of consequences.
A clear and compelling vision for your future life.	No dream, no vision, no image of the future.
A clear and compelling purpose for your life.	No purpose to live, or die, for.
Taking care of your health.	Poor self care, self-induced health problems, no exercise, smoking, drugs, alcohol, diet, etc.
More education.	Less education.
Gratitude and appreciation.	Envy and resentment.
Trust in others.	Mistrusting and suspicious.
Taking responsibility for, and control of, your life.	Being a victim who, is not responsible for or in control of, your life.
Confident, competent, and evolving.	Hesitant, incompetent and stagnant.
Judge your happiness by how well you are meeting your own needs, wants and aspirations.	Judge your happiness by how well you're doing compared to your "reference group".
Giving generously to people in need, and your favorite causes.	Being stingy and telling yourselves others aren't worthy of your generosity.
Save every month.	Spend more than you make.
Simplify your life.	Complicate your life.
Close, caring relationships.	Uncomfortable, manipulative relationships.
Appreciate what you have.	Believe you'll only be happy when you get the right "stuff" or earn more money.
Believe focus and hard work are the keys to success.	Believe luck and connections are the keys to success.
Focus on the solution.	Focus on the problem.
Persistent and resilient.	Give up easily.
Takes action to maximize your health, wealth, happiness, and sustainability.	Complain forever but can't get started to improve your life.
Have meaningful goals and plans to achieve them.	No goals, no plans, no accomplishments.

About the Author

Steve Moeller is an entrepreneur, speaker, management consultant and retirement strategist. For more than two decades, he has trained investment advisors to provide holistic retirement planning and wealth management services to affluent clients. He also helps successful individuals and couples flourish in retirement.

An expert in business optimization, personal finance, and the science of human flourishing, Steve spent ten years researching the emerging field of positive psychology, including positive emotions, positive neuroscience, peak performance, optimum health, and life satisfaction.

In addition to speaking, writing, and consulting, Steve is the Director of Flourishing for Blue Dolphin Investment & Retirement Strategists. The firm applies many of the insights and recommendations in this book. It's mission is to help successful people make smart decisions that enhance their financial independence and quality of life, now and in the future.

Steve lives with his wife, Brooke, in Southern California.

Join the Endorphin Zone Community, to Help Yourself and Others Flourish

Discover links, additional resources, and a community of people who are using the science of human flourishing to create happier, more successful lives for themselves and a better world for all.

Visit EndorphinZone.com for information on the following:

- Subscribing to the Endorphin Quest newsletter and blog
- Joining the Endorphin Society
- Free special report on flourishing in retirement
- Forming a book study group around *Endorphinomics* and the science of human flourishing
- Ordering bulk quantities or customized versions of this book
- Workshops and other programs to help you implement the strategies in this book
- Training and licensing programs, business opportunities, and strategic alliances
- Hiring Steve Moeller as a speaker or workshop leader for an upcoming conference or meeting
- Consulting, coaching and business-development services

You will also find a bibliography and links to other useful sites.

Join us on Facebook at https://www.facebook.com/steve.moeller.

ENDORPHINOMICS: The Science of Human Flourishing
QUICK ORDER FORM

	Qnty.	Price	Total
Single books (less than five)		$29.95 ea	
Six Pack, Buy five (5) books and get one (1) book free!	6	$149.75 for 6	
California Residents Add 8.00% sales tax		Sales Tax	
Shipping and handling, in Continental USA $5.00 for one book. $15.00 for the Six Pack. One (1) book free		S & H	
		TOTAL (US$)	

Bulk orders and customized books with a foreword by YOU!! (For business executives, financial advisors, coaches, counselors, etc. to use with your clients and prospects.)

For details, see our website, www.endorphinzone.com, call 800-678-1701 or email us at info@endorphinzone.com.

PAYMENT INFORMATION

Check # _____ enclosed ☐ American Express ☐ Mastercard ☐ Visa

Credit Card #: _____ Exp. Date __ / __ CVV # _____

CUSTOMER INFORMATION Please use address where credit card statement is received.

Name	Co.
Address	Suite #
City / State / Zip	Day Phn.
E-Mail	Signed

Call: (800) 678-1701 or (714) 505-8030
Email: info@endorphinzone.com
www.endorphinzone.com

Email completed form to: info@endorphinzone.com
Mail to: Endorphin Zone New Media
1131 E Main St., Suite 203, Tustin, CA 92780

www.ingramcontent.com/pod-product-compliance
Lightning Source LLC
Chambersburg PA
CBHW071856290426
44110CB00013B/1168